A Great Moral and Social Force

A HISTORY of BLACK BANKS

By: *Tim Todd*

A Great Moral and Social Force
A History of Black Banks

Published by the Public Affairs Department of
the Federal Reserve Bank of Kansas City
1 Memorial Drive • Kansas City, MO 64198

Diane M. Raley, publisher
Tammy Edwards, executive advisor
Lowell C. Jones, executive editor

Tim Todd, author
Casey McKinley, designer
Cindy Edwards, archivist

Special thanks to Shennette Garrett-Scott, Ph.D.; Barbara Krauthamer, Ph.D.; and Christopher Robert Reed, Ph.D. for their contributions to this work.

ISBN 978-0-9744809-6-1

First Edition, 2022.

Contents

Foreword

" ... (A) BANKING INSTITUTION IS SOMETIMES A GREAT MORAL AND SOCIAL FORCE. " *

At the Federal Reserve Bank of Kansas City we have produced a number of publications focused on historical explorations of several important banking-related topics including the founding of the Federal Reserve, a history of the payment system and the lessons from past banking and financial crises. We believe a knowledge of history can hold a key to understanding the current environment and is a necessary step in efforts to address some of our most difficult economic challenges.

In 2019, we published "Let Us Put Our Money Together: The Founding of America's First Black Banks." The book focused on the formation of the earliest African American banks and the important work of the institutions and their leaders in providing access to credit and financial services for a population who had been unserved and marginalized.

Our motivation was twofold.

In researching the role of community banks in U.S. economic history it was clear that the history of our nation's African American banks was not broadly available nor widely known.

We also believed that the publication was an important and meaningful contribution amid a continuing decline in the number of Black banks. The loss of these banks hurts communities and households, who lose the benefit of economic leadership and engagement that these banks can bring.

We quickly discovered there was significant interest in this topic. Many readers, in fact, encouraged us to expand our exploration of this history with another publication bringing the story forward. We agreed, believing a consideration of events that happened across a more extended timeframe would prove valuable.

This publication seeks to appeal to a broad audience by examining some key communities and their banks at important points in U.S. history: Richmond, Virginia; Boley, Oklahoma;

* *The Houston Post*, Sept. 9, 1906.

Chicago, Illinois; Memphis, Tennessee; Detroit, Michigan and finally, a look at more recent efforts to provide financial services via handheld mobile devices.

Rather than providing a comprehensive history of Black banking, our goal here has been to move across time, examining some of the communities where banks played a dual role, fighting for both economic opportunity and social equality. Readers will find that the motivation to create many Black banks, regardless of the time period, was rarely a purely financial endeavor or business opportunity. Instead, many were created with a primary mission of public service. This focus on the community is similar to the motivation behind many of our nation's small and mid-sized banks today. Community banks are the local catalysts in helping families and individuals establish businesses, buy homes and pay for education that can open doors to opportunity. They are community leaders.

One example of this from the early history of our nation's Black banks relates to the story of William Pettiford, founder of Birmingham's Alabama Penny Savings Bank in 1890. Pettiford said in creating the bank he recognized that Birmingham had a large African American population whose earnings, after being deposited in a bank as savings, could be used as a source of credit for the city's growing African American community. In later telling the story of the bank's creation, he would often discuss something he had observed years earlier while serving as pastor of the city's historic 16th Street Baptist Church. A husband and wife died leaving two orphan children. The couple's estate of around $10,000 – more than $250,000 in modern-day amounts – was lost because no one among the couple's family or friends had the financial resources to post a bond that was required of anyone acting as administrator.

"When I saw (the) helplessness to help orphan children in saving the property earned by their parents, it occurred to me that if we had a strong financial institution (we) could make bond and save the property left for the benefit of the heirs," Pettiford said.

We have drawn the title of this volume from a 1906 newspaper account of this event. The reporter recognized the story illustrated very clearly the reach of a bank extends well beyond that of many businesses and "reveal(ed) the fact that a banking institution is sometimes a great moral and social force."

That role is evident throughout this publication. Banks and bankers were and are centrally involved with some of the most important individuals and events in America's history of race relations. Readers of our previously published history told us they were particularly appreciative of the way that book presented the social environment around the earliest institutions. With this volume, we believe it is even more important to place the histories of the institutions we examine within the context of their times given that economic opportunity is a necessary element in equal opportunity. Such context improves our understanding of these institutions while also potentially increasing understanding of how this history has shaped our world and continues to influence our communities in significant ways yet today.

For some readers, this inclusion of a contextual landscape will provide an introduction to historical events of which they may not have previously been aware. One example of this within the region served by the Federal Reserve Bank of Kansas City pertains to the establishment in America's Plains of a number of Black towns, particularly in Oklahoma. Related to this, of course, is the painful story of the Tulsa race massacre, and the violent and horrific assault on that city's Greenwood community in 1921, which is discussed here as well.

America's history of race relations is an often uncomfortable topic that includes many painful chapters. Some sections of this publication may be difficult to read. However, history shows that times of turmoil often intersect with banking and the central role of community banks in multiple ways: There were times when banks provided their communities with urgently-needed resources in the face of uncertainty; in other instances, racial tension and violence were catalysts for establishing a bank to serve the community. Notably, at key junctures in the fight for civil rights, bankers were among those leading the fight for social justice.

As I have seen firsthand throughout my nearly 40-year career, community banks are a critical facilitator of local stability and opportunity, and their influence on a community's well-being extends well beyond the parameters of financial considerations. Many of the banks within this volume exhibit these qualities to an exceptionally high degree. Applying their lessons in the face of modern challenges has the potential to pave a path for progress.

Esther L. George
President and Chief Executive Officer
Federal Reserve Bank of Kansas City

Author's Note

This publication offers a historical consideration of Black banking in the United States by focusing on some key individuals, banks and communities. While it is in no way a comprehensive history, it does include background that is essential to understanding each financial institution, its time, the events that led to its creation and the community of which it was not only a vital part, but very often a leader. Much of this history frames the world we find today.

Within the confines of a book focused on banking, however, it is not possible to comprehensively explore all of the issues and events that are referenced. Recognizing this, we have extensively sourced this publication to assist readers interested in fully examining some of the topics that are introduced within. Many of the source materials used in this work are of significant cultural and historical importance, while more recent works provide important insight and perspective.

This publication would not have been possible without the assistance and contributions of Shennette Garrett-Scott, Ph.D., associate professor of History and African American Studies, Arch Dalrymple III Department of History, University of Mississippi; Barbara Krauthamer, Ph.D., dean of the College of Humanities and Fine Arts, professor of History, University of Massachusetts Amherst; and Christopher Robert Reed, Ph.D., professor emeritus of History at Roosevelt University and general secretary of the Black Chicago History Forum. The work of each is highly recommended to anyone seeking an understanding of American history.

Any errors or misinterpretations in this publication are the sole responsibility of the author.

About the author

Tim Todd is an executive writer with the Federal Reserve Bank of Kansas City. This is his eighth book examining banking history and follows the previously published "Let Us Put Our Money Together: The Founding of America's First Black Banks," which is also available from the Federal Reserve Bank of Kansas City.

Richmond, Virginia

I.

Alden McDonald sits in the back of a van on his way to talk with federal banking regulators about the importance of African American banks and the troubling decline in their numbers.

He is the dean of the nation's African American bankers. Born in a crowded two-bedroom house in New Orleans, McDonald put himself through school and on a path that led him in 1972 to the presidency of a new Black-owned bank at age 29. In 2005, he led that institution, Liberty Bank and Trust, through Hurricane Katrina and its aftermath with a response that gained national attention from *The New York Times* and other publications. As the community reeled, the bank allowed depositors to each withdraw as much as $500 in needed cash from ATMs, despite the bank having no way of knowing whether the accounts held sufficient funds. Meanwhile, grace periods on loans were extended and interest on credit was deferred. McDonald focused on rebuilding.

"[Some say] a banker is someone who gives you an umbrella when the sun is shining and takes it away when it starts to rain," he later tells a reporter.[1] "We try not to be that banker."

Fifteen years later, on Feb. 5, 2020, the conversation in the van is not about that storm, but what might be considered another – the exploitation of individuals and families by payday lenders. This is an issue closely intertwined with America's declining number of Black banks that serve minority communities. When any minority-owned bank location is lost, it is unlikely to be replaced by another, creating fertile new ground for a group of entities known as alternative financial services (AFS) providers – payday lenders, title loans, pawnshops and the rest.[2] These firms are more likely to be located in neighborhoods of color with low-to-moderate income levels.[3] Black neighborhoods may be particularly attractive targets because African American households are more likely to be either unbanked or "underbanked."[4] Without established access to other sources of credit, these households can be especially susceptible to exploitive AFS interest rates and fee structures in times of emergency or any time when expenses exceed income.

As the van arrives at the meeting site, the conversation revolving around all of these issues pauses, but it is never really over for McDonald. The driver, silent throughout the ride, speaks up as he helps McDonald and the other riders out of the van and hands them their bags.

"Don't be talking bad about payday loans," the driver says. "That's how I survive sometimes."

The driver chuckles, perhaps not out of humor, but out of the unease of revealing his financial struggle to strangers. If he is expecting a sympathetic smile in return, it does not come. Instead, McDonald pauses monetarily and asks the driver for details. The driver reveals he has two maxed out credit cards with interest rates well above 20 percent. His reliance on payday lenders is necessary for the purchase of food or other essentials when ends are not meeting.

Hearing this little bit, McDonald hands the driver one of his business cards and tells him to contact the bank. Mention this conversation, McDonald says, and the bank will work it out. The driver looks stunned as McDonald continues: The bank will consolidate the debt, lower the payments and get him back on his feet. McDonald explains very carefully how this could work. He presses the driver to make certain he understands all the details. The driver appears overwhelmed by all of this. When McDonald started talking the driver seemed to think this was some kind of con or joke. Now he sees that is not the case.

The driver says a prayer of thanks for bringing this opportunity into his life – something so random on a damp February morning. After he gets back in the van and heads off to find his next passenger, a bystander asks McDonald if this type of thing happens often. "Yes," he says, lifting his bag.[5]

It is significant that these moments unfold in Richmond, Virginia. Here, where Patrick Henry in 1755 said he would welcome death over a life without liberty, where in 1861 the Confederacy made its capital, and where, before that war's end, more than 300,000 men, women and children were bought and sold. Here, where history is always looming.[6]

On the morning of the meeting, the past weaves with the current day in a way that makes this very brief discussion into something symbolic of the American experience with providing minority communities – particularly Black households – access to credit and financial services.

Consider the following:

- Richmond, after the Civil War, was the cradle of Black capitalism, especially Black banking. On the day before this one, and only a mile away, McDonald toured the Maggie Walker National Historic Site, the former residence of the Black woman who was the first female bank president in the United States of any race. Near the home is a vacant lot that was once the location of the nation's first chartered Black bank. The Savings Bank of the Grand Fountain, United Order of True Reformers was an economic catalyst that helped the city's Jackson Ward neighborhood earn national renown as "Black Wall Street" and the "Harlem of the South" in the early years of the 20th century.

- Virginia today has one of the largest African American populations in the United States, yet the state's last Black-owned bank, after struggling financially, was sold to white ownership in 2017. The former First State Bank was immediately rechristened as Movement Bank with an eye toward becoming "a largely digital bank."[7]

- Virginia also had what have been deemed "unusually weak" consumer protections for those who borrow from payday and title lenders.[8] In 2019, the state's average payday loan annualized percentage rate (APR) was 251 percent and one out of every eight title loan borrowers ended up with their car repossessed – both levels among the worst in the United States.[9] In the city of Richmond, which encompasses around 60 square miles of land, there were 37 separate licensed locations offering a payday loan, a title loan or both. The list of Richmond businesses happy to charge a fee for cashing a check has too many entries to count.[10]

When William Washington Browne obtained a charter to establish the Savings Bank of the Grand Fountain, United Order of True Reformers, in Richmond on March 2, 1888, he realized a dream older than his 38 years. The idea of a Black-owned bank had been formerly discussed as early as an 1847 meeting in Troy, New York, and was likely a topic of informal consideration well before that. In such a bank, supporters saw a mechanism for both fostering economic opportunity in the northern United States *and* creating a powerful symbol of equality for the nation. With many in the discussion involved in any number of other efforts in the fight against slavery, the bank discussion did not advance.

In its stead, after the Civil War, there was the Freedman's Savings and Trust Company. Although modern-day discussions of minority-owned depository institutions (MDIs) sometimes point to Freedman's as the nation's first MDI – that statement is not accurate. While the government-created bank was intended to serve formerly enslaved individuals, the levers of control and governance remained firmly in the hands of powerful, influential and wealthy white Americans. Rather than serving its depositors – the bank did not even offer loans to its customers – Freedman's collapsed in failure amid rampant abuse. Much of that abuse was at the direction of Bank President Henry Cooke, a white financier who made Freedman's into little more than a dumping ground for the problematic and failed deals of his other financial interests. While Cooke was fighting to save himself financially, he decimated Freedman's savers. Around one-half of the Freedman's 61,000 depositors lost everything in the collapse. None of the depositors ever received more than a total of 62 cents on the dollar after a distribution process that lingered for years and was paid out on an irregular schedule.[11] More than two decades later, former Freedman's depositors continued to meet in their communities in hopes of devising a strategy to obtain a full recovery.[12] Those efforts proved futile.

Freedman's 1874 failure was one of a series of developments that compounded the difficult conditions facing many Black Americans after the Civil War and later, after the end of Reconstruction in 1877. These included, but were not limited to, the establishment of Black Codes, which essentially reinstated the South's slave-like labor structure; and the creation of Jim Crow laws legalizing segregation, which had effectively received the U.S. Supreme Court's blessing under the *Plessy v. Ferguson* "separate but equal" decision. In addition to the mechanisms that turned the legal structure into a weapon against Black Americans, there was the rise of racist paramilitary organizations including not only the Ku Klux Klan but also other groups whose names may be unfamiliar in mainstream modern America including the Knights of White Camelia and the Red Shirts.

It was in this environment that Browne formed his bank in 1888 as an affiliate of a Black fraternal beneficiary institution that he helped found in the 1870s, the United Order of True Reformers. The True Reformers functioned as something of a rudimentary insurance provider with local chapters, known as "Fountains," which provided financial assistance to members through a fund created by their dues. Payments to members in need ranged from $1.50 per week for illness to as much as $125 in funeral expenses.[13]

As created, this structure mirrored a system used by the enslaved in secret societies dating back perhaps to the earliest days of slavery on the North American continent in the 1600s. In these systems, small contributions from individuals who had been able to hire out their time or sell their own goods created combined funds that would be allocated to a member at a time of need. These systems were often known as burial societies since it is believed that they were originally created to help pay for the elaborate funerals mandated by religious tradition. Later, systems of this same design expanded to provide funds for other purposes.[†]

From a financial perspective, the key difference between the True Reformers' system and the design of a modern insurance provider is apparent. Insurance firms, rather than tapping a pool of purely contributed funds, receive premiums on a regular schedule that they then invest, generating profits for the firm while also increasing the amount of funds available to pay claims. True Reformers Fountains, meanwhile, generally kept their funds entirely liquid, placing the accumulated cash in what members hoped was a safe location until it was needed.

In some instances, this only compounded the danger for an enterprise already fraught with risk. Any effort at formal organization within the Black community was likely to draw the attention of white supremacists and introduce the specter of violence. According to a True Reformers history, in 1886 the risks were heightened for a Fountain in Charlotte County, Virginia, as racial tensions rose in the aftermath of the mob lynching of a Black man.[14] This was very likely the hanging of Dick Walker. On May 5, 1886, Walker was arrested and accused of striking a white girl after briefly holding her at knife point as she walked along a road near her rural home. Walker was arrested far from the site of the alleged attack – perhaps more than 20 miles – and was on foot, according to newspaper accounts, suggesting he was very likely innocent.[‡] He never got his day in court. The night of his arrest, a mob stormed the jail, nabbed Walker and killed him.

At the time, the Charlotte County True Reformers Fountain was holding around $100 in the safe of a local white storekeeper. After the attack, the storekeeper informed his neighbors of the funds, fueling speculation that the group would organize an effort to retaliate in some fashion for Walker's murder. The Fountain members, fearful for their own safety, considered disbanding and reached out to Browne for guidance. Browne returned to an idea he had considered but rejected earlier in his life – the creation of a Black-owned bank that would hold True Reformers' funds. The idea was adopted and expanded into a general banking business.[15]

The bank opened in Browne's Richmond home on April 3, 1889, and moved in 1891 into a newly constructed, three-story brick headquarters in the city's Jackson Ward on North Second Street. As the community grew around it, the building remained the neighborhood's

---

† A more structured version of this system was later used to form rotating credit associations where each member contributed an agreed-upon amount on a regular schedule and then had a turn receiving an agreed-upon amount of the combined funds. These systems are still in use today in some low-income minority communities. See Todd, Tim. *Let Us Put Our Money Together: The Founding of America's First Black Banks.* Federal Reserve Bank of Kansas City. 2019.

‡ Many newspapers reported details of the event, including *The (Raleigh, N.C.) News and Observer,* May 7, 1886. Brief items about the lynching appeared in major newspapers, including on the front page of *The Washington Post,* May 7, 1886.

most prominent with the organization expanding into other areas of the United States and with a wider scope of activities in Virginia, including the opening in Richmond of a hotel in 1894 and a store around 1900.[16, §, *]

§ The Hotel Reformer was located at the intersection of Sixth and Baker Streets. The area today is the I-95/I-64 interchange. The store was near Sixth and Clay Streets, which became the location of the Richmond Coliseum.

* Around the same time Browne was establishing his bank, not far away in Washington, D.C., Black community leaders began the work establishing the Capital Savings Bank in that city. See Todd, Tim. "Let Us Put Our Money Together: The Founding of America's First Black Banks." Federal Reserve Bank of Kansas City. 2019.

2.

In the 15 years after the True Reformers bank opened for business, the nation saw an average of about one new Black-owned bank opening for business annually. Three of these banks were in Richmond.

The first, Nickel Savings Bank, was founded in 1896 by Richard Fillmore Tancil.[17, ††]

Born enslaved in 1852 in northeast Virginia near Washington, D.C., Tancil went on to earn a medical degree from Howard University in 1882. He worked at the Central State Hospital near Richmond before opening a medical practice in the city's Church Hill neighborhood.[18, 19, 20, 21]

Tancil was known for his extensive work with the poor. He operated a soup kitchen out of his home for at least two winters, founded the People's Relief Association of Virginia and provided free medical services to those unable to pay.[22]

"He has a peculiar way of never pressing a bill for professional services and many a visit has he made for which he never received one penny," a local reporter wrote.[23] "In cases where his patients were in destitute circumstances he also furnished the medicine free of charge."

He established several professional and civic organizations, and he served as president of the Richmond Hospital Association, which opened a hospital for the city's Black population. Even while bank president, he continued his medical practice.

The motivation for founding the bank, he said, was "nothing but to help our people to help themselves."[24]

To encourage regular deposits, Nickel Savings implemented a system that had not been used previously in the South.[25] Depositors were provided with small, nickel-plated banks into which they could place coins and currency. Once every three months, depositors were required to bring the banks to Nickel Savings where a bank official with a key would remove the deposits and credit the amounts to a pass-book savings account. A minimum initial deposit of $1.50 was required to participate in the program.[26, ‡‡]

Despite its name, the bank was not purely focused on holding savings but also provided

†† The bank was located at 601 N. 30th Street, less than a mile east of St. John's Church, where Patrick Henry gave his legendary address on the eve of the Revolutionary War.

‡‡ While the Nickel Savings system may have been unique, the development of U.S. banks focused on serving low-income depositors began in the 1850s. The institutions were based on a European model where, initally, financial services were only provided to governments, the wealthy and large firms.

a range of financial services including lending to depositors and clearing checks. The latter service, however, was not without its challenges. When Richmond's first Black banks opened, they were not members of the local clearing house, the entity that handled interbank transactions. Without this connection, there was no mechanism for exchanging checks among the banks, which resulted in white banks refusing to accept checks written on accounts with the Black institutions. Eventually, local white merchants who served Black customers became the force for change when they threatened to close their bank accounts if the banks would not cash the checks. In response, one of the city's national banks stepped in to act as a clearing house agent.[27]

Nickel Savings' success eventually led to its expansion in the city with the opening of a branch location at 311 N. Fourth Street, the same building that was home to one of the era's most important and loudest voices in the fight for civil rights – *The Richmond Planet*.[28] There, the bank's story intertwines with the founding of another of the city's early Black banks.

The idea that *The Planet* would have its own building, let alone one with a bank branch, may have seemed highly unlikely only a few years earlier. In 1884, the publication was being operated out of the boardinghouse room of 21-year-old John Mitchell Jr., a former teacher, and future banker, who was fresh into his first publishing endeavor.

Born enslaved near Richmond in 1863, Mitchell was taught to read by his mother before attending private and public schools, graduating from Richmond's Normal and High School.[§§] His teaching career was brief – he was one of 10 Black teachers fired en masse by the school board – driving him to become editor, and effectively the publisher, of the then-upstart publication.[29]

The Planet was unsparing. Its articles revealed a degree of brutality unleashed by white supremacists that is difficult to read more than a century later. In its July 22, 1899, edition, as only one example, *The Planet* published a photo of three hanging bodies above a list of all of the known lynching victims in the United States between Jan. 5, 1897 and Jan. 5, 1898. It is a record of nearly 130 entries with each victim's name, race and the alleged transgression. All but 10 of the victims were "colored," with charges ranging from the serious – although perhaps manufactured – such as alleged murder and arson; to those where the reason listed

§§ Before attending public schools, Mitchell was a student at the private school of Baptist minister Anthony Binga Jr., who was a cousin to Jesse Binga, later founder of Chicago's Binga Bank. McCrery, Anne, Errol Somay and the Dictionary of Virginia Biography. "John Mitchell Jr. (1863–1929)." Encyclopedia Virginia. Virginia Humanities, 6 May. 2019.

was simply "nothing." In a number of instances, the supposed offense was little more than a minor affront. These included "troublesome," "wanted [to] drink soda water," "talked too much," "bad character," and "in white families [sic] room." One victim was noted to be an 8-year-old boy.[30]

Providing these types of details, as well as lengthy stories about individual hangings including those administered under the guise of the legal system, with photographs and sometimes Mitchell's own hand-drawn illustrations was not without risk. Coverage of the 1886 hanging of Dick Walker – the same event that is believed to have led the local True Reformers Fountain to nearly disband – prompted an anonymous letter to the paper, threatening to kill Mitchell if he dared to visit the community.

Mitchell published the threat in *The Planet,* along with a response that quoted a line from Shakespeare's "Julius Caesar":

There are no terrors, Cassius, in your threats, for I am armed so strong in honesty that they pass me by like the idle winds which I respect not.[31]

And then, with a pair of revolvers, he traveled more than 80 miles to visit both the jail where Walker had been held and the tree where he was murdered. No one challenged him during the visit.[32, 33, **] A contemporary later described the then-editor as "courageous, almost to a fault."[34]

Mitchell, who also won pardons for multiple individuals sentenced to death, became increasingly active in politics around 1890 and served on the city's board of aldermen. He joined Browne's True Reformers early in that organization's history and later took a leadership role with another fraternal order, the Virginia Knights of Pythias. This role, along with his influence in other related organizations, were pivotal to Mitchell's creation of the Mechanics Savings Bank in 1902. Deposits by the Knights provided the core around which the bank developed. As a result, it was sometimes known colloquially as the "Knights of Pythias Bank."[35, 36]

More than a decade earlier, during an address made to a True Reformers meeting, Mitchell offered some insight to his views on banking and business.

"Colored men, be your own masters, save up your money, love the mighty dollar,"

** As a result of this event, Mitchell is sometimes known as the "Fighting Editor." The name is on a historic marker erected in his honor in Richmond in 2012.

he said.[37]

"Rely upon yourselves. Freeze to the mighty dollar. Set up each other in business. Be honest, as you have always been. You have never been charged with stealing anything more than a chicken while the white brother has stolen a bank."

The bank's creation, and Mitchell's vision for its future, in some ways mirrored what Browne had done with the True Reformers, although initially the two men were of somewhat opposing views on achieving racial equality. Mitchell, as evidenced by the flexed muscular arm and clinched fist that appeared on *The Planet's* masthead, was more militant. The two men's views, however, came into closer alignment after Mitchell established the bank and through *The Planet* began to increasingly call for the creation of Black-owned businesses.[38]

Only two years after opening the bank, Mitchell was the first Black banker to attend the American Bankers Association's (ABA) annual convention in New York City in 1904.[39]

During the convention, Robert Foster Maddox, a white Atlanta banker who would later serve as that city's mayor, made a statement to the assembly that elicited an impromptu speech by Mitchell that made headlines nationwide.

Maddox's comments, which some onlookers saw as a clearly racist attempt at humor:

We the people of the South believe there is a middle course between social equality and lynching. The one is contrary to the law of nature, and the other contrary to the law of the land. Both tend to elevate the negro above his sphere and separate him from his friends.[40]

According to newspaper accounts, the statement received no reaction from attendees, other than Mitchell. He engaged the convention for 30 minutes with remarks that were:

- Fact filled: Black banks, he told the ABA's members, held $300,000 in deposits while Black workers produced goods worth more than $232 million in the past year.

- Pointedly humorous: After starting what appeared to be a likely verbal assault on Maddox, he stopped himself, paused and then said, "I like to hear a white man talk. No matter what he is talking about, there's something musical in his voice, even when he's abusing us. How I do like to hear a white man talk!"

- And affecting: "When I hear them abuse us – when the last day comes, the sunset sheds its last light on our earthly work, I shall say: 'Father, forgive them, for they know not what they do.'"[41]

At his conclusion, ABA members gave Mitchell a standing ovation.

While John Mitchell was making history in New York, another banker was making history in Richmond.

Born July 14, 1864, in Richmond, Maggie Lena Mitchell was raised by a single mother after the death of her stepfather. The girl, unrelated to John Mitchell, helped her mother, who worked as a laundress. She attended Richmond's segregated public schools where, at the age of 14, she became active in the Independent Order of St. Luke – a society established in 1867 with a mission similar to other societies that provided sick and burial benefits for their members.

After graduation, she taught for three years before marrying Armstead Walker Jr., turning her focus to raising her children. In her work with the order, Maggie Walker established councils in Virginia and West Virginia as a traveling organizer. In 1899, she was elected the society's national executive secretary treasurer – a position that was functionally the head of business operations, including membership and finance.

At the time of her election, the organization was in a precarious position. It had suffered the loss of a longtime leader and had $400 in outstanding debt against $31 in its treasury.

Wendell P. Dabney, a prominent writer during the era and a high school classmate of Walker's, said that she made St. Luke's successful "almost immediately."

"[Her] earnestness, diplomacy and oratorical ability … served as a magnet."

The organization's membership doubled within two years. At the order's 1901 annual meeting, Walker proposed a number of changes to the organization and a major expansion of its initiatives, many similar to what had occurred with the True Reformers and, to a lesser degree, the Pythians. The meeting also included what were likely Walker's first public remarks about creating a bank.

"We need a savings bank. Let us put our moneys together; let us use our moneys; let us put our money out at usury among ourselves and reap the benefit ourselves," she said.

"Let us have a bank that will take the nickels and turn them into dollars."

Under Walker's leadership, her vision was realized with the opening of the St. Luke

Penny Savings Bank in November 1903 in the St. Luke headquarters building at 900 James Street in Richmond. On the bank's first day, it received more than $8,000 in total deposits from 280 depositors, with amounts ranging from a few dollars to hundreds.

At the bank's helm, Walker almost immediately became a national figure.

Her travels to some of the country's major cities and speeches at numerous churches made headlines in *The Boston Globe, The New York Times, The Washington Post* and others.

She was one of the era's most prominent voices for Black equality and women's rights, including suffrage.

"We are Negro women … and we must make history as Negro women and make such history as will cause posterity to rise up and call us blessed," she told an audience in Newark, N.J.

Similar to the way the bank was only part of Walker's life, it was also only one of several initiatives created by the Independent Order of St. Luke. Over time, its operations expanded to include a store, a formalized insurance business, a printing press and a weekly newspaper, the *St. Luke Herald.* Each entity employed a number of Black women at Walker's direction, and the women were encouraged to save toward homeownership.

"When any one of our girls is advanced to making as much as $50 a month we begin to persuade her to buy a home," Walker said. "As soon as she saves enough for the first payment, the Bank will help her out."

In addition to its broader focus on homeownership, St. Luke Penny Savings was also involved in educating children about the importance of saving money. Similar to the nickel-plated banks used by Nickel Savings, St. Luke Penny Savings created small cardboard banks that could hold 100 pennies, creating the dollar necessary to open an account.

Notably, Walker provided a steady hand. The bank began construction on a new building at the corner of First and Marshall streets that opened the following year. In 1929, Walker led a merger with another Richmond Black-owned bank, the Second Street Savings Bank, creating Consolidated Bank and Trust. In 1931, the new bank merged with a third local Black-owned bank, Commercial Bank and Trust. Walker remained chair of the bank until her death in 1934. Consolidated, meanwhile, was acquired by Abigail Adams National Bank in 2005. It became Premiere Bank after a 2009 merger.

During Walker's lifetime, she served on numerous civic boards including the National Association of Colored Women and the Virginia Industrial School for Girls. She also helped locally organize the National Association for the Advancement of Colored People (NAACP) in Richmond and served on that organization's national board.

3.

That Richmond's Jackson Ward became one of the era's most renown economic and cultural hubs, was a testament to the Black bankers, entrepreneurs and artists who built it. That it existed as a defined district, however, was due in part to the efforts of the city's established white leadership trying to limit the influence of a burgeoning Black population on what was then the South's second largest city behind only New Orleans.

For emancipated slaves seeking jobs, Richmond was an attractive option, despite the city's Civil War history. Not only was it a significant transportation hub with prominent milling, iron and tobacco industries, but the city in the war's aftermath was also in desperate need of construction workers. In the war's final days, retreating Confederate soldiers hoping to thwart the Union Army's advance had set fire to military supplies and bridges across the James River at the city. Soon, the out-of-control blaze spread from the riverfront and into the city's core, destroying as much as 90 percent of the central business district.[42] The effort to slow the troops was, of course, unsuccessful and days later, Robert E. Lee surrendered to Ulysses S. Grant, ending the war.

Even then, Richmond already had a substantial Black population, accounting for nearly 40 percent of its total population, about one in every five living freely, primarily along the city's fringe.[43] With the ending of the war and the beginning of Reconstruction, many Black families began to move into an area northwest of the city's central business district.

The extension of voting rights to Black men during Reconstruction upended generations of whites-only control at all levels of Southern government. Between 1866 and 1880, around 1,300 Black politicians ranging from local school board members through governors won various elections, creating the South's first-ever multiracial governments.[44] In Richmond, white lawmakers in 1871 sought to limit the increasing government diversity by creating a new "Black" voting district, or ward, in the area that was home to 40 percent of the city's Black population. It was christened Jackson Ward, likely after either Joseph Jackson, who built a home there in the 1790s, or after James Jackson's beer garden, which was a popular neighborhood location in the 1820s.[45]

When Jackson Ward's boundaries were drawn, about 45 percent of Richmond's total population was Black. Jackson Ward had more Black voters than any of the city's six wards for much of the late 1800s, and its boundaries effectively capped Black representation in city government at one out of every six seats on the city's two publicly elected municipal boards.[46, 47, †††] And even that was not assured, because both politicians and voters still faced a long list of challenges including political opposition, violence and trumped-up legal charges that were used as a mechanism to disenfranchise voters.[48] The range of machinations took on nearly unimaginable forms. For example, in 1896, a Black man, J.W. Madison, apparently without any foreknowledge or involvement on his part, was listed on the ballot as a candidate for Richmond mayor by white supremacists who hoped such a move would ensure a large turnout by angry white voters.[49, ‡‡‡] In the same election, Black voters were delayed by around 20 minutes each as they attempted to vote in a single booth for the entire ward. "Gray headed men were asked all kinds of questions to delay time, and in many instances, the judges refused to vote colored men on their oaths."[50]

In spite of all of this, it appears Jackson Ward's Black officeholders and their few allies were able to wield a degree of political power in the late 1800s. During this period the city improved street lighting in Black neighborhoods, established an armory in Jackson Ward for the Black militia – albeit a significantly smaller building than similar facilities in other wards – and constructed a new school in the city's segregated education system.[51, 52, 53]

The forces that sought to limit Black participation in city government, however, were relentless. All Black candidates lost in a fraudulent 1900 election.[54] Soon, officials took another try at drawing district lines. This time, Jackson Ward was gerrymandered into a meandering ward that became known as the "shoestring district" because of its distorted shape. As a result, none of the city's voting districts then had a Black majority, thereby effectively eliminating the likelihood that even a single Black alderman could win election.[55, 56]

During this same time period, predominately white state governments throughout the former Confederacy, including Virginia in 1902, were rewriting state constitutions to disen-franchise Black voters through the implementation of measures such as poll taxes, educational requirements for voting and other restrictions that, in practice, would circumvent the voting rights granted to Black men under the 15th Amendment to the U.S. Constitution.[57] It

††† Richmond's municipal government included a mayor, a 30-member common council and a 12-member board of aldermen.

‡‡‡ This manipulation introduced a risk that likely surprised its perpetrators. Madison was running against the city's white mayor, R.M. Taylor. Under quirks of Virginia election law at the time, if Taylor had lost his life before the election, Madison would have won by default as the only name on the ballot. Newspaper accounts suggest this realization made Taylor fearful that he would become the target of a violent assault. *The Norfolk (Virginia) Virginian.* May 12, 1896.

would be nearly a century before a Black politician, Douglas Wilder, would win election to the Virginia Senate in 1969 and 15 additional years before Yvonne Miller broke the color barrier in the state's House of Delegates in 1984.

The many painful ramifications of the loss of franchise were perhaps best elaborated by W.E.B. Du Bois in his seminal work, "The Souls of Black Folk," published in 1903:

> To-day the Black man of the South has almost nothing to say as to how much he shall be taxed, or how those taxes shall be expended; as to who shall make the laws, and how they shall be made. It is pitiable that frantic efforts must be made at critical times to get law-makers in some States to even listen to the respectful presentation of the Black man's side of a current controversy. Daily the Negro is coming more and more to look upon law and justice, not as protecting safeguards, but as sources of humiliation and oppression. The laws are made by men who have little interest in him; they are executed by men who have absolutely no motive for treating the Black people with courtesy or consideration; and, finally, the accused law-breaker is tried not by his peers, but too often by men who would rather punish ten innocent Negroes than let one guilty one escape.[58]

It is in no way coincidental that this was the time that John Mitchell became involved in banking.

"You men of business told us negroes to eschew politics and take to business," Mitchell said at the 1904 ABA meeting. "Before that, we had tried religion first, but we had found out we weren't ready for heaven. Then we had tried politics, but after 30 years you drew us out of that. Now we have tried finance and business. Here we expect no discrimination. A man is judged by his worth. The colored man is respected just in proportion as he respects himself. That is so in the South as it is elsewhere. We have found that the way for us to reach success and respect is through finance."[59]

While the Jackson Ward political district was redrawn to thwart Black political will, the *community* of "Jackson Ward" remained as it was previously defined. It was home for a substantial Black population, the majority of which were confined to low-level jobs at the city's white-owned businesses and firms, particularly industrial jobs. In response, the Jackson Ward "community embraced the admonition not to shop where they could not work," and instead embarked on a process that "developed a vibrant and commercial economy that was their own."[60]

In this transition, the creation of the city's four Black banks "proved to be the most important event in the … principal 'incubator of black capitalism,' in the United States."[61] The result was that "within the context of an uncertain political situation," Jackson Ward as a community was able to develop "considerable economic and social strength," which included the emergence of a Black middle class.[62]

The Black banks, meanwhile, continued to provide leadership in the push for civil rights, including standing at the forefront in a boycott of the city's segregated streetcar system.

In America's civil rights history, the Montgomery, Alabama, bus boycott of the mid-1950s is a watershed moment. Rosa Parks' refusal to relinquish her seat to a white passenger while on her way home from work sparked one of the nation's most prominent large-scale civil rights protests, which in turn led to an eventual Supreme Court ruling mandating integration of the Montgomery's public buses under the 14th Amendment. It also introduced to the world the then 26-year-old minister Martin Luther King Jr., who was president of the Montgomery Improvement Association.

More than a generation earlier, however, similar boycotts were organized in many Southern cities to fight streetcar segregation measures implemented around 1900. These measures followed the even earlier segregation of public horse carts during the Reconstruction era.[63]

The segregation of the Virginia Passenger and Power Company's Richmond streetcars was mandated by state legislation passed in 1904 and immediately prompted action by the city's Black community. While other communities in the South responded similarly, in other cities it was church leaders who were at the forefront, as was the case in Savannah, Georgia.[64] In Richmond, the city's four Black banks led with a particularly bold step: They collectively pledged financial support for any initiative that would create an alternative mass transportation system. While the announcement of this offer caused a stir at a Jackson Ward community meeting held in a packed True Reformers auditorium, at least as important, if not more, was the urging of peaceful protest.

Mitchell believed that part of the motivation behind streetcar segregation was to "goad the colored people" into confrontation. Streetcar operators basically had carte blanch to implement the law as they saw fit on their vehicles. They were armed and many were considered "ill-tempered men" who had only recently become conductors, hired as replacements for regular drivers who had gone on strike the previous year. Mitchell feared that if Black passengers resisted orders to move to the back of the car, they risked not only arrest, but also their lives.[65]

"The 'Jim Crow' street car service for Richmond is an innovation to which the progressive, independent colored people of this city will hardly care to submit," Mitchell wrote. "Walking is good now – let us walk."[66]

Across the South, the boycotts had varying degrees of success, ranging from reduced profitability – systems in both Savannah, Georgia, and Houston, Texas, noted they were particularly hard hit – to decisions by some local operators to simply ignore segregation statutes, which happened in Jacksonville, Florida, and for a brief period in Mobile, Alabama.[67]

In Richmond, widespread support of the boycott in the Black community, coupled with the fallout from the previous year's worker strike that had increased operating costs, wound up bankrupting the system by summer 1904. At the time of the bankruptcy, only one Black passenger had been ticketed on a streetcar in the three months since the start of the boycott – a woman who was fined $10 because she wanted to sit near an open window.[68]

4.

Richmond's Black business district was burgeoning in the years before and after the streetcar segregation issue. In 1902, the city was home to several Black-owned grocers, restaurants, multiple newspapers of various publication schedules and a 150-bed hotel. These businesses were in addition to the banks and other providers of financial services, including insurance firms, as well as a number of sole proprietorships in the services sector such as barbershops, carpenters and professionals including attorneys, doctors and dentists.

The True Reformers, the organization with the most extensive operations during this period, had not only its Richmond grocery store but also similar stores in four other cities. Combined, the independently operated stores had total sales in 1901 of around $3 million in modern amounts and 335 employees.[69]

In the years that followed, Jackson Ward economic development continued with more Black entrepreneurs "doing business in Richmond on their own account than any other city of similar size."[70] For comparison purposes: According to an 1899 survey, the city was then home to a total of 28 Black businesses, but by 1910, nearly as many firms were located along a single four-block stretch of North Second Street – known as "The Deuce" – including the True Reformers Bank, three Black-owned insurance companies, three benevolent societies, two attorneys, a doctor, a dentist, three real estate offices, a funeral home, four grocery stores, three confectionaries, barbers, tailors and shoemakers.[71, 72] Jackson Ward was by this time a financial and cultural Main Street for a thriving city-within-a-city spanning more than 40 blocks that included at least 10 churches. Brick row houses and town homes with intricately designed cast-iron porch rails and fences lined many of its residential streets. Meanwhile, its business community included numerous theaters and social clubs. Over the years, the legends who performed for Jackson Ward audiences included Billie Holiday, Cab Calloway, James Brown and many others.

Virginians were among the nation's strongest adherents of "racial parallelism." This social construct, which was supported by some within both the Black and white communities, was based on the idea that interracial harmony was best achieved with separate social and economic structures for each race. To a degree, such a social contract both created and limited the opportunities for Black business owners. While Black businesses might be assured of a customer base within their communities, they would be left unable to expand beyond a certain level.[73] Thus, as America's industrial engine started to crank to life in the earliest years of the 1900s, "Black business remained on the periphery, a shadow economy, its profits eclipsed by the financial giants of the age."[74]

At the dawn of the 20th century, the Census Bureau pegged the U.S. Black population at 8.8 million residents while total Black wealth at that time was around $700 million, which equates to about $80 each, or a little over $2,000 in modern amounts.[75]

Nationally, some were able to achieve substantial financial success, but their numbers were few. Probably the most well-known was Madam C.J. Walker's cosmetics and hair care products business. Sarah Breedlove, who started the business in 1905, was believed to be the nation's first self-made female millionaire of any race by the time of her death in 1919. Lists of other large Black-owned businesses from this era that might be considered a tier or more below Breedlove's include a large silk plant, a foundry, multiple stores and several agricultural enterprises.[76]

"The Negro has no Morgans, no Rothschilds, no Mantel Brothers, no Mark Hannas, nor Rockefellers," said Giles B. Jackson, the first Black attorney to argue before the Virginia Supreme Court of Appeals and author of the True Reformers Bank charter. "Every Negro started with nothing, worked himself up slowly, and by strict attention to business, and by sometimes the severest deprivation attained his present height."[77]

Thus, for local Black banks, not only were savings accounts small, but lending opportunities were limited. While the economic development of the Jackson Ward neighborhood was impressive relatively few potential borrowers needed regular access to credit for things like inventory or expansion.[78] Nationally around this time, it was believed that 80 percent of all Black-owned businesses had less than $2,500 in capital.[79]

Absent other opportunities to provide credit, much of the lending by Richmond's four Black banks was concentrated in real estate. Like any bank, the True Reformers' lending portfolio varied over time. In general terms, the bank was significantly involved in mortgage lending and real estate development, especially in the few years after 1900. A substantial focus, and one that reflects the catalyst behind its creation, was its heavy investment in financing the various True Reformer subsidiary operations including the store and hotel.[80] During the financial turmoil of the late 1800s – including recessions from January 1893 through June 1894 and another from December 1895 through June 1897 – the bank was more resilient than many financial institutions of a similar size. Perhaps most famously, in September 1893, when Richmond's other banks refused to provide currency for the school district to pay its janitors in cash at the height of the crisis, True Reformers cashed the district's checks.[81]

The Mechanics Bank, meanwhile became one of the era's largest Black enterprises. At its height in 1919, the bank had more than $500,000 in deposits, or the equivalent of more than $7.5 million in modern amounts. While it was a small bank, it is important when considering total deposits to keep in mind the era's environment for a Black financial institution. A majority of its accounts held less than $100, or the equivalent of around $1,500 for a modern saver. Still, the bank was an important source of credit. Like the True Reformers Bank, Mechanics was heavily involved in real estate, and it also provided financing that funded the Black Woodlawn Cemetery and other endeavors.[82]

The banks were also important in one of the most prominent events of the era. In 1902, Jackson Ward hosted the third annual meeting of the National Negro Business League (NNBL), which was founded by Booker T. Washington in 1900 to further Black economic development. This particular meeting was the organization's first gathering in a Southern state, with its previous annual events held in Boston and Chicago.[§§§]

Washington's opening night address was the highlight of the three-day session. Standing before more than 2,000 attendees packed into the third-floor auditorium of Browne's True Reformers headquarters, Washington urged the group to embrace the leadership mantle:

> The type of minister who heretofore has spent his time in merely traveling from one community to the other, without a home of his own, without a bank account, without financial credit, will more and more lose his influence as a leader. The people are beginning to look for leadership in the type of man who owns his home, who has a bank account, who has the respect and confidence of not only the Black people, but the white people in the community where he lives. By the side of every church I want to see well cultivated farms owned by our people. By the side of every certificate of church membership I want to see a bank book.[83]

§§§ In the mid-1960s, the NNBL was reincorporated as the National Business League.

Boley, Oklahoma

I.

Hollie I. West may have put Boley, Oklahoma, on the modern-day map in a figurative sense.

His family helped to do it literally.

West was born and raised in Wewoka, Oklahoma, a small town east of Oklahoma City and capital of the Seminole Nation of Oklahoma. It is smaller now than it was when West was a child, but even then it seemed an unlikely starting point for one of *The Washington Post's* most well-known journalists. He covered Martin Luther King Jr. He was with Stokely Carmichael, the civil rights icon and original Freedom Rider who coined the race slogan "Black Power," on the streets of Washington D.C. in the hours after King's assassination.[1] An extensive interview with fellow Oklahoman Ralph Ellison produced a lengthy three-part article that is an essential read for those wanting a full understanding of the "Invisible Man" author. The numerous other important social and civil rights icons interviewed by West ranged from author James Baldwin to "The Greatest," Muhammad Ali. West had a strong affection for jazz and spent time with and writing about many of the genre's legends including Duke Ellington, Miles Davis and Dizzy Gillespie.

West's work was extremely popular with *Post* readers. In turn, *Post* editors afforded him column inches to a degree the paper's other journalists no doubt envied.

"I was interested in writing about how Americans interacted with each other and the only way to do that was through a feature piece or a long piece," he said.[2]

In 1975, one of those pieces focused on Boley.

"It's 40 miles from where I grew up," he later said. "In fact, I used to visit this town regularly when I was a kid."

His mother was raised there. And his grandmother was a McCormick, a prominent family of local community leaders. Although Boley of the mid-1970s was past its prime, West convinced his editors it was worthy of a *Post* story. The readers loved it.

"They hailed it. [The editor] said, 'If we can get a story like that once a month, we'd love you.' I said, 'It's hard to get one of those.'

"It was a thriving community back in the '20s, '30s and '40s."

As he wrote in 1975:

The time was ... when Boley couldn't be missed for the filling stations and cafes dotting the highway, trucks and horse-drawn wagons exiting the town. Boley was a mecca in the early part of the century for hundreds of Blacks fleeing the racial persecution and terrorism of the post-Reconstruction Deep South.[3]

His article begins with the words to a poem, or perhaps lyrics to a song, written by E.J. Pinkett, a man known locally as Uncle Jesse around the time of Boley's founding:

Say, have you heard the story,
   Of a little colored town;
Way over in the Nation,
   On such lovely sloping ground?
With as pretty little houses
   As you ever chanced to meet.
With not a thing but colored folks,
   A-standing in the streets?
Oh, tis a pretty country
   And the Negroes own it, too,
With not a single white man here
   To tell us what to do – In Boley.

The Civil War's end presented the nation's emancipated slaves with essentially two options for finding employment: They could stay in rural areas, labor in agriculture and, in some cases, start their own small farms; or they could head to one of the nation's cities to find work – for many this initially meant a Southern city like Richmond. Others, however, focused on a third option: fleeing the former Confederacy. This path became especially popular after the failure of Reconstruction in 1877. When the last federal troops departed the South, they left open a door to racial violence, segregation and discrimination that would continue unabated for generations.

"We had much rather stayed there [in the South] if we could have had our rights [but] in 1877 we lost all hopes ... we found ourselves in such condition that we looked around and we [saw] that there was no way on earth ... that we could better our condition there ... " said Henry Adams, a former Louisiana slave. "The whole South – every state in the

South – had got into the hands of the very men that held us as slaves...

"Then we said there was no hope for us and we had better go."[4]

J.L. McCormick Jr., who would spend much of his adult life as a lawman in Oklahoma, recalled in 1975 why his family had fled Alabama in 1891 for Indian Territory:

> My father looked down the road one morning and saw a bunch of white people leading a negro boy tied to a buggy. He was the son of a man accused of molesting a white woman. Dad saw his family doctor driving the buggy. He was a white fellow. And my father respected him – thought he was quite a man. But they lynched this colored boy. So my father said, 'Wife, I'm going to gather this crop and leave this doggone place.' And he did.[5]

This initial post-war exodus from the South was more than a generation before the start of the more well-known, and far more substantial, Great Migration of Black workers and families who migrated to urban centers, particularly in the upper Midwest, in hopes of securing manufacturing jobs. These earlier Black migrants, referred to as "Exodusters," saw their opportunities not in northern factories and foundries, but in the open spaces of the American West, starting with the windswept Kansas plains before developing elsewhere.[*]

There, they began to establish towns where most, if not all, of the population was Black. Among the most notable of these were Nicodemus, Kansas, Dearfield, Colorado; and settlements in central and western Nebraska with names that have long since been lost to time.[6]

No state, however, rivaled the area that is now Oklahoma. More than 50 Black towns and settlements were established in the state before the 1920s, and perhaps the most successful of these was Boley.[7]

The development of a large number of Black communities in Oklahoma was in part a result of the state's location and its proximity to the Confederate South. However, there were other factors involved that are specific to the Sooner state. All states have their own histories, but Oklahoma's is no doubt unique – perhaps rivaled only by Louisiana in the mixture of cultures that compose its heritage.

---

[*] Although the term "exodus," when used to describe the movement of southern Blacks to the Great Plains, is often used in historical discussion to refer only to the wave of activity in 1879, the actual migration was not limited to a single year.

Before exploring Boley – and specifically its two Black-owned banks – it is first beneficial to understand Oklahoma's history and other aspects of America's often painful racial history including the federal government's treatment of Native Americans and, along with that, tribal slavery structures.

2.

The land that would later become modern-day Oklahoma was the established home to a number of Native American tribes when it was acquired by the United States with the Louisiana Purchase in 1803. Wichitas, Plains Apaches, Quapas and Caddos had all called the area home during the Spanish and French colonial period. By the early 1800s, some Chickasaws, Osages, Kiowas, Comanches and others had either migrated into the area or relied on its resources, particularly the state's rich hunting grounds.[8]

In 1830, the United States government began forcing additional tribes from the eastern United States onto this land, known as Indian Territory. To free areas in the East for white settlement within established states, the Indian Removal Act gave the president the authority to grant Native American tribes land west of the Mississippi River – effectively within modern-day Oklahoma – in exchange for tribal homelands east of the Mississippi River. The following year, the Choctaw Nation, which had already ceded some lands a decade earlier, left central Mississippi for Indian Territory, beginning a process that would continue for years with President Andrew Jackson signing around 70 removal treaties to move 50,000 Native Americans. Among the more prominent events in this period was the forced removal of the Cherokee along what became known as "The Trail Where They Cried" or the "Trail of Tears," where an estimated 4,000 Cherokees died.[9]

Perhaps less well known is that Native tribes were slave owners who, in the case of the Cherokee, brought their slaves with them West to Oklahoma. There, slave labor was used to establish Native communities in the new territory.[10]

Prior to the arrival of Europeans, some native North American societies, such as the Aztecs, had practiced forms of slavery or forced labor for some time.[11] Eventually, however, some North American tribes began to implement a more European-style slave culture, enslaving Black individuals instead of members of rival tribes or those taken as prisoners of war. This transition may have been initiated by tribe members of mixed European and Native American heritage.[12] Similar to the way a Southern plantation owner might point to his large number of slaves as a status symbol, Native tribes may have owned slaves both for the work they could do, but possibly also as a tribal symbol of wealth and status.[13]

At the time the Civil War began, the Oklahoma Indian Territory was home to around 86,000 Native Americans and likely somewhere between 8,000 and 14,000 slaves.[14] While the Territory was not officially a part of the Confederacy in the way that individual states were, by late 1861 the Confederacy had negotiated treaties with the Cherokee, Choctaw,

Chickasaw, Creek and Seminole nations in Indian Territory. Collectively, this was the group referred to by U.S. officials as the Five Civilized Tribes – the demeaning term drawn from the adoption, to varying degrees, of what were considered European social structures and their engagement with European settlers.[15]

It should be emphasized that, despite these agreements with the Confederacy, not all Native Americans implemented slavery in the same fashion. Even today, debate continues about how slavery among Native American tribes differed from the practices of Southern plantation owners. One way this difference has been described by academics and historians is a "slave society," versus a "society with slaves." In the Confederacy – a true "slave society" – slaves were the dominant labor source and, as a result, influenced every other social relationship within that society. In a "society with slaves" – such as those existing in some Native American tribes – slaves were one part of a labor structure that included other workers, mitigating the influence of slavery on other social relationships.[16] This is a very fine distinction and also one that may be vulnerable to overgeneralization since the treatment of slaves varied widely by tribe. The Choctaw and Chickasaw, for example, were generally viewed as the most extreme in alignment with Southern ideals, while the Creeks and Seminoles were far more liberal, allowing intermarriage and letting fugitive slaves live on their land unmolested. Some Cherokees, meanwhile, formed a secret abolitionist organization and had more soldiers fighting in support of the Union than with the Confederacy.[17, 18] It should be no surprise that this issue was a source of disagreement within some tribes to the point that some tribal members fled the territory rather than align with Confederates.

The pacts between the tribes and the Confederacy were thus not purely about the institution of slavery. They also were based in a shared distrust of the United States government among the tribes and a concern that, if there were not agreements with the Confederates, the tribes could be vulnerable to a Confederate military attack.

Regardless of the reasoning behind the pacts, the United States government viewed them each as essentially a declaration of war that nullified all previous agreements between the United States and the tribes. Because of this, new treaties were drawn up that set in motion sweeping cultural changes.

The treaties required that tribal slaves be not only emancipated, but that they also were recognized as tribe members, although the administration of the latter was entirely at the discretion of each tribe. There was significant variance. While the Creek and Seminole, for example, awarded full citizenship, the Cherokee, who had emancipated their slaves in

1863, granted citizenship only to those meeting certain residency requirements. At the other extreme, the Chickasaw and Choctaw implemented their own version of "Black Codes" in the war's aftermath, very similar to what occurred among white governments in the South.[19]

From a modern-day perspective, the reasoning behind the tribal membership provision, as opposed to simply granting the former slaves freedom, may not be apparent. The decision reflected the belief that some enslaved people owned by Native Americans may have had very little in common with slaves held on Confederate plantations. Instead, their lifestyle reflected Native American culture in innumerable ways including language – many did not speak English – food, clothing and community structure. To differentiate between the slaves and the Indians, the term Freedman was applied to the tribal name. For example, a former Creek Slave became a Creek Freedman.[20, †, ‡]

The Reconstruction treaties also marked a major step toward eventual white settlement. Tribes were forced to relinquish a significant amount of the land they had been allocated and provide rights-of-way for railroad construction through tribal lands. The railroad was an area where the region severely lagged developments in the rest of the United States and the nation's other territories. Although surveying for an east-west rail line across the territory had been completed 1853, the Civil War had prevented any actual construction.[21] When the federal government awarded construction rights to begin building the first rail line in Indian Territory in 1870, not only were neighboring states far along in rail building, but also the first trans-continental line across North America had already been completed.

The arrival in Oklahoma of railroad workers from other areas of the United States, the migration of homesteading "Sooners" who came to the territory ahead of the opening for settlement, and the eventual 1889 Land Rush of settlers to what is today central Oklahoma and the later opening of other areas to migrant settlers, all soon brought increasing numbers of non-Native Americans to what were then the "twin territories" of Oklahoma Territory and Indian Territory.

Meanwhile, the federal government began the process of allotment which saw, over a number of years, the division of communal tribal lands into individual properties. In addition,

† This designation of former slaves as tribe members was at the crux of a legal battle in the 2000s involving the Cherokee Nation and the descendants of the former slaves, known as Cherokee Freedmen.

‡ A far more detailed discussion of the various tribal differences in this era can be found in: Grinde, Donald A., Jr., and Quintard Taylor. Red vs. Black Conflict and Accommodation in the Post Civil War Indian Territory, 1865 – 1907. American Indian Quarterly. Vol. 8, No. 3., (summer 1984) pp. 211-229.

tribes were forced to sell or cede land – including some that were opened for settlement – to the federal government. For example, the Five Tribes were forced to relinquish land for western tribes including the Cheyenne, Arapaho, Kiowa, Comanche and Apache.[22]

3.

For years, the idea of a Black territory in North America had "never been far from the center of Black thought."[23, §] At one of the earliest meetings about potentially forming a Black bank in the United States, held in 1851 in New York City, there was discussion about how a bank could provide a source of funding for establishing Black homesteads, particularly in the American West.[24, **] Later, perhaps as many as 40,000 Black settlers relocated to the West with the help of individuals including Nashville's Benjamin "Pap" Singleton and Louisiana's Henry Adams.[25] These relocations were in addition to small settlements established in Canada and the Great Lakes region of the United States.

Among the proposals for an organized initiative to create a dedicated Black territory, there were legislative proposals that received at least a degree of attention in both 1864 and 1879, while in 1874 a Black convention in Alabama formally established a committee to study the potential of creating a Black state.

As might be anticipated, such proposals were divisive. While supporters in both races saw in them the potential for creating communities that would spotlight Black resilience, independence and success, there were others who saw them as a means to make Black Americans "virtual outcasts" outside of the parameters of America's mainstream social and economic structures.[26] Such concerns aligned with the views of Frederick Douglass who, in considering the creation of a Black territory, said he believed that the "business of this nation is to protect its citizens where they are, not to transport them where they will not need protection."[27]

This debate aside, the number of Black settlers on America's central Plains continued to grow in the years after the Civil War, particularly in Kansas. Between 1870 and 1880, the state's Black population more than doubled from 16,000 to more than 43,000 – nearly a quarter of them not migrants, but Kansas-born.[28]

During this period, a key figure in the later Black migration to Oklahoma arrived on the Plains: Edward P. McCabe.

§ These initiatives were separate from the American Colonization Society's creation in the early 1800s of a colony on Africa's west coast that later became Liberia.

** These efforts did not advance. For more about efforts to establish the first Black banks in the United States, see: Todd, Tim. "Let Us Put Our Money Together: The Founding of America's First Black Banks." Federal Reserve Bank of Kansas City. 2019.

Born in Troy, New York, in 1850, McCabe moved often as a young man and earned a law degree in Chicago before coming to Kansas in 1878.[29] He made a home near Nicodemus, the western Kansas town then being founded by Black settlers from Kentucky. Soon, he was elected county clerk and, in 1882, state auditor, making him Kansas' first Black elected state official.

Around the same time that McCabe's political fortunes were rising, the idea of establishing a Black region within the Oklahoma and Indian territories began to receive some support. A group of Black petitioners from Kansas and other states unsuccessfully sought Congressional approval to move into unoccupied areas of Indian Territory in 1882.[30] Meanwhile, the idea of a Black state or territory was backed by Kansas' Republican press with Black colonization of the region actively promoted by immigration societies, including most notably the Topeka-based Oklahoma Immigration Association. Among other efforts, these groups sent agents across the South, promoting Oklahoma as "as land where you will be free and your rights respected."[31]

McCabe became a central figure in the initiative around 1890 when he arrived in Oklahoma after spending time in Washington, D.C., where he had focused on Black voting and civil rights initiatives while also likely trying to gain for himself a leadership position in Oklahoma, perhaps as territorial governor.[32]

As might be assumed, the various issues that had emerged in earlier discussions about creating exclusively Black enclaves in other areas of the United States became even more contentious and complex in Oklahoma where there was opposition among both white settlers and Native Americans. Additionally complicating the issue was the belief that the Black state initiative, led by an established politician in McCabe, was possibly more concerned with creating a Republican political base in Oklahoma than an opportunity for Black Americans.[33] The influence of political interests in the initiative is supported by the fact that McCabe initially focused on locating Black families across political districts in such a manner that they would eventually form a voting majority in each – effectively a reverse version of what had occurred with Richmond's voting wards. Much of the administration of this fell to associates and relied to a degree on utilizing previously abandoned dwellings and properties for Black families who were "willing to undergo all kinds of hardships if they could secure forty acres of land, freedom and 'independence.'"[34]

McCabe's vision of a Black state obviously did not advance and was finally abandoned, although he was by no means a failure, regardless of his motivation.[††] One noteworthy accomplishment was his involvement in establishing Langston in 1890, northeast of Oklahoma City and named for Black Virginia congressman John Mercer Langston. The community is home to Langston University, founded in 1897, Oklahoma's only historically Black college or university.[‡‡] Also, although newspaper reports from this era are notorious for exaggeration, one account credited McCabe's effort with attracting as many as 10,000 Black settlers to the state.[35] His promotional efforts had very much opened a door, and among those who came through was Thomas Haynes.

Born in 1869 in northeast Texas, Haynes grew up near the banks of the Red River, dividing Texas from Indian Territory to the north. The environment was similar to what was found in much of the South with increasing Black political involvement of the post-war era countered by white supremacists, often with violence. In 1899, Haynes left Texas for Oklahoma Territory, settling temporarily perhaps near current-day Oklahoma City before migrating in 1901 to the Creek Nation, south of Tulsa. There he constructed a dugout while selling wood cut from the property.[36, 37, 38]

For construction workers building the nearby Fort Smith and Western Railroad, Haynes' dugout became a popular gathering place. The nearest settlements were 15 miles away, so workers generally camped in the area or stayed with Haynes in one of two rooms he offered for rent.[39, 40] Among them was a white overseer named John Boley.

Boley was friends with Lake Moore, one of three founders of nearby Weleetka, Oklahoma[41, 42] The two were considered "progressives by the standards of the period" – especially Moore, who was known to confront local racists and "engage in arguments in defense of the ... [Black] race."[43] When one of the arguments focused on Black self-government, Boley suggested to Moore the establishment of a Black town as a way of proving the doubters wrong.

[††] It is not clear, based on media accounts from the era, whether McCabe profited financially from his initiative. Some suggested McCabe was significantly involved in land speculation while others said he simply promoted the idea of a Black community. "Regardless of his motives, McCabe did much to promote Black immigration to Oklahoma." Littlefield, Daniel F., Jr., and Lonnie E. Underhill. "Black Dreams and 'Free' Homes: The Oklahoma Territory, 1891-1894." Phylon, Vol. 34, No. 4 (Q4 1973) pp. 342-357.

[‡‡] Langston was also home to a bank, but the institution is not found on any contemporaneous lists of the era's Black banks. This may be an oversight on the early lists. It is also quite possible the institution was partly owned by white investors, as was most likely the case with a bank in Nicodemus, Kansas, and other communities. In many instances, the establishment of Black towns involved white speculators. See Walker, Juliet E. K. The History of Black Business in America: Capitalism, Race, Entrepreneurship. Macmillan/Prentice Hall International: New York, N.Y./ London, 1998, pp. 173.

In putting forward this idea, Boley almost assuredly knew this was something that Haynes had attempted to establish previously but had been thwarted by land ownership restrictions, which had since been eased. It was Haynes' view that "the excellent soil and pure water in a country which needed development" had made for an ideal location for an all-Black community that he hoped to found near his property and name Oxford.[44]

Moore decided to move forward with the idea. He leased 80 acres from James Barnett, a Creek Freedman and widower who made the agreement on behalf of a young daughter who had been allotted land near the rail line.[45, §§] This 1903 agreement would be followed a year later by a purchase of the land and other deals with the Barnetts as the town of Boley, Oklahoma emerged.

§§ The decision to name the community Boley, instead of Barnett, was reportedly the result of a coin flip. Haynes called "heads" and won the right to name the town.

4.

Thomas Haynes, the obvious choice for townsite manager, essentially built Boley. And while he certainly had help from James Barnett among others, it is hard to overstate Haynes' involvement. He cleared the ground for streets by hand, but more importantly he "was particularly vocal in articulating a vision of Boley that elevated the pedestrian and arduous tasks of forest clearing and lot surveying to the loftier status of Black civilization building. Haynes imagined that he and those who joined him could create … a 'modern Jerusalem,' of the 20th century for African Americans."[46] Boley drew families from Texas, Alabama, Florida, Georgia, Mississippi and Louisiana the following year. It was officially incorporated in spring 1905 with the first town election in May – an event where many Boley residents voted for the first time in their lives.[47]

Almost immediately, a community bank was established.

Local newspaper accounts suggest the idea for a bank was something community leaders had been discussing for some time. During a March meeting of the Business Men's League of Boley, the Farmers and Merchants Bank of Boley was organized with plans for $15,000 in capital stock. At the time, there were around 20 Black banks in the United States; however, most of the others had been created either in conjunction with or closely affiliated with a fraternal organization or insurance provider. Farmers and Merchants was among the first of a new kind of institution – one purely focused on the traditional business of banking, which would determine its viability.

"The corporation is composed of some of the best farmers and business men of Boley, and as a colored institution, in a town exclusively designed for colored people, there seems to be no reason why it should not be as prosperous a bank as any in the Indian Territory," read an article in Boley's local newspaper, *The Weekly Progress.*[48]

Among the founders were Haynes and D.J. Turner, a longtime acquaintance.

Turner had come to Indian Territory as a boy in the 1880s, likely living with an older brother who had married into a Native American family.[49] Haynes convinced him to move to Boley soon after its founding where Turner opened Turner's Drug Store. In addition to serving as a pharmacy and retailer, the store also provided something of an informal bank for the community. Turner owned a safe, and local residents as well as newcomers would take their money to Turner for safekeeping. It is unknown whether Turner provided additional services, such as lending, although there are mentions of Turner operating with some type of structure over the financial services businesses, potentially as a trust company.[50] If so, this structure may have closely reflected those used by early merchant bankers in the United States. [***]

When the Farmers and Merchants Bank opened it served a community that included around 20 businesses.[51, 52] Around this same time, Booker T. Washington visited Boley as part of a weeklong journey through the territory and said the community was "the most enterprising and in many ways the most interesting of the Negro towns in the United States."[53]

In late 1907, the town added another bank, Boley Bank and Trust, founded in large part by E.L. Lugrande. Originally from Denton County, Texas, Lugrande came to Boley after selling Texas land that had increased in value nearly tenfold since his purchase of it. In Boley, he was again engaged in real estate and farming as well as later opening an insurance business.[54, 55] Boley Bank and Trust merged with Farmers and Merchants Bank in early 1910.

Each institution was a true community bank in every sense of the term, with not only local officers and shareholders, but also in providing community leadership. Haynes had convinced Hilliard Taylor, a former Houston, Texas, city alderman, to open a cotton gin in Boley instead of another city in Oklahoma, as had been his original plan.[56, 57] Turner, meanwhile, was a driving force for all kinds of development.

"There has never been an enterprise that has succeeded at Boley that has not had his cooperation," wrote Theo Baughman, a traveling reporter for the *Topeka Plaindealer*. When it came to developments that would help the community, Turner was "ready to work and spend his money to make it a success."[58]

Baughman, who reported on Boley regularly, described Turner as "a character who will curse you out and then turn right around and do more for you than anyone else."

As would be expected, the banks were heavily involved in agricultural lending and real estate.[59] In the 1910s, typical Farmers and Merchants loans were for a few hundred dollars at 2 percent monthly interest.[60] Anecdotally, around 75 percent of the farmers around Boley were Black, and the average farm was less than 100 acres.[61] For these producers, Farmers and Merchants would most likely have been the only option for obtaining financing.

In 1910, a local resident named B.F. Brown wrote an article for the city's *Weekly Progress* newspaper, urging local patronage of the bank, specifically noting farm financing.

"When you do business through your local bank you are laying the foundation on which you will be able to secure money to make your crop or buy your farm," Brown wrote. "To have a greater Boley, we must have a substantial bank."[62]

[***] As Turner's role with the bank increased, the pharmacy was operated by California Taylor.

Thanks to aggressive marketing across the South, including a network of traveling agents and promotion through numerous Black churches, Boley continued to grow.[63]

"In 1905 and 1906 people came to Boley by the train loads. In some instances eight to ten families would alight from the same train," Hallie S. Jones, an early Boley resident, later recalled. "Their luggage would fill the depot platform and would be piled six and seven feet high. Gangs like that started Boley off in a big way."[64]

One newspaper account touted the arrival of about 500 migrants to the region by train over only a few days in December 1910.[65]

By 1920, the community was home to 82 businesses.[66] The following year, another bank was established. The First National Bank of Boley became the first Black-owned bank in the United States with a national charter when it opened for business in September 1921. Among its founders were J.D. Nelson, a longtime local educator who had become school superintendent, and Sebrone Jones King.

King, who served as bank president, was a successful businessman near Kilgore in east-central Texas, operating a peach orchard and sawmill, in addition to other business interests. He came to Boley in 1910 after a dispute over a boxcar that King had reserved to ship peaches from his Texas orchard. When a white man tried to claim the boxcar for his own use, King produced the necessary paperwork and won the dispute. That evening, however, a posse of men in white hoods paraded past his home. Fearful for his family's safety, King loaded everything he had on five rail cars: his wife, children, furniture, farm equipment, animals, and enough lumber to build an Oklahoma home and a new beginning.[67]

Near Boley, King acquired nearly 500 acres of land – a parcel nearly five times the size of the average area farm. In town, he established a cotton gin, referring to himself in newspaper advertisements as the "old reliable ginman," while also working as a vet.[68, 69]

The bank was "born of the desire to help develop the resources of our community and assist in the realization of a Boley commercially awake, progressive and strong," according to one account.[70]

The banks, King's cotton gin and some of the town's other businesses were not only important for the local economy; the ownership of such economic engines by men who were not white was of extreme symbolic importance.[71] For those who came to the Boley area from rural areas of Texas, Arkansas and Mississippi in search of cheap land and an opportunity to farm, they instead found a vibrant community to a degree that might be difficult for 21st century Boley visitors to fully appreciate.

For example, the modern era's one-story post office building on Pecan Street with its covered-over windows and face of concrete block was originally a three-story Masonic Temple that, around the time of its 1915 construction, was one of the tallest buildings in eastern Oklahoma.[72, †††] City leaders worked aggressively to convince the Masons to construct the building in Boley with Haynes and Turner both among the largest contributors to a building fund for a construction project that would total about $1.3 million in modern amounts.[73, 74] Once completed, the facility included offices for the justice of the peace and the telephone company. Other local businesses lining Pecan Street, the city's main business throughfare, included hotels, grocery stores, restaurants and multiple retailers. At a time when America's stores stacked merchandise to the ceiling behind the service counter, one Boley retailer employed 12 clerks to assist shoppers on weekdays and more on Saturdays. The town was also home to an undertaker, a movie theater, a lumber yard, a soft drink plant, numerous churches, a large high school and, for a few years, the Creek-Seminole College and Agricultural Institute. Service providers included an electrical company, Boley Lights & Power, a waterworks and the phone company. These businesses were all in addition to multiple professionals including doctors, lawyers and dentists.[75]

Although Boley was located in rural Oklahoma and some of its roads were dirt, it was not necessarily of the frontier variety small town that some might imagine. This becomes apparent in portions of a film reel that was recorded in the community in the early 1920s by Rev. Solomon Sir Jones, a Baptist minister and amateur filmmaker.[‡‡‡] In the film, many town residents are seen in formal apparel including hats, ties and dresses. Pecan Street is wide and fully lined with businesses, many with sweeping awnings to protect shoppers from the brutal Oklahoma sun. The buildings of both the Farmers and Merchants Bank and the First National Bank make brief appearances.

Henrietta Hicks was born near Boley in 1935, near the end of what might be considered its heyday. Yet, memories from her childhood offer some indication of what the community had been like at its height:

On Saturday nights you could not find a parking place on the streets because there

††† The original Masonic Temple structure was destroyed in a March 1955 fire. *The Miami* (Oklahoma) *Daily News-Record,* March 17, 1955.

‡‡‡ Today, the film is in the collection of the National Museum of African American History & Culture. Those interested in watching can access it online at https://nmaahc.si.edu/object/nmaahc_2011.79.3.1abc.

were the places they called the juke joints ... where the music was played of all genres, mostly blues. Then there was the area where the youngsters went at The First and Last Chance to dance...

The grocery store stayed open until very late because people would buy their groceries late on Saturday night. There were places where you ... could go and eat on a Saturday night. If you wanted to go and look for your hat for Sunday, the millinery shop was open. Everything was booming on Saturday nights.[76]

In 1914, Booker T. Washington returned to Boley, a far more developed community than the one he saw only a few years earlier. On this visit, he was accompanied by 400 National Negro Business League (NNBL) members. In Washington's view, "Boley, like the other negro towns that have sprung up in other parts of the country, represents a dawning race consciousness, a wholesome desire to do something to make the race respected; something which shall demonstrate the right of the Negro, not merely as an individual, but as a race, to have a worthy and permanent place in the civilization that the American people are creating."[77]

Boley, Langston and other smaller Plains communities "provided an attractive social, political, and economic alternative to racial subordination in the New South's agricultural-based economy," wrote historian Juliet E.K. Walker. "Still, given the reality of the interdependence of the national economy, the late nineteenth-century decline of traditional market towns nationally, and an expanding industrial infrastructure developing in an increasingly hostile and racially segregated America, few Black towns had the economic viability to survive."[78]

As fate would have it, the 1921 founding of Boley's First National Bank came at a particularly unfortunate time economically. The same year, at least 20 Oklahoma banks failed with another 500 failures nationwide amid turmoil in agricultural and commodity prices.[79]

As with many small American communities, the agricultural base that provided the foundation for Boley's initial growth was also the town's vulnerability.

"Boley was built on the idea that farming would last indefinitely as an economic base," one resident told a reporter in the 1970s. "That was a mistake."[80]

Since 1908, Oklahoma officials had urged the state's farmers to diversify away from cotton – between 1900 and 1910 cotton acreage in the state nearly tripled with about half of the state's farms engaged in some amount of cotton production.[81]

In the area surrounding Boley, around one out of every three farm acres was planted in cotton. In many cases, the farmers were not the landowners, but tenant farmers who were extremely vulnerable financially when cotton prices sank in 1920 and early 1921. By March 1921, Oklahoma cotton prices were around 25 percent of what they had been a year earlier – moving them below the cost of picking and ginning. As a result, there were many farmers who simply plowed the crop under.[82, 83]

It is impressive that, despite the turmoil, both Boley banks survived in the face of severe economic challenges. One newspaper account lauded First National in particular as a "God send to the ... farmers and business people around Boley. Had it not been for this ... [they] could not have withstood the hardships."[84]

An account of Farmers and Merchants' performance noted that "when scores of banks in Oklahoma were forced to close their door because of business depression, this bank continued its business and has been adjudged one of the strongest banks in Okfuskee County. The survival of this institution is due to the keen economic point of view of its president [Turner]"[85]

5.

Measuring the economic impact of a rural agricultural hub can be difficult. The community it serves extends not only well beyond the city limits but also perhaps across county lines. During Boley's prime years contemporaneous newspaper accounts and promotional materials talked about a Boley population of anywhere from 4,000 to 15,000 residents.[86] These numbers were of course ripe for wild exaggeration. Town building was very much about aggressive promotion and marketing a community as *the place* everyone wants to be. Even Black newspapers in other U.S. cities that had no economic interest in boosting Boley would sometimes substantially exaggerate Boley's size in using it as a model worth emulating.

Officially, as a municipality, Boley proper at its largest covered only several hundred acres of land with a recorded population that around 1910 barely nudged its way above 1,000 before falling below that level at some point after the 1920 census.

However, there is no question that several thousand Black families relied on Boley's banks and businesses for years. In 1910, Okfuskee County had nearly 20,000 residents, more than 8,000 of them Black and, based on anecdotal evidence, many lived in what might be considered the greater Boley area. In addition, the county was near the midpoint of a cluster of east-central Oklahoma counties that each had sizable Black populations during this period including Okmulgee and, further east, Muskogee. All of this likely contributed significantly to Boley's position as an economic hub because segregation limited access to stores, facilities and opportunities in many other communities either through statute or intimidation.

This combination of opportunity and the risk of violence was something discussed by the author Ellison, who grew up in the state after his parents' arrival in Oklahoma City in the early 1900s:

[In] the late [18]90s and the early 1900s you had a heck of a period there – say 30 years in which to feel enthusiastic and hopeful, and during which you could build something for yourself. For instance, people are surprised when I tell them I knew a few millionaires who were Black. Some had made their fortunes on farming, one man on making cosmetics. There were a number of wealthy doctors who were land poor and then had oil discovered. People who traveled and had a lifestyle that was rather elegant considering that they lived much better than many of the whites and they possessed a higher degree of culture than many of the whites who had an opportunity to make more money, because you did have discrimination and you did have whites who were trying to keep Negroes under control.[87]

As Ellison's comments suggest, the economic opportunities found by some were not accompanied by the hoped-for safe haven from racially driven violence and oppression.

When the area that became Langston, Oklahoma, opened for settlement, there was an armed standoff between white detractors and Black settlers staking out claims and putting up tents.[88] In 1907, as Oklahoma gained statehood, it immediately implemented four Jim Crow statutes related to education and voting rights – some of this very likely in response to the growing political influence of those living in communities such as Boley.[89] Soon, law-makers would add similar statutes governing a number of matters related to race including segregating rail cars and banning interracial marriage.[90]

The downturn in the cotton market in the early 1920s can be seen in hindsight as the first in a series of developments that kept Boley from perhaps recognizing the economic potential envisioned by its founders. By 1928, the state was wrestling with rising farm foreclosures that likely contributed to First National's merger with Farmers and Merchants. The Great Depression would follow soon after and, in early 1939, the collapse of the Fort Smith and Western railroad.

Beyond agriculture, Boley was of course vulnerable to the same problem that has confronted small towns since time immemorial – young people seeking their fortunes else-where, usually a larger city that offers more opportunities. As far back as a 1913 newspaper article, Turner had lamented that Boley was successful in nearly all areas except one: "The only thing we lack … is employment for our young men."[91] Boley's largest employers were the cotton gins along the rail line at the edge of town, but work there was largely seasonal. Before the community could address the need for more stable jobs, perhaps by luring a full-time employer such as a large-scale manufacturer, the nation saw the rise of the automobile, which made it even easier to travel to bigger cities in search of work or, as it impacted local retailers, purchase goods from stores that offered wider selections and lower prices than what was possible in Boley.

"The complaint advanced by many … at meetings of the city's business league is that the chain stores in surrounding towns and cities, together with modern means of transportation just as in other parts of the United States create such a competition that it is almost impossible for them to attract and hold local trade" reads one local report from the late 1920s.[92]

This was before the state was faced in the 1930s with severe drought, the Dust Bowl and the Great Depression.

It was during this period, late in the morning of Nov. 23, 1932, that George Birdwell, a well-known close associate of infamous bank robber Pretty Boy Floyd, walked into the Farmers and Merchants Bank. Over the next few minutes, events would unfold that would be retold time and again – essentially whenever anyone mentions Boley – for generations to come.[§§§]

After Birdwell and at least one of two associates with him that morning demanded money, bank President Turner pulled an alarm, setting off what was described by one witness as "a regular war" of gunfire.[93]

Birdwell, cursing Turner for the alarm, fatally shot the bank president. Herbert Mc-Cormick, the bank's bookkeeper, who had fled to the vault when the men entered, came out with a shotgun, opening fire and killing Birdwell. The other robbers attempted to flee but were confronted by armed townspeople who began shooting, killing one of the robbers and wounding the other.

"The boys here kind of expected that thing to happen," McCormick's brother J.L. explained in an interview more than 30 years later. "A lot of these people here had rifles. Several burglar alarms on Main Street connected to the bank.

"I remember I was walking down the street … And somebody ran up to me and said, 'The bank's being robbed.' Well, I went over to the American Legion hall and got some rifles and took off down the alley, jumping over fences. And by the time I got there, the shooting was on."[94, ****]

It made headlines nationwide.

§§§ Boley nearly had other historic moments. While Muhammad Ali was trying to engineer a return to boxing after he was banned from sanctioned fights for refusing to report for the Vietnam War draft, a fight between Ali and tenth-ranked Billy Joiner was planned for Jan. 12, 1970, inside a large tent in Boley. Ali, however, backed out, saying he did not like the outdoor conditions and Joiner was not a worthy opponent. (*Jet,* Jan. 22, 1970. p. 46.)

**** In the aftermath of Turner's death, the bank failed, but it was reorganized and reopened with new ownership in 1935. It remained in business for nearly three decades. Herbert McCormick, meanwhile, was honored by the Oklahoma governor as a breveted major for his bravery. He was later elected Boley's mayor. An interesting sidenote: Herbert McCormick was married to Abigail Barnett, who, as a young girl, owned the property Boley was founded upon.

6.

Boley and the other small Oklahoma communities that relied on agriculture could not hold a candle to the economic engine that powered Tulsa: oil.

The discovery of oil near Tulsa, first in 1901 and later with the massive Glenn Pool oil field in 1905, put what had been a small frontier community on a path that would soon make it the proclaimed "oil capital of the world." For Black Americans fleeing the South and lured by the promise of opportunity on America's plains, the Tulsa area offered something not widely available in farm communities like Boley – readily available jobs.

Between 1910 and 1920, Tulsa's population, not including outlying areas, increased nearly fourfold, and it doubled again by 1930. The boom economy had innumerable spill-over effects, thanks to the wealth generation. By 1910, for example, it was not uncommon for middle class white families to have a Black employee working as a maid or nanny—many particularly well paid when compared against similar positions in other cities.[95]

On the eve of this boom, O.W. Gurley saw the coming opportunity and grabbed it. Gurley, a Black school teacher from Pine Bluff, Arkansas, had initially come to Oklahoma during one of the land runs and settled near Perry, where he was an educator and operated a store. Around the time of the 1905 boom, he visited Tulsa and acquired a sizable parcel of land on the city's undeveloped northern outskirts, where he made a home and opened a grocery, the first of several small business ventures developed in the neighborhood to serve a Black population that was prohibited from shopping in white-owned stores.

Soon, Gurley informally partnered with John the Baptist "J.B." Stradford, a Black attorney originally from Kentucky, who also acquired land in the area. The pair subdivided their properties into individual parcels on which they began to build an exclusively Black community that drew many Black migrants from the Deep South. The area's main thoroughfare, Greenwood Avenue, was named for the Mississippi hometown of many of the community's first residents.[96, ††††] The area emerged as a beacon, not only for Black Oklahomans, but also nationally. Where Richmond had the legendary Jackson Ward, northeast Tulsa was home to the Greenwood neighborhood, a 35-block area centered on the corner of Greenwood Avenue and Archer Street.

The Greenwood economy not only grew, but it also thrived. By some estimates, when

†††† Some suggest that the name Greenwood may also be drawn from Greenwood, Arkansas.

a dollar came into Greenwood, it would move as many as 26 times within the community, perhaps more, before exiting back to "white" Tulsa.[97]

Estimates of the number of businesses in Greenwood at its economic peek vary. One of the more comprehensive reports on the Greenwood business community, the result of extensive historical research done in the early 1980s, identified more than 70 Greenwood business establishments ranging from auto repair through retailers, with additional numbers of skilled professionals, craftsmen, services providers and churches.[98] Another report pegged the number at nearly 200.[99]

Among them was the office of Dr. A.C. Jackson, a surgeon lauded for his skill by the founders of the Mayo Clinic and John Williams' renown auto repair shop. Williams' success in serving Black and white customers allowed him to construct two Greenwood landmarks: the three-story building that included Williams' Confectionary and the nearby 800-seat Dreamland Theater.[100, 101]

Absent from the list of Greenwood's many businesses, and especially conspicuous for an area widely known as "Black Wall Street," are any Black-owned banks.

This is, of course, surprising. Given the essential role of banks in community building, and the historical record of Black-owned banks in Jackson Ward and elsewhere, it is tempting to think that the omission of a bank or banks from a list of Greenwood businesses is an oversight. It appears, however, that is not the case.

Business directories from the era, including a city directory from 1920, the year when Greenwood was at its height financially, show no banks with a Greenwood address. The Tuskegee Institute's annual and extensive Negro Year Book makes no mention of a Black bank in Tulsa. It also appears there were no Black bank advertisements nor articles during this period in the Black The Tulsa Star or other Black newspapers. The well-known Black economist Abram Harris compiled a listing of all the Black-owned banks in the United States, which includes even banks that may have had partial white ownership. This list indicates Oklahoma's only Black-owned banks during this era were in Boley and Muskogee.[102]

How is this possible?

In considering this question, it is first important to understand that very often in the United States the creation of a bank is something that happens in response to a community's need for capital. Banks fill this need by providing access to credit through the lending of a community's pooled resources, or its savings, on which the depositors then earn interest. The bank is thus providing a service for both borrowers and lenders to a degree that they would not be able to accomplish individually.[103] This is a model that functioned well not only in the development of Jackson Ward and Boley historically, but in innumerable communities nationwide still today.

In Tulsa, however, conditions were different. Despite segregation, at least some of the city's white banks served Black customers.[104] Exchange National Bank and the National Bank of Commerce both promoted their services to the Black community with sizable ads in *The Tulsa Star*.[105, 106] Gurley, one prominent example of Black wealth, was known to keep his money in accounts divided among several of the city's white banks.[107]

Outside of the white banks, within Greenwood, individual lenders also provided credit, albeit not via a bank, including both Gurley and Stradford. Gurley offered financing for those buying real estate from him and also loaned to Black entrepreneurs looking to establish businesses.[108, 109] Stradford, meanwhile, offered loans and investment services, in addition to selling real estate, from an office in his impressive Stradford Hotel, at 301 N. Greenwood, which was believed to be the largest Black-owned hotel in the United States.[110, 111]

Almost no details are available about the business practices of Greenwood's private lenders, although it appears they ran the gambit in how they treated customers. Newspapers advertisements make it apparent that some were little more than pawn shops and at least one, The Protective Investment Building and Loan Association, was later accused of charging borrowers as much as 10 percent interest.[112] It seems reasonable to assume that both Gurley and Stradford were at the other end of this spectrum.

Both were not only extremely prominent and successful, but they were also deeply focused on building a Black community. While little may be known about Gurley's ideologies or activities outside of his businesses, Stradford was a renowned community builder and civil rights advocate. In addition to his various businesses, he established and operated a Black library in Greenwood.[113] More than once while traveling by train, he was arrested after refusing to relinquish his seat to a white passenger.[114] On at least one of these instances, he filed a lawsuit against the railway company.[115] As it relates to finance, some articles written later about Stradford noted that he was an especially strong believer in the idea of using a community's pooled resources as the fuel to drive its growth. If he followed this ideal in his business practices, he was operating under what is essentially a textbook definition of a community bank, albeit one with a single depositor whose resources were used to the benefit of many borrowers.

By 1921, Greenwood was home to perhaps as many as 15,000 Black residents and somewhere around 100 businesses if not more. These numbers provide some important and necessary perspective to the scale of the Greenwood massacre, one of the most violent, painful and troubling events in United States history.

After World War I, the United States saw a surge in organized racial violence with a reborn Ku Klux Klan due, in no small part, to the film "Birth of a Nation." The 1915 D.W. Griffith silent picture may have been something of a blockbuster of the silent film era from a technical perspective, but the storyline makes it arguably the most racist motion picture in U.S. history with its denegation of Black Americans while portraying Klansmen as heroic saviors. Within a few years of its release, the Klan had returned on a scale seen during Reconstruction, and the nation witnessed racial violence in at least 25 U.S. cities during a period known as the "Red Summer" of 1919.[116] What happened in Tulsa was at a scale beyond what happened in all other communities.

The violence started after the arrest of Dick Rowland, a 19-year-old Black man accused of assaulting a white girl named Sarah Page in a Main Street office building elevator on May 30, 1921. The idea of such a brazen attack in a public setting made little sense, and Rowland was later acquitted of all charges. Today, it is generally believed that Rowland likely only stepped on Page's foot, which caused her to exclaim in surprise or pain.[117] During a later trial, there was discussion of the elevator being jolted as it started to move, causing both its passengers to slip.[118]

The suggestion of an assault, however, fit comfortably within the vile and favored narrative of white supremacists: that white women were regularly at risk of being assaulted by Black men. This racist trope, which was used across the South to justify violence against Blacks by white mobs, however, made little sense. As teacher and journalist Ida B. Wells explained in her Memphis newspaper in 1892, "nobody in this section of the country believes the old threadbare lie that Negro men rape white women." Soon after the statement was published, a white mob destroyed Wells' printing press, forcing her to the safety of New York City where she later elaborated on her statement, "the thinking public will not easily believe freedom and education [are] more brutalizing than slavery, and the world knows that the crime of rape was unknown during the four years of the Civil War," when many Southern white men were away from home.[119]

As Wells' logic makes apparent, there were underlying causes – especially economic, ranging from the job competition that Black workers presented to white laborers to the white jealousy of Black financial success.[####] Many who were killed by violent white mobs had "committed only the social crime, in white thinking, of showing talent [and] ambition."[120]

At the time, few places in America were a more visible beacon of Black economic success than Oklahoma. In 1921, the state was home to at least three Black millionaires, and Greenwood proper included "a number of men and women" whose worth would be valued at more than a million dollars in modern amounts.[121]

"This fact has caused a bitter resentment on the part of the lower order of whites, who feel that these colored men, members of an 'inferior race,' are exceedingly presumptuous in achieving greater economic prosperity than they who are members of a divinely ordered superior race."[122]

In addition, and as became apparent later, the Greenwood neighborhood was in an area of Tulsa that leaders at the time viewed as well-suited for the expansion of the city's white business community and industrial development.[§§§§]

Regardless of the motivating factors, on May 31, white and Black mobs met outside the Tulsa County Courthouse, the building where Rowland was held captive, and exchanged gunfire. The brief skirmish was followed by a full-out assault on Greenwood early the next morning.

It is difficult to capture, to any appropriate degree, the violence. Perhaps as many as 10,000 armed whites assaulted the community with an attack so extensive that it included small planes firebombing the neighborhood.[123]

Tulsa attorney B.C. Franklin, father of historian and civil rights advocate John Hope Franklin, later wrote one of the rare firsthand accounts of the massacre. Within hours of seeing his neighbors head to work on a beautiful late-May morning, he witnessed them dying on Greenwood's streets. Among those he saw on the run for shelter was John Ross, a young World War I veteran trying to protect his wife and mother. Ross told Franklin that he had been outside of the community and saw that all of the Greenwood neighborhood

---

[####] Wells' motivation to expose lynching and its true motivations was the lynching of her friend Thomas H. Moss and two others. Moss, the Black owner of a successful grocery near Memphis, was viewed by competitors as an economic threat.

[§§§§] For a further exploration of this issue see the following: Messer, Chris M. "The Tulsa Race Riot of 1921: Toward an Integrative Theory of Collective Violence." *Journal of Social History,* summer 2011, Vol 44. No. 4. Pp. 1217-1232.

was surrounded.^{*****}

> When young Ross and his family left me … I thought of those stirring words of our war president, 'We must fight to make the world safe for democracy.' I repeated those words aloud and they sounded liked hollow mockery.

> During that bloody day, I lived a thousand years … I lived the whole experiences of the race; the experiences of royal ancestry beyond the sea; experiences of the slave ships on their first voyage to America with their human cargo; experiences of American slavery and its concomitant evils; experiences of loyalty and devotion to the race, to this nation and its flag in war and in peace; and I thought of Ross back yonder … in his last stand, no doubt for the protection of his home and fireside, and of old Mother Ross left homeless in the eventide of her life. I thought of the place the preachers call hell and wondered seriously if there was such a mystical place. It appeared, in this surrounding, that the only hell was the hell on this earth, such as the race was then passing through.[124]

Greenwood was burned to the ground.

By some estimates, as many as 1,000 buildings were destroyed including businesses, homes and churches. More than 800 people were injured and historians today believe as many as 300 people were killed – either shot or burned. Some were very likely buried in unmarked mass graves.[125, 126] Among the most prominent casualties was the surgeon A.C. Jackson, who was shot after surrendering. Nearly all Greenwood residents were left destitute. With no local Black-owned bank, there were reports that most kept their life savings at home, where it was lost to the fire or looters ahead of the blaze.[127] As a result, many spent the winter in tents. Some recalled later passing white Tulsa residents on the street who were wearing clothes or jewelry they recognized as stolen from their own homes.[128]

It has only been since the formation of a statewide commission in the 1990s that there has been what might be considered an attempt to publicly reckon with the Greenwood massacre. For 70 years the event was so rarely mentioned that some Tulsa residents grew to adulthood unaware that it had even happened.

***** According to Franklin, all three of the Ross family members survived the attack. John was left blinded and committed to an asylum after suffering a mental breakdown. Franklin's full manuscript recounting his experiences, written in 1931, is available online through the National Museum of African American History & Culture at https://nmaahc.si.edu/object/nmaahc_2015.176.1.

"Black folks lived with the fear that the whites who had come once might come again," said Don Ross, a local resident and state lawmaker who led efforts to generate interest in the massacre's history in the late 1990s.[129]

Stradford was finally pardoned in 1996, 61 years after his death, for grand jury charges of inciting violence in 1921. He had been in the midst of the standoff outside the courthouse where he was trying to act as a peacemaker and calm the armed Black men. Facing charges, he fled the area and lived in Chicago until his death.[130]

The Greenwood of the pre-massacre era never returned. Nationally, in the massacre's aftermath there were fundraising efforts promoted within the Black press. Those making contributions were asked to send them not to a Tulsa bank, but to the Black-owned First National Bank of Boley.[131]

Under William Washington Browne's leadership, the Savings Bank of the Grand Fountain, United Order of True Reformers became the first Black bank in the United States to obtain a charter. Soon, the Richmond, Va. bank was joined by others, making the city's Jackson Ward neighborhood the cradle for Black financial services.

By the time Dr. Richard Filmore Tancil established Richmond's Nickel Savings Bank in 1896 he'd already built an impressive legacy of community service. In addition to a medical practice where he often waived fees for the poor and needy, he operated a winter soup kitchen out of his home and led the creation of several professional and civic organizations while serving as president of the Richmond Hospital Association.

JOHN MITCHELL, JR.

John Mitchell Jr. founded Richmond's Mechanics Savings Bank in 1902. A former teacher, Mitchell was a newspaper publisher who was at the forefront of numerous civil rights battles.

The Planet newspaper office in Richmond featured the same flexed muscular arm that appeared in the paper's masthead. Under the leadership of John Mitchell Jr., the paper was relentless in exposing racial violence in the South.

The Planet Office
Mr. John Mitchell, Jr., Editor
311 North 4th Street

Maggie Lena Walker is perhaps the most well-known of America's early Black bankers. Modern day visitors to Richmond, Va. can tour her Jackson Ward home, which has been preserved as a national historic site.

The three-story Masonic Temple in Boley, Okla. included offices used by the local justice of the peace, the phone company and others. When it was built in 1915, it was one of the tallest buildings in eastern Oklahoma.

D.J. Turner was a pharmacist and retailer in Boley, Okla. before he became involved in founding Farmers and Merchants Bank and serving as its president. He was a key figure in developing the Oklahoma community.

John Williams' success as an automobile mechanic in Tulsa's Greenwood neighborhood provided him and his wife Loula with the capital to construct two of the community's landmark buildings – the Williams' Confectionary and the 800-seat Dreamland Theater, a showplace for film and live performances.

Greenwood Avenue was main street for Tulsa's 35-block Greenwood neighborhood, one of the nation's most vibrant Black communities of the early 20th century. By some estimates a dollar that came into Greenwood would circulate through 26 of its Black businesses before exiting back to "white" Tulsa.

O.W. Gurley (front row, second from left) was a Greenwood founder and one of the community's wealthiest individuals. Here, he is with members of the Colored Citizens Relief Committee and East End Welfare Board.

Jesse Binga, who founded Binga Bank in 1908, was heavily involved in Chicago real estate, both as an investor and in providing mortgage financing. Much of his work was along and near South State Street, expanding the city's Black Belt neighborhood.

MR. JESSE BINGA.

Crowds gathered along Chicago's South State Street in front of Binga Bank after racial violence erupted in the city during the summer of 1919. Banker Jesse Binga is believed to have played an important role in bringing food into the neighborhood when deliveries stopped amid the turmoil.

Anthony Overton was a successful and well-known businessman whose investment and acumen were essential in building Chicago's Douglass National Bank out of the failed Merchant's and Peoples Bank. Under Overton's leadership, the Bank was heavily involved in lending to home buyers and businesses.

Wayne Cox founded Delta Penny Savings Bank and Mississippi Beneficial Life Insurance Company in Indianola, Miss. in the early 1900s. Cox, who was believed to be the wealthiest Black man in the Delta region, said the businesses were "monuments of protest to the injustices" he and his wife had suffered from racists.

W. W. COX

Joseph Walker, here with his wife Leila, founded Memphis' Tri-State Bank in 1946. Walker got his start in banking after Wayne Cox convinced him to serve as president of Delta Penny Savings Bank in 1913. Prior to that, Walker was a doctor with a medical practice in Indianola, Miss.

A. Maceo Walker founded Tri-State Bank with his father after being denied a $1,000 loan from another Memphis, Tenn. bank. A. Maceo succeeded his father as head of Universal Life and president of Tri-State Bank.

Jesse Turner Sr., chief executive officer of Tri-State Bank, accepts a deposit from the Masons, including civil rights leader Benjamin Hooks. During Turner's tenure, bank offices were sometimes used for demonstration planning meetings and bank officials were available after hours to provide bail money for protestors who had been arrested.

REV. R. H. BOYD, D. D.

Rev. Richard Henry Boyd was a founder of Nashville's One Cent Savings Bank in 1904. He originally came to the city in the late 1800s to establish a Baptist publishing house. Both the Bank, under the name Citizens Savings Bank and Trust Co., and the publisher, under the name R.H Boyd, were still in business more than a century later.

James Carroll Napier established a National Negro Business League chapter in Nashville that hosted the organization's national convention in 1903. The event was key in generating local support for One Cent Savings Bank, which Napier helped to found the following year.

Dr. Robert Fulton Boyd was president of People's Savings Bank and Trust Company when it opened in 1909. Boyd was one of Nashville's most prominent residents and a founder of the organization that later became the National Medical Association.

R. F. BOYD, President
People's Savings Bank and Trust Co.

Don Davis was a guitar player and studio musician who bought Detroit's United Sound Systems Recording Studios in the 1970s. Within a decade, he'd amassed enough wealth to buy a controlling interest in the failing First Independence Bank and began work turning it around.

William T. Johnson was believed to be the first Black man to own a cable television franchise when he purchased the Columbus, Ohio system in 1977. When cable television boomed in the 1980s, he sold some of his holdings and invested in River Rouge Savings Bank near Detroit with attorney and activist Kenneth Hylton. They rebranded the institution OmniBanc and engaged in an aggressive growth strategy.

Charles Allen was a Washington D.C. banker helping Don Davis work through problem loans at First Independence Bank when Davis convinced him to serve as the Detroit bank's president. Under his tenure, the bank assets more than doubled while the institution built a national reputation for its innovation in providing low-cost financial services.

Chicago,
Illinois

I.

Frederick Douglass silenced the hecklers. How many times in his more than 70 years had he encountered their kind and many others who were far worse? This afternoon, Aug. 25, 1893, these few voices among an audience of 2,500 had no chance of frustrating a speaker who had so often feared for his life. Instead, they could only stoke the old abolitionist's fire.

The 1893 World's Columbia Exposition, popularly known as the Chicago World's Fair, was a celebration of Christopher Columbus' arrival in the Americas. Visually, the Fair's neoclassical buildings were a nearly luminous white, earning it the name "White City."

It is possible, however, to draw from that nickname another connotation. Organizers had entirely rejected minority involvement in the planning and decision making. Some in the Black press labeled the event "the white American's world's fair."[1] The fair's exhibits not only actively promoted white cultural superiority, but they also denigrated other races with dehumanizing caricatures and gross racist stereotypes. The most prominent Black exhibit, for example, was a "village" of around 80 people from the West African Kingdom of Dahomey, replete with huts and residents presented as barbarians.[2, †] This overt racism occurred in the same summer and same city where a Black surgeon, Dr. Daniel Hale Williams, performed the world's first ever successful open-heart surgery.[3, ‡]

When fair organizers scheduled "Colored People's Day," for Aug. 25 to appease Black critics, there were calls for protest within the Black press. Such fair days were scheduled for any number of marketing-related reasons. In addition to innumerable celebrations for various nations around the globe, special days were held for stenographers, confectioners and others.[4]

Despite the frustrations of some, Douglass accepted an invitation to offer what was effectively the day's keynote address and urged others to attend, arguing that foreigners visiting the fair "do not stop to think that for 250 years the wealth, the science, the inventions of the South were the product of our brain and brawn. All the races of the earth are represented

† The Kingdom of Dahomey ended in 1904 when the king was defeated by the French. Today, the region is within the nation of Benin. The Dahomians had a contract with a promoter and were paid in some fashion for their participation in the Fair. Eventually, as the Chicago weather began to turn cold, they went on strike for higher pay. *The Chicago Tribune,* Sept. 24, 1893.

‡ Williams' patient, James Cornish, went on to live more than 20 years after the July 1893 surgery that included the repair of a coronary artery.

at the Fair, but the colored American is simply an on-looker. We have not been given the prominence our numbers in the country warrant. There is no member of the [fair] commission whose skin is the color of mine. There is prejudice against the Black man. We must acknowledge it. It is the natural product of 250 years of slavery. Yet we are given one day at the Fair in which we may lay our case before the world. Let us take this chance. Let us not sulk but show to the world what sort of men and women are the product of but 30 years of freedom."[5]

Douglass' willing participation in the event concerned many of his allies, who feared that the aging icon would be used as a mere spectacle for the pleasure of white fairgoers. This concern appeared particularly well founded when fair visitors that day arrived to find a number of watermelon stands had been erected.[6]

If those who packed the fair's Festival Hall, however, expected to find an icon past his prime, they were surprised. When the heckling started, Douglass, spoke in "tones compelling attention, drowning out [the] catcalls as an organ would a penny whistle."[7]

He cast his written remarks aside to confront the full depth of the nation's racism, prejudice and the disregard of Black lives as he stood essentially center stage of a fair that highlighted white accomplishment while casting minorities into the supporting role of sideshow attractions.

We fought for your country. We ask that we be treated as well as those who fought against your country. We ask that you treat us as well as you do those who love but a part of it.[8]

Today a desperate effort is being made … to brand [the Black American] as a moral monster. In 14 states of this Union, wild mobs have taken the place of law. They hang, shoot, burn men of my race without justice and without right. Today, the Negro is barred out of almost every reputable and decent employment.

But stop. Look at the progress the Negro has made in 30 years. We have come up out of the Dahomey unto this. Measure the Negro. But not by the standard of the splendid civilization of the Caucasian. Bend down and measure him – measure him – from the depths out of which he has risen.[9]

The Great Migration out of the rural American South is without equal in its cultural and socioeconomic impact on the United States. Between 1910 and 1970, around 6 million Black Southerners left the largely rural South for the industrial centers of the Upper Midwest, Northeast and later the West.

For American manufacturers, the outbreak of World War I in Europe created a labor crisis. Since around 1880, European immigrants willing to work long hours under often harsh conditions had been the key source of labor in the industrial centers of the Northeast and Midwest. Between 1900 and 1914, the U.S. received nearly 1 million immigrants annually – 1.2 million in 1914 alone – almost half from central and eastern Europe.[10] When the War started, however, transatlantic immigration came to a halt. By 1918, the number of immigrants had dwindled to a low of around 110,000; meanwhile, some European immigrants who had already become established in the U.S. returned to their homelands to join the fight overseas. The American labor squeeze tightened further with entry of the U.S. into the War in 1917 as around 5 million men served in the military, either through enlistment or conscription, while demand on the nation's factories rose to support the war effort.

To find workers, Northern agents headed into the Deep South, where they recruited Black workers, sometimes buying railroad tickets north for those willing to fill jobs in factories, steel mills and any number of other industries.

While an opportunity to earn income was important, for many, the paycheck was often a secondary motivation – an indication of just how dire conditions in the South had become.

Unlike their ancestors who had seen an improvement in living conditions in the post-Civil War era through the end of Reconstruction, many of those in the first wave of the Great Migration had come of age in the post-Reconstruction era. Throughout their lives, the environment in the South had only grown progressively worse in many regards. Some of the rights that they had seen their families afforded when they were young were now being taken away via Jim Crow laws, racism, segregation and violence.

Adam Clayton Powell Sr., the clergyman who made Harlem's Abyssinian Baptist Church the largest congregation in the United States, explained it to a *New York Times* reporter:

> To say that the negro is coming North for higher wages is to grossly misinterpret the spirit of the exodus. The negroes are leaving the South because life to them has been made miserable and unbearable.

They are tired of being kept out of public parks and libraries, of being deprived of equal educational opportunities for their children, for which they are taxed; of reading signs, "Negroes and dogs not admitted." The men are tired of disfranchisement, the women are tired of the insults of white hoodlums, and the whole race is sick of seeing mobs mutilate and burn unconvicted negro men. These migrating thousands are not seeking money, but manhood rights. All the people coming here are not poor. If the 350,000 negroes who have recently left the south were offered $5 a day and free transportation back, not 10 percent would return in a whole year. If they were assured that these horrible injustices would be removed, especially the hellish institution of lynching, 80 percent of them would return almost as quickly as they came away."[11]

More than 500,000 went North between 1910 and 1920, moving to cities such as Chicago, Detroit, New York City and Philadelphia in the first decade of a migration that continued into the Civil Rights era. They followed around 194,000 others who had found homes in places as diverse as New York's Harlem neighborhood to Plains communities like Boley.

In Chicago, the wartime demand for workers finally brought an end to the longstanding discrimination practiced by many of the city's industrial employers.

The "same factories, mills and workshops that have been closed to us, through necessity are being open to us," Publisher Robert Abbott wrote in *The Chicago Defender,* arguably the nation's most important and influential Black newspaper.[12] "We are to be given a chance, not through choice but because it is expedient. Prejudice vanishes when the almighty dollar is on the wrong side of the balance sheet."

The reluctance of Chicago firms to hire Black workers until the start of World War I might surprise even those who are knowledgeable about the Windy City's history. At the time of the war's beginning, Chicago was already home to a well-established Black community with its foundation predating the Civil War by around 20 years. Jean Baptiste DuSable, a Black man, was the Chicago area's first permanent settler when he established a trading post and farm near Lake Michigan in 1779 and did business with Native Americans as well as British and French explorers. The first Black politicians were elected in the city in the late 1800s; a Black newspaper, *The Conservator,* was established in 1878; and Provident Hospital and Training School, the nation's first Black hospital, opened at 29th and Dearborn in 1891. By 1905, there were 25 Black churches, including at least one that operated a penny savings bank of which little is known, as well as local chapters of the True Reformers, Knights of Pythias and other fraternal societies and organizations.[13]

Efforts to end formalized segregation in the city had started in the 1870s but made little in the way of tangible improvement. Employment within the white community was possible, but generally limited to service jobs, either as household staff or at a low level in a white-owned business. Factory work, civil service and most unions remained off limits until the war, when the number of Black men employed by factories finally exceeded those in service jobs.[14, 15]

Amid the wartime labor shortage, the white workers who had been mired in the city's least desirable jobs moved up, capitalizing on vacancies in better paying and higher status work.[16] As a result, newly arriving Black migrants filled the city's most dangerous and grueling jobs where they were frequently underpaid when compared against white co-workers. Many found employment in the city's legendary packinghouses, often on a killing floor of "nauseating smells, the cries of stricken animals, the streams of warm blood and tons of raw meat."[17]

Not only were the conditions deplorable, but the jobs were often dangerous. Because the government did not accurately track work-related injuries, it is difficult to fully measure the degree of risk that faced industrial workers at that time. The available reports, however, are appalling. In 1917, for example, one-half of the workers at a single Chicago packing plant suffered work-related injuries or illness within a 12-month span.[18]

Still, for many, the risk was offset by the return. For those who had been tenant farmers, the idea of a regular paycheck instead of an existence of near continual debt to a landowner was a welcome change. Even those migrants who had earned regular pay in the South found Northern wages to be significantly higher than what they had earned previously, even if those earnings were still very low by Northern standards.

Not surprisingly, many wrote home to friends and family about the opportunities, urging them to come to the city. Between 1916 and 1918, the city's Black population nearly doubled from around 58,000 to nearly 110,000.[19]

The changes in the city were substantial, not just in the packing plants and on the factory floors.

In the late 1800s, a Black professional class had started to emerge in a long, slender region along South State Street and neighboring blocks. This area of the "Black Belt," later known as Bronzeville, saw increasing growth in the 1900s as Black businesses extended from around 18th Street south to as far as 55th Street. Among them were retailers who sold necessities, such as grocers, as well as those who dealt in luxury items like high-end clothing. Services providers included beauty parlors, barbershops and real estate agents. Stores were open 24 hours a day along what the *Chicago Defender* called "the greatest thoroughfare for the race in the world."[20]

Also, like Richmond's Jackson Ward, the area was also well known for entertainment, in this case, jazz in particular. The blocks between 26th and 39th streets were known as "The Stroll," home to clubs, restaurants, bars, theaters and hotels. It was said that during the Jazz Age, a trumpet held into the night air along The Stroll could play itself.[21] Luminaries to perform in the nightspots during this era and later included Duke Ellington, Louis Armstrong, Gertrude "Ma" Rainey and Cab Calloway among a long list of others. Only a few blocks to the west, the Chicago American Giants, one of the Negro League's most dominant teams, played home games at Schorling Park under the leadership of Rube Foster, a player, executive and manager known as the "father of Black baseball."

Poet, author and activist Langston Hughes later recounted his first visit to the city in 1918 when he was 17 years old:

South State Street was in its glory then. A teeming Negro Street crowded with theaters, restaurants and cabarets. And excitement from noon to noon. Midnight was like day. The street was full of workers and gamblers, prostitutes and pimps, church folks and sinners.[22]

As individuals and families sought homes in the area, the population influx began to push beyond the Black Belt's traditional racial barriers and into nearby white neighborhoods Starting around 1917 and increasing in the years that followed, this period saw the introduction of restrictive covenants barring the sale of homes, primarily to Black buyers but also to other minorities, and a rash of bombings of Black residences. These incidents, as well as a number of street fights and brawls with sides drawn along racial lines, would later be seen as a preamble to the most violent and deadly episodes of racial violence in U.S. history.

2.

In a hot Chicago summer, Sunday, July 27, 1919, was another hot day. Temperatures were headed well into the 90s and there was little respite except for that available along Lake Michigan. That's where 17-year-old Eugene Williams, a smart, athletic and good-looking young man with a job at the grocery store, headed with friends.[§]

At some point on that afternoon, Williams was alone on a raft that drifted across an invisible, although widely acknowledged, line into what was considered the white section of the lake. From the shore, stones were thrown at the boy, with at least one hitting him with enough force to leave him disoriented and causing him to plunge into the water. Would-be rescue efforts were blocked by whites and fighting erupted across the shore as Williams drowned.[23, *] Soon, the violence spread across areas of Chicago's South Side.

From the next morning's edition of *The Chicago Tribune*:

So serious was the trouble throughout the district that Acting Chief of Police Adcock was unable to place an estimate on the injured. Scores received cuts and bruises from flying stones and rocks, but went to their homes for medical attention.

Minor rioting continued through the night all over the south side. Negroes who were found in street cars were dragged to the street and beaten.

They were first ordered to the street by white men and if they refused the trolley was jerked off the wires.[24]

Provident Hospital treated 75 victims who were beaten, stabbed or shot in the first 24 hours of the turmoil. "Cots were placed in the wards and in the emergency room until every available space was occupied; then the victims had to lie upon the floor."[25]

§ Very little is known about Williams beyond the details of his tragic death. Some hints of what his life was like, however, can be found in Lorezel, Robert. "Searching for Eugene Williams." Chicago. Aug. 1, 2019. The article can be accessed online at: http://www.chicagomag.com/city-life/August-2019/Searching-for-Eugene-Williams/

*There are a few slightly different versions of what transpired on the beach around Williams' drowning. Some accounts suggest an incident on the beach as preceding the throwing of stones into the water, while some suggest fighting erupted after he went into the water.

Across five days of violence 38 people were killed, 23 of them Black, and more than 500 were injured. Homes near the stockyards were burned. The end finally came with the arrival of the state militia that roughly coincided with a period of summer rain that may have discouraged some from heading outdoors. Later, a white man, George Stauber, was arrested and charged in connection with Williams' death. There was no conviction.

During the violence, thousands made their way to South State Street, fearful that an assault on the community would begin soon. While it did not materialize, in the days that followed, many returned to South State, this time seeking provisions for their families, crowding delivery trucks to buy food after shipments into neighborhood stores came to a halt.[26]

At the time, South Side was home to three Black banks, each of which responded to the crisis. The institutions, all named for their founders, were Binga Bank, established by Jesse Binga in 1908; R.W. Hunter Banking Company, which also included a real estate brokerage, established by its namesake in 1917 with branch offices in Chicago and other cities; and Woodfolk Banking Company, established by former Hunter employee Roger Woodfolk in 1918 but not officially open for business until late May 1919.[27]

The Woodfolk and Hunter banks were short-lived – both failed in 1919 – due in no small part to their willingness to place community needs above their own financial interests. The Woodfolk bank cashed around $20,000 in checks, the equivalent of $300,000 in modern-day amounts, for individuals who did not have deposit accounts with the bank and, in some cases, did not have identification.[28] The amount nearly equaled its total deposits at the time.[29] Hunter, meanwhile, extended about twice that amount in loans, providing money to tide families over until it was safe for the breadwinner to return to work. Hunter's other actions were detailed in a newspaper report:[30]

[Bank] officials from the President R.W. Hunter down ran the gauntlet with their fleet of automobiles, carrying their brave … men and women employees to and from the banks. Money was passed out to the hundreds who were caught in this terrible storm. There were those who had money somewhere in some bank, that money [could] not be reached only by facing death to enter or get to a white man's bank. There were those who had hard-earned money over there somewhere across that death line. There were those who had no money but were in distress. All were given the assistance of this … bank that was on the ground with resources and willing and able under the direction of its president to do for the race what no other institution could do … not even the city, county, Red Cross or even the big banks downtown.[31]

Of the two institutions, the Hunter collapse was likely the most shocking to the community and bank depositors.

Since its establishment, Hunter Banking Company had been aggressive in both its vision and promotion – the latter to an almost uncomfortable degree in some instances.

The bank promised depositors 8 percent interest and touted that it handled more than a half million dollars over a nine-month span.[32] It supported the claim by publishing a list of 25 recent deposits, including the names of each of the depositors *and the amounts deposited.* Thus, readers of the Nov. 2, 1918, issue of *The Chicago Defender* could learn that Pharmacist William H. Huff deposited $4,377.74.[††]

The bank also claimed to be the only bank in the United States where the "wage earner and salaried people [are] on a business rating where they can borrow … just as responsible business men and women can borrow from their banks."[33]

The bank's goal was "to be to the Colored people of the United States what J.P. Morgan & Co. are to the white people of the United States."[34] Eventually, the plan was for the Chicago bank to serve as a clearinghouse and depository for a network of affiliated Black banks located in a dozen U.S. cities.[‡‡] Early steps taken between mid-year 1918, when it

[††] William Henry Huff's accomplishments and importance lie well beyond the scope of this work. However, because his name is largely unknown to many modern-day Americans, some additional detail is warranted here. Huff came to the Chicago area from Oglethorpe County, Georgia, in 1908. After his pharmacy struggled during the Great Depression, he returned to school and earned a law degree, embarking on a career where he became one of the nation's most important legal voices in the fight for civil rights. Huff, through the auspices of the National Association for the Advancement of Colored People (NAACP), won more than 100 cases where Southern authorities sought to extradite individuals back to the South, many who had escaped peonage or chain gangs to which they had been sentenced for misdemeanor offenses or crimes for which they had been wrongly arrested. Among his other notable legal work, Huff was heavily involved in the Emmett Till case, serving as the attorney for Emmett's mother Mamie after the 14-year-old boy was murdered by white racists in Mississippi in 1955. Beyond Huff's numerous legal accomplishments, he was a songwriter and poet, with hundreds of poems appearing in daily editions of *The Chicago Defender* for many years. He recorded at least two of his songs: "You Better Leave that Moon Alone," and "Please Don't Tell the Truth on Me," in 1962. More about Huff can be found in *The Chicago Defender,* July 6, 1963, and in the *Atlanta Daily World,* Nov. 27, 1963, among other era newspapers.

[‡‡] Communities identified by R.W. Hunter Banking Co. in addition to Chicago were Gary, Indiana; Pittsburgh, Pennsylvania; New York City's Harlem; Detroit; Los Angeles; Cleveland; Oklahoma City; St. Louis; Washington, D.C.; Louisville, Kentucky; and Baltimore, Maryland. *The Chicago Defender,* July 12, 1919. Later newspaper articles suggested as many as 18 locations may have been under consideration.

was operating out of a single location at 28th and State streets, and the eve of its collapse in late 1919, included:

- Opening two additional Chicago locations, including one at 48th Street and State Street and another on West Lake on the city's West Side.
- Opening, or nearly opening, banks in Detroit; Gary, Indiana; and Pittsburg, Pennsylvania.[35] The Gary bank, which was only open for a few months, was the first Black-owned bank with a state charter in the northern United States.[36]
- Purchasing the Angelus Building at the corner of 35th Street and Wabash Avenue, a landmark seven-story structure that was the largest apartment and office building on the city's South Side. The bank issued $150,000 in bonds to finance the purchase.[37]
- Beginning the process of seeking a national charter.[38]
- Paying shareholders a whopping 21 percent dividend out of the bank's surplus funds, with the dividend checks going into the mail about two weeks before violence erupted along the lakefront.[39]

By the end of the year, the bank was urging Black Belt residents to pull their money from white banks and deposit the funds with Hunter. "The riot has taught the race a lesson," a Hunter bank newspaper advertisement headline proclaimed. The ad explained how white-owned businesses in the Black Belt had closed during the turmoil, abandoning their customers. Meanwhile, many Black Belt residents had deposits in banks located in other areas of the city they were unable to reach to make withdrawals.

"Let us get wise in this country like the white races and bank our money with our … banks and do business with one another, the same as the white races do. Let us boost our own business enterprises."[40]

Absent detailed historical records, it is difficult to determine the strength of the two banks at the time of the crisis. Whether Hunter would have been able to realize its vision without the 1919 riot is not clear. The riot may have erupted at a time when the bank was overextended and in a precarious financial condition. The Woodfolk bank was likely under-capitalized, not unusual for a new bank at the time, but later events suggest that at the time of the crisis it may have been the stronger of the two institutions.[41] Notably, the Woodfolk bank loaned the Hunter bank at least $6,000 during the 1919 bank runs, and likely far more.[42] During later court hearings, it was discovered that Woodfolk, not Hunter, had at some point become the owner of the Angelus Building.

Hunter Banking customers and creditors appear to have suffered substantial, if not total, losses. Both the bank and Hunter individually were bankrupt by the end of 1919, and as late as early 1921, bank trustees published a notice saying they were "having the fight of their lives" trying to generate revenue through an asset sale that could be paid out to creditors.[43]

The Woodfolk bank's post-failure assets, meanwhile, went to a court-appointed receiver, generally a step that would be followed with the failed bank's assets going to an established local institution. In this case, however, Woodfolk Banking customers turned to a seemingly unlikely source whom they urged to intervene.

3.

P.W. (Pearl William) Chavers did not have banking experience, nor was he a longtime Chicago resident. Although he had come to the city, his wife's hometown, only in 1917, by 1919 he'd already made a place for himself, establishing a trade school where Black girls learned to produce fabric goods – generally uniforms and aprons used by the city's many meatpacking firms.[44, 45] In addition, he was a well known community leader who was involved in establishing the Black Chicago Business League.[46]

Both efforts aligned with initiatives he'd led in his previous hometown of Columbus, Ohio. There, he founded the Lincoln-Ohio Industrial Training School for Colored Youth, which included job placement services, and he was involved in The Colored Business Men's Association of Ohio.[47] He also spent a few years publishing *The Columbus Standard,* a Black newspaper, in which he advocated for Black business development, and he authored at least one book on Black economic challenges.[48]

In Chicago, Chavers may have also been working with Woodfolk bank leaders late in 1919 in efforts to try to keep the bank viable.[49] If so, it would have undoubtedly been a key consideration of the depositors who turned to him for help in preserving the community bank.

For Chavers, the plea from Woodfolk depositors presented a dilemma that was explained by historian Christopher Robert Reed in his study of Chicago's Black community in the 1920s:

> He could either take a plunge and start a banking operation based on his personal assessment that the time was right (in regard to his own talents to learn the business on the run and amass the capital) or wait for a day that appeared to never come in a society geared toward delaying Black progress and deferring full citizenship on a level playing field upon which to compete. If Black banks and building associations did not lend money to prospective African American homeowners, what entities would, given the racist climate in lending?[50]

In March 1920, the receiver transferred the Woodfolk bank's assets into a new institution operating under Chavers' leadership, the Merchant's and People's Bank. To keep a sense of continuity with the previous institution, the bank opened in the old Woodfolk bank building near the corner of 32nd and State streets.[51]

"More of us should get into community affairs to make a place for our people," Chavers reportedly told a family member.[52] "It is not enough that I am doing well for myself ... We have to fit into the scheme of things in the big city ... [and] the only way is for us to venture for survival, using our brains in the business world. That is how others got established in this country. We have to gain respect from people in business and one of the better ways is through banking." Before Chavers decided to enter banking, however, he consulted with a man who was the dean of Chicago's Black bankers and the city's most well-known Black business leader at that time: Jesse Binga.[53]

"Jesse Binga was the money man ..." reads one biography.[54] "Every man, woman and child in Chicago's Black Belt knew that name."

Binga was born in Detroit in 1865, one of 10 children. His father was a barber, and his mother managed the family's real estate business. Their tenants included some of the many families that had returned to the U.S. after fleeing to Canada and living as refugees across the Detroit River from the city in the years after President Filmore signed the Fugitive Slave Act in 1850.[55, 56]

After completing high school and briefly studying law under attorney Thomas Crisup, Michigan's first Black lawyer, Jesse Binga worked as a Pullman porter and at least a part-time barber, traveling the rails across the West. He landed in Chicago in 1892.[57] According to legend, all he had at the time was a shoeshine kit and $10 in his pocket.

In the city, he set up shop as a peddler, one of perhaps as many as 30,000 in Chicago selling fruit to tourists near the train station around the time of the 1893 World's Fair. Binga likely later returned to work as a Pullman porter and probably engaged in other ventures, possibly some outside the city, before entering Chicago real estate in 1902.[58, 59] His first steps were funded with savings generated by his other various endeavors. He later told a reporter "I never borrowed a dollar in my life."[60]

In real estate, Binga relied on skills he likely learned from his mother's experience in property management and his own willingness to take matters quite literally into his own hands. He did all of his own repairs and maintenance, and also sometimes renovated rented properties that he could then sublet at a higher rate, pocketing the difference.[61]

He benefitted, he said, because "the average white man ... [would] underestimate my knowledge of real estate values. They wouldn't believe that a colored man could take almost any old building and whip it into shape."[62]

Soon, the white landlords recognized it was in their financial interest to hire Binga to manage the properties they leased to Black tenants.[63]

Binga's move into real estate came at a particularly important time. Between 1890 and 1900, the number of Black residents more than doubled to 30,000 – a figure that likely undercounted transient single men and seasonal labor.[64] By the time the population influx of the Great Migration was getting ready to pick up steam, Binga was well established with perhaps more than 2,000 South Side residents already making their monthly rent payments to him.[65] In addition, the amount of real estate owned by Black residents, as measured by its value, roughly doubled to $4 million over this same period – the equivalent of around $130 million in modern amounts. Across this span, Binga would have been one of perhaps as few as four real estate dealers who handled transactions with Black buyers.[66]

For many of the Black Belt renters, particularly newcomers from the South seeking a new beginning, the landlord was the wealthiest individual they knew and one of the few potential sources of money in an emergency. As a result, Binga was sometimes asked to provide credit, not only in the form of delayed rent payments, but also for financial emergencies or other unexpected expenses. It is unclear when Binga began to capitalize on this informal form of banking, but it was likely very early. By 1907, in a newspaper ad where he listed 10 houses and flats for sale and another six for rent, he also advertised loans to those interested in buying one of his properties.[67] By this time, his eventual move to banking had become all but inevitable.

4.

Before a new bank opens, the would-be startup bankers have to complete an extensive process of regulatory review that examines everything from financing and capital adequacy, to risk management policies and the backgrounds of its senior managers, among other items. To protect future customers and the federal safety net that will be called on in the event of a failure, bank regulators must be convinced that the bank has a reasonable chance of succeeding in a safe and sound manner even if it should suffer some amount of unexpected loss. After meeting these standards to get the doors open, the new institution – known as a De Novo bank – operates under regulatory restrictions for a period of years.

In 1908, the process that Binga and others followed was a bit less onerous:

"You just put [the word] 'Bank' in the front window and you were a bank," a Binga relative later recalled.[68]

In this case, Binga's bank was in a building along South State Street that had been home to the white-owned McCarthy Bank until its 1907 failure.[69] Although the Binga Bank would later fall under state regulation – a step Binga supported as early as 1912 – it was born as an unregulated private bank.[70] At the time, such banks were not at all unusual, particularly in the Midwest. For example, Illinois was home to at least 135 private banks – most likely many more – in 1900.§§ In comparison, at the same time, the state had 155 banks with state charters and 240 nationally chartered banks.[71]

From a modern perspective, an unregulated bank might seem to be incredibly risky for depositors and comparable to a dangerous loan shark for borrowers. While there is no doubt that some private banks operated with unscrupulous management, there were also a number of private banks that treated their customers fairly. In these cases, the institutions remained private simply because they were too small to meet minimum capital requirements, which could range from $25,000 in small towns to more than $200,000 in cities, depending on whether the bank was seeking a state or national charter.[72] At the time Binga Bank opened for business, the average capitalization of an Illinois private bank was around $22,000 compared to more than $125,000 for those with either a state or national charter.[73]

§§ Because private banks were not required to complete an annual regulatory filing, the number of private institutions may have been significantly higher than the number that was officially tabulated. For example, data compiled by other organizations in the late 1800s and early 1900s suggest the actual number of private banks in Illinois may have been twice the number appearing in some reports.

Generally, private banks fell into one of two categories as far as business operations. In rural areas, they were community banks, providing credit and deposit accounts to a population that was too small to merit its own chartered bank – thus the significant number of private banks in the Midwest. In urban areas, meanwhile, private banks were often created as an offshoot of an established business that sought to generate additional income from its financial resources.[74]

Binga Bank fell a bit into both categories. The bank, at the time of its creation, was definitely an outgrowth of Binga's established real estate business, but it was also providing financial services to an underserved local population.

When Binga Bank opened on the southeast corner of South State and 36th Street, it was Chicago's first Black-owned bank and one of around 50 operating in the United States at the time, almost all of the others in the South.

The bank was housed in a three-story building that was also home to Binga's real estate business. With marketing savvy, rather than simply propping a "Bank" sign in the window, Binga painted "Jesse Binga Banker" in letters 10 feet tall on the side of a neighboring building towering far above the bank.[75] Passersby could be forgiven if they were confused as to which building was the bank, but there was no mistaking who was the banker.

On weekdays, the bank was open until 3 p.m., and between 6 p.m. to 8 p.m. on Wednesdays and Saturdays. Customers could open checking accounts with a $100 deposit. Savings accounts, which could be opened for $1 – "Begin with one dollar" being a Binga Bank slogan – earned 3 percent interest payable semiannually in January and July. Safe deposit boxes could be rented for $3 a month.[76]

Although it would later become one of the largest Black banks in the United States, the majority of Binga Bank's earliest depositors were not Black, with whites accounting for perhaps as much as two-thirds of the initial customer base.[77]

This, of course, soon began to change, as evidenced in this 1912 newspaper account about the bank's role as the South Side's economic engine for an emerging Black economy:

The development of this section of the city may be largely attributed to the influence of this financial house. A reliable bank, well managed, may be called the foster-parent of its community. It not only furnishes a nucleus around which the business interests of the section can assemble and operate, but, on the other hand, it creates a standing fund which is always open to the launching of legitimate new enterprises. The presence of such a fund makes business expansion possible in that community.[78]

As a real estate investor and landlord, much of Binga's work directly involved the expansion of the Black Belt to the south. Eventually, his portfolio included the so-called "Binga Block," which spanned more than 500 feet of South State Street between 47th and 48th streets with 21 stores and more than 50 flats; and the six-story Binga Arcade at the corner of 35th and South State streets, home to offices and stores, and topped by a reception hall with 20-foot-high ceilings, eight glass chandeliers and an inscription reading, "Let peace and contentment enter into the hearts of all who gather here."[79]

In residential development, Binga was well acquainted with the opposition white neighborhoods presented to Black homebuyers. As a banker, real estate investor and – perhaps even more importantly, the most prominent Black businessman in Chicago – Binga was "frequently called on … to defend the rights of Negroes," particularly families as they moved into these previously segregated neighborhoods.[80]

Some insight to the malice behind the opposition these families encountered can be found in the remarks made by white real estate agent L.M. Smith around the time of the 1919 violence:

We want to be fair. We want to do what is right. But these [Black] people will have to be more or less pacified. At a conference where their representatives were present, I told them we might as well be frank about it, "You people are not admitted to our society," I said. Personally, I have no prejudice against them. I have had experience of many years dealing with them, and I'll say this for them: I have never had to foreclose a mortgage on one of them. They have been clean in every way, and always prompt in their payments. But, you know, improvements are coming along the lake shore, the Illinois Central, and all that; we can't have these people coming over here.

Not one cent has been appropriated by our organization for bombing or anything like that.

They injure our investments. They hurt our values. I couldn't say how many have moved in, but there's at least a hundred blocks that are tainted. We are not making any threats, but we do say that something must be done. Of course, if they come as tenants, we can handle that situation fairly easily. But when they get a deed, that's another matter. Be sure to get us straight on that. We want to be fair and do what's right.[81]

Some additional details may be helpful in interpreting Smith's comments. The denial of any role in the bombings was in response to reports in the city at the time that the bombings may have been done under the direction of a couple of white neighborhood organizations. The reference to tenants as something that can be handled "fairly easily" refers to the eviction of Black renters, which sometimes occurred without notice, leaving entire families homeless.

Confrontations were of course inevitable. One that directly involved Binga occurred in early May 1915, when Charles A. Davis, a 20-year postal service employee and his wife, a longtime teacher, were met by a white crowd as they tried to move into a home they'd purchased at 4506 South Forrestville Avenue.[82] The home's previous resident had been a white male renting the property from an estate. When the man moved, the estate's trustee sold the house to a woman who may have worked at a real estate agency. She almost immediately sold the property – perhaps without ever setting foot inside – to the Davises. This somewhat unusual ownership/tenant history may have fostered an already likely conflict because, while the Davises held the title, the neighbors still had the keys that they'd been given by the tenant before he left.[83, 84]

The neighbors, among them two municipal employees including a city attorney who may have organized the effort, argued that they had a prior agreement to collectively purchase the home as "community property." To protect their interests, they had gone so far as to install a 6-foot-tall, 200-pound white man inside the house as "custodian of the property," while convincing a white police officer to station himself outside to meet the Davises.[85, †††]

Encountering this, the Davises alerted Binga, who arrived at the scene while neighbors called for additional police, who also responded. Eventually, the matter ended up at a police station.[86]

"While there seems to be considerable speculation among the neighbors ... as to whether a bona fide sale exists between Mr. Davis, who purchased the property and the agents as represented, it must be remembered ... the restrictions amongst the owners

––––––––––

††† The Black *Chicago Defender* published a list of names, and, in some cases, the employers of the white residents who lived on the street. Readers were advised to exhibit patience in regard to the list, but to keep it for future reference with the suggestion that some of the individuals might be politically connected. To be sure, innumerable events such as this and much worse occurred but did not receive media attention. In this instance, the involvement of a city attorney likely piqued the interest of the press.

against selling to negroes are generally promoted by politicians, real estate men, etc.... to achieve notoriety by blaring their trumpets at the expense of the Negro race," Binga said.[87] "This, like all other residential districts which have been secluded for years, must change with the times, the same as the business districts in an enterprising city like Chicago."[‡‡‡]

Many incidents were no doubt unreported as the city was confronted by the practice of "blockbusting," a scheme used by unscrupulous real estate speculators willing to make "a business of commercializing racial antagonisms."[88]

More than a century later, the scars of blockbusting, racially restrictive real estate covenants and "redlining," remain on America's cities and arguably on modern-day families even if their ancestors moved away from the affected neighborhoods years ago.

Blockbusting schemes, which date back to at least the early 1900s, exploited Black individuals and families seeking homes in an overcrowded housing market while leveraging racial prejudice to create panic-selling among nearby white property owners. It was not only openly fanning the flames of existing racism, it was in some ways encouraging prejudice by actively creating racist stereotypes among the white public.

In a typical case of blockbusting, a real estate speculator would come to a white neighborhood abutting a Black community and start by simply suggesting the homeowners might want to consider selling their home before it is "too late." The time frame suggesting that Black families living a street or two over were either considering a move or encouraging their friends and family members to live nearby. Sometimes, the agent would pay Black individuals to participate in the scheme, either in the role of a potential home buyer who might ask to see a house or to begin regularly traveling through the neighborhood in a highly visible manner.[89]

Eventually, through "panic peddling," a property would almost inevitably be purchased, often at a reduced price, by an agent who either rented it or resold it at above-market prices to a Black family who was willing to pay a premium to simply find a place to live.[90] Because Black buyers could often not obtain credit, because of racism or, in other cases, because the

[‡‡‡] It is not clear whether the Davises ever moved into the home. Newspaper coverage of the incident implied they were preparing to, but if they did, they did not remain long. It is not known why they left, but it would not be unheard of at this time for white neighbors to pool their money and purchase a home from a Black family to get them out. Violence and threats would be another means of encouraging a Black family to leave. Regardless, the 1920 Census shows the home as the residence of Jacob and Eva Rosenberg and their five children. A few years later, the house was home to Leroy and Mabel Johnson, married Black attorneys who hosted many prominent social events at the address.

selling price was exceptionally high to the point it distorted risk/return relationships in financing, it was common for the agent to sell the property on an installment plan, which the agent would finance. Such an arrangement provided the agent with additional leverage and the ability to evict the tenants, sometimes without notice because, unlike a mortgage, the buyer was building no equity until total ownership was achieved with the final payment. Faced with the looming threat of losing their homes, it was not uncommon for the home buyers to rent out spare rooms as a means of supplementing household income or to secure additional employment to the degree that it left little time for regular home maintenance.[91]

All of this would then be exploited by speculators to create an impression that an entire neighborhood was rapidly deteriorating because of its Black residents, thus potentially motivating other white homeowners to sell their properties at below-market levels, which, in turn would start the cycle again as it expands to a new property.

Although Chicago blockbusting was particularly aggressive, the practice was pervasive in U.S. urban centers ranging from New York City and Philadelphia to Cleveland and Kansas City, particularly in the period after World War II. It was eventually outlawed under the Fair Housing Act of 1968, although the practices no doubt continued in many communities for years after.

The racist stereotypes that allowed blockbusters to prosper were supported and reinforced by racially restrictive real estate covenants. The covenants, either drawn up by residential developers at the inception of their projects or retroactively implemented by the residents of established neighborhoods and placed in property deeds, barred the future sale of real estate to Black buyers. Here, the private sector was working to implement a type of segregation that was similar to previous municipal segregation ordinances – the first of which might have been deployed in Baltimore in 1910 and was soon mirrored in various forms elsewhere.[92] While the Constitution, including importantly the 14th Amendment, created a legal standard many of the municipal ordinances could not meet, the same was not necessarily true of the real estate covenants. Instead, these restrictions that white homeowners and housing associations began to implement relied on the legal system for enforcement under the same mechanism that home associations turn to when they mandate things like building design standards or requirements on maintaining an orderly lawn – things that are seen as affecting the values of neighborhood properties.

A 1930s government housing report explained the difference between the ways that the public and private sector could implement such measures:

Whereas it is … unconstitutional to legislate against one element of citizens, the law permits individuals to enter contractual relationships and offers machinery for punishing violators of contracts. Thus, these covenants have become widespread through the North, and these exclusion methods have been reinforced by violence in Chicago, Detroit [and elsewhere].[93]

The covenants, and the racist views within, were self-perpetuating. For example, after covenants were implemented in affluent neighborhoods, those living in other areas began to believe that similar measures were necessary for protecting the value of their neighborhoods. Soon, covenants were supported even by middle- and lower-income white homeowners who otherwise bristled at the idea that any outside limitations might be imposed on how they sought to use their property.[94] In Chicago, where covenants became increasingly popular in the 1920s, efforts to implement the restrictions within some neighborhoods found support not only from groups of homeowners, but also from a wide range of institutions including businesses, banks and churches which became actively involved.[95]

As one later analysis explained:

In the context of covenant law in the 1920s and later, it seemed entirely obvious that … race by itself was indeed relevant to property values. Why? Simply because white owners thought so … [and] their view was supported by a steadily increasing drumbeat from surrounding institutions. Real estate professionals' appraisal manuals reported that property values dropped for white people if African Americans or other nonwhite persons moved into a neighborhood. Real estate boards, no doubt many sincerely believing they were serving their customers, stated that it was unethical to introduce racial elements that would be "detrimental" to property values in a neighborhood...

With all these respectable institutions asserting that racial mixing would cause property values to drop, and acting on that asserted belief, it should not be surprising to find that property values would in fact drop when neighborhoods were integrated.[96, §§§, **]

Among the most notable of these institutions was the Federal Housing Administration (FHA), which encouraged racially restrictive covenants in its underwriting manuals.

Among the raft of New Deal initiatives implemented after the Great Depression were policies designed to remake the nation's mechanism for mortgage financing. While the government had sought to encourage home ownership among middle income families for years, many would-be homebuyers were unable to meet the terms of a then-standard mortgage: 50 percent down and interest-only payments with the full loan repaid within seven years or less. In 1933, the government created the Home Owners Loan Corporation (HOLC), which purchased mortgages at risk of default and then transitioned them into a mortgage structure that is more familiar to modern-day homebuyers: longer-term loans with amortized payments that allowed homebuyers to build equity. In 1934, the government took the additional step of establishing the FHA, which insured bank mortgages in hopes of further increasing home ownership.[97]

These programs, however, were not for all potential homebuyers. In connection with the government initiative, the HOLC created maps that were used to identify risks associated with individual neighborhoods. Those deemed the highest risk or "hazardous" for lending, as determined in part by the appraisals of local real estate agents, were colored red, or "redlined." While the designation could be used for areas with aging homes in desperate need of upkeep, a neighborhood *automatically* "earned a red color if African Americans lived in it, even if it was a solid middle-class neighborhood of single-family homes." By doing this, the government was, in effect stating that all Black households, and all Black homebuyers, were poor credit risks.[98]

In addition, as noted by academic and author Richard Rothstein and others, the government programs created, for all practical purposes, a "state-sponsored system of segregation,"

§§§ For an extensive and detailed exploration of restrictive covenants see: Brooks, Richard R.W. and Carol M. Rose. *Saving the Neighborhood: Racially Restrictive Covenants, Law, and Social Norms.* Harvard University Press. Cambridge, Mass. 2013.

** Likely unbeknownst to many homeowners, it is not necessarily unusual to find racial covenants still in place in real estate deeds a century after they were first implemented. As one example, in 2021 the state of Washington ordered additional research into real estate deeds in that state after a University of Washington study found 20,000 properties with racial covenants still in place in King County. See: *The Seattle Times.* May 1, 2021.

fostering the growth of white suburbs via government-supported mortgages. Black home-buyers, including those capable of affording a home in one of these suburban communities without having to rely on a mortgage, meanwhile were blocked by restrictive covenants that permitted only white homeowners in many developments.[99]

Property values and homeownership sank in redlined areas where mortgage financing was for all practical purposes unavailable for large swaths of urban real estate. Those seeking to purchase homes in a redlined area – sometimes the only option available – were then vulnerable of being forced into the same installment payment arrangements used by blockbusters.

A comprehensive understanding of how deeply this has affected families and communities is well beyond the scope of this work. Redlining, although long since outlawed, is an oft-cited significant contributor to the ongoing racial wealth gap.[100] In addition to research showing the way redlining affected generations in terms of educational opportunity and access to services, there are other issues that are only now beginning to emerge through research. For example, some particularly interesting research has revealed that previously redlined neighborhoods have been shown to have higher summer temperatures because of a lack of trees that have been lost and replaced by large swaths of pavement. This, in turn, affects not only comfort during the hottest months of the year but also overall health with a higher potential risk of cardiac arrest or respiratory complications such as asthma.[101, ††††] The issues, it appears, may be very nearly endless.

Jesse Binga, to be clear, was not a blockbuster. A family moving into a neighborhood that had, up to that period, been entirely white was not blockbusting. Although Binga was able to purchase homes at what were generally considered below-market values as a result of so-called "white flight," he did not employ blockbuster tactics nor engage in the exploitive practices used by blockbusters. His reputation within the community was generally impeccable.

†††† Even those familiar with the history of redlining might be surprised by its depth and scope. Redlined neighborhoods included Black neighborhoods in large urban centers such as Chicago as well as in significantly smaller cities including such places as Rochester, Minnesota, and St. Joseph, Missouri. Those with an interest in this issue can access historic Home Owners Loan Corporation "redlining" maps and some supporting materials that have been digitized through an effort hosted by the University of Richmond in partnership with a number of other universities, individuals and contributors. The maps are available at: https://dsl.richmond.edu/panorama/redlining.

For more on redlining's lingering impact on communities and race into the 21st century, see: Aaronson, Daniel. Daniel Hartley and Bhashkar Mazumder. "The Effects of the 1930s HOLC 'Redlining' Maps." Federal Reserve Bank of Chicago. REVISED Aug. 2020.

One of Binga's core beliefs was that homeownership was an essential step in strengthening the community – "to become a good citizen, it is necessary to own a home."[102, ####]

In a later interview, he talked about blockbusting as a "commercializing of a deadly passion by dishonorable and dishonest real estate dealers," something that he became very much acquainted with.[103] Days after the 1919 riot, Binga received a letter whose sender was listed only as the "Headquarters of the White Hands":

> You are the one who helped cause this riot by encouraging Negroes to move into good white neighborhoods and you know the results of your work. This trouble has only begun and we advise you to use your influence to get Negroes to move out of these neighborhoods to Black Belt where they belong and in conclusion we advise you to get off South Park Ave. yourself. Just take this as a warning. You know what comes next.[104]

In the years around the riots, the homes and businesses of at least 40 Black Chicago families were firebombed. Some counts place the total at nearly 60 assaults on Black homes with at least two people killed. There were no prosecutions.[105] These attacks were in addition to the innumerable rocks and bricks thrown through windows and other incidents that were left unreported.

Binga was bombed six times over this span – four times at his home and two at his real estate office. In addition, there were at least two instances where a bomb thrown at his house failed to explode, including one incident where melting snow extinguished a fuse.[106]

Eventually, the attacks on Binga became so commonplace that, after one explosion at his home, a *Chicago Tribune* article about the damage described it as such: "As usual, the pillars of the front porch were blown out of place and scores of window panes in the neighborhood were shattered."[107]

Throughout this period, Binga was not one to live in fear. While he did eventually employ an armed bodyguard, the attacks only appeared to firm his resolve:

> My idea of this bombing of my house is that it is an effort to retard the Binga State Bank which will take over the mortgages of colored people now buying property

For more details on Binga's life and career, see Hayner, Don. "Binga: The Rise and Fall of Chicago's First Black Banker." Northwestern University Press. Evanston, Ill. 2019. The book served as an important source of information for this publication.

against which effort is being made to foreclose. I will not run. The race is at stake and not myself. If they can make me move they will have accomplished much of their aim because they can say, "We made Jesse Binga move; certainly you'll have to move," to all the rest. If they can make leaders move, what show will the smaller buyers have? Such headlines are efforts to intimidate ... [people] not to purchase property and to scare some of them back South.[108]

While Binga's prominence placed him at the center of a target, his connections in the city also proved beneficial for some of the South Side's residents during the 1919 turmoil.

Binga is believed to have done substantial work behind the scenes to a degree that may not have been possible for others. These activities likely included such things as ensuring the delivery of food and other essentials into the Black Belt during this time.[109] Local union heads had ordered their drivers to stop delivering ice, milk and perhaps other goods into the neighborhood out of fear for the drivers' safety.[110] Families, of course, were caught unprepared and some were willing to risk starvation rather than venture to another part of the city, prompting Binga to ask the state militia for help.[111]

"My people have no food," Binga told a reporter. "Retailers in the district have run out of stocks and outside grocery and butcher men will not send their wagons into the district."

Like the city's other Black banks, Binga Bank also took action beyond the parameters of normal business operations. The bank was an emergency pay station, providing a location where employees of Armour & Co., and perhaps other stockyards firms, could obtain and cash their paychecks without having to risk traveling to other areas of the city.[112] Later, in 1921, Binga stepped up to coordinate a Chicago fundraising effort for the Greenwood victims.[113]

These steps, along with some of the actions by the Hunter and Woodfolk banks, were taken despite a reality that had to frustrate all of the bankers – many of the South Side residents who did have bank accounts, chose to deposit their funds not with one of the Black institutions but instead with one of the city's established white banks.[114]

5.

In the aftermath of the 1919 violence, Illinois Governor Frank Lowden established the nonpartisan interracial Chicago Commission on Race Relations to study the riot's causes and race issues in the city. The resulting report, at nearly 800 pages, provided the community with something it had not seen previously – an exploration of race in Chicago drawn not from a single perspective but with nearly equal input from all sides racially and politically.

Economic issues were, of course, a key concern. While the commission examined the problems of real estate and home ownership that had proven volatile, it also considered the economic environment from a broader perspective including various labor-related issues, as well as banking and access to financial services.

Before considering what the report says about financial services available to Black Chicagoans during this period, it must be stressed that this was not a comprehensive banking report from this era. A limited number of banks were involved, and it was a voluntary survey. It offers a peek into financial services access, but not a highly detailed look. There is no resulting quantifiable data.

With that caveat, the findings are still informative, sometimes by their contradictions. They are also frustrating in that some matters are not further explored. However, this should not be a considered a fault of the committee who wrote the report. Recall that the focus was on the riot and race relations. As a result, financial services, while extremely important, was but one part of a larger review of such things as population density, labor markets, the role of the press and even rumors.

The report is, however, particularly illuminating considered through the lens of the traditional role of any community bank – an institution that uses a community's combined resources, or its savings, as a catalyst for community improvement by extending loans and services to businesses, individuals and families. In this light, it is hard to reach any conclusion other than that a potentially significant opportunity had been missed for economic improvement because Black Belt depositors chose to not use local financial institutions but instead took their money outside of the community to banks that did not reciprocate by lending funds back to the community.[115]

This was of course a key issue for the Hunter and Woodfolk banks. Whatever other issues the banks may have had, a larger depositor base would have been beneficial at the time of the crisis. While there is not a direct correlation between a bank's size and its stability –

certainly history has shown time and again that a large bank can have any number of problems – Hunter and Woodfolk were providing services, and in some cases extending loans, to individuals who did not support the banks with their deposits. In addition, had a larger number of local residents had money on deposit with the banks, there is some potential they may not have been as concerned about their ability to access those funds during the violence. Some who turned to the local banks during the crisis were no doubt fearful of heading into predominantly white areas of the city to access their money.

This is all reinforced to a degree by another finding that was apparently unexpected by the committee, which wrote that "in spite of contrary opinion it appears the resources of [Black Chicagoans] are astonishingly large." Given the committee's low expectations, this statement is difficult to quantify and the report provides relatively little banking data.§§§§ Anecdotally, one white bank said it had total Black deposits of around $20 million in modern amounts while another had around $13 million. What was apparently a third institution said it had around 4,000 Black depositors.[116]

Perhaps more noteworthy than the number of depositors or the size of their accounts are the views that some of the white bankers expressed about the Black community and the broader implications that may have been a result.

In response to a survey question about their institution's willingness to hire a Black employee for a skilled position, only one of 14 white banks that answered the question responded with an unconditional "yes."[117] The employment question was connected to a concern the authors raised about the lack of practical experience with banking or other financial matters and how such experience could be obtained. The suggestion was that one solution might come from employment within banks. The need for financial education and experience was an issue raised by many. Binga had sought to address it in part through a weekly newspaper column published in *The Chicago Defender* where he talked about any number of issues, often from an educational perspective.

In terms of how white banks viewed Black depositors, the report found "that in only a few of the banks are [Black customers] welcomed and in most of them they are only tolerated."[118] The word "tolerated," of course, cries for further explanation, particularly as it pertains to the extension of credit and a willingness to finance home purchases.

§§§§ One table does show the size of average accounts comparing all accounts versus those of Black depositors. However, the figures include an unknown number of corporate or other accounts, which can greatly distort the averages, thus the table provides almost no amount of valuable insight.

In response to a question about lending to Black borrowers for real estate or commercial purposes, nearly all of the banks responded positively with some offering details including an unnamed national bank that said it "buys commercial or collateral paper on its merits, without regard to color."[119]

The rest of the report, however, found otherwise.

Binga's bank, and two apparently white institutions are mentioned in the report as significantly involved in financing Black home purchases, but the committee believed even combined they were not able to achieve the scale necessary to make a substantial dent in demand. The report further noted that "many of the [white] banks that are the depositories for Negroes' funds *do not make loans to them, giving as their reason that they do not lend on the class of property purchased by Negroes* [emphasis added]." While there were certainly some exceptions, the committee also found that "most large real estate firms and loan companies decline to make loans on property owned or occupied by Negroes."[120]

However, as it pertained to credit risk, the report included anecdotal accounts from two lenders who financed mortgages for borrowers of all races and said that their Black borrowers typically asked for less money than white borrowers *and* sought loans for a smaller percentage of the property's value than was the case with most white borrowers.[121]

The rampant prejudice of white lenders against Black borrowers was, of course, in no way unique to Chicago.

"There are white banks in Texas, in Atlanta and in Black Harlem that with millions of Negro money would sooner lend to the devil than to a negro business enterprise," W.E.B. DuBois wrote in an article discussing the then-upcoming Chicago Commission on Race Relations report.[122]

A more comprehensive examination on banks and lending within the Black community came a few years later from Howard University. The report noted the difficulties businesses had in borrowing money from white banks even when those banks accepted Black customer deposits, hampering economic growth and offering "little inducement for an attempt to develop new enterprises."[123]

The Howard report also included partial results of a survey of Black bankers who noted that their most important role in the community was providing credit to purchase homes, property and establish businesses that, in turn, became catalysts for job creation. The report also found that, around the same time that Binga established his bank, the nation's Black banks in general were turning more toward commercial lending whereas most of the earlier lending had been focused on home purchases.[124] Thus, the availability of credit was expanding, although not sufficiently to meet demand.

Finally, in considering the issues of mortgage lending and the ability of Black banks to foster community economic growth during this era, the work of Mehrsa Baradaran raises a particularly disturbing observation. Baradaran, a law professor and author who has engaged in a significant exploration of the racial wealth gap and its root causes, notes that in a strictly segregated environment, such as Chicago during this era, the money multiplier effect was often muted in the Black community when it came to home buying. To understand this, recognize that when a bank finances a home purchase, it deposits money into the seller's bank account. The seller's bank, with an increase in its deposits, is then in a position to increase its lending by some amount. In pre-Great Depression Chicago, however, when a Black homebuyer purchased a home, it was very often from a white property owner. As a result, that purchase money would very likely leave the Black community and be used by a white bank to loan to its predominantly white customers. "White banks had the advantage of circulating and growing money, and Black bank loans just fed into that circulatory system."[125] In addition, from the perspective of the lending bank and the borrower, racism and the later redlining further reduced the actual value of the property, often below the price that was paid.

6.

Private banking in Illinois was abolished effective Jan. 1, 1921. The measure, which came after depositors lost millions in savings held by the institutions, required Chicago banks to obtain state or national charters.

About 40 Chicago banks were unable to raise the funds necessary to meet the minimum capital requirements and closed.[126] Binga's bank, meanwhile, was reorganized as Binga State Bank with $125,000 in capital.

Binga explained his vision for the bank during a shareholder meeting the previous April, when he talked about the institution's role in educating, building confidence and eliminating the suspicions that many had of financial institutions:

> We have a unique task to perform, which we alone can work out in our own peculiar way for the good of our community. By stopping money loan sharks who are doing business in the rear of every saloon, the mortgage loan brokers who are robbing our people in commissions for placing loans on their homes and the pawnbroker on every block with his three bullets for a sign. It is said by one of our prominent bankers in Philadelphia that the Negro bank is breaking up this evil and is the happy medium between the large white banks and the money loan shark.

> We must get together, encourage a good fellowship and work in harmony. We want it distinctly understood that the Binga State Bank will not be a one-man institution, but a state bank under state supervision, operated by our people and for our people and the success of this bank will be balanced only by the energy that every member of the race, as well as every officer, director and stockholder performs his duty.[127]

On opening day, the bank received $200,000 in deposits and welcomed 1,100 new depositors – each receiving a Binga State Bank birthday card to mark the occasion.[128] By October 1924, the bank's deposits had grown to around $1.2 million.[129]

At Merchant's and Peoples Bank, meanwhile, Chavers had embarked on the process of transitioning that institution to a national charter, christening it Douglass National Bank after the abolitionist icon. Chavers apparently received preliminary approval for a federal bank charter in April 1921, but the United States Office of the Comptroller of the Currency

(OCC) questioned Chavers' lack of banking experience and a similar lack of experience among his board members. In addition, as a nationally chartered institution, the bank needed to secure twice the capital of Binga's state-chartered bank before it could open for business.[130]

It is not clear why Chavers did not pursue a state charter instead. While a national charter afforded the ability to conduct business with customers in other states, the higher capital requirements were a nearly insurmountable obstacle for Chavers who, while trying to raise capital, was also still trying to resolve about $30,000 in debt related to the Woodfolk default.[131] Rather than backing away from his vision of a national charter, Chavers took some seemingly unusual steps to try to generate more financial backing. He operated an informational booth about the bank at community events, offered prizes to current stockholders who could convince others to invest and traveled to Detroit, Indianapolis and St. Louis in hopes of securing additional capital from Black investors living in those cities.[132]

"This is to be a people's bank," Chavers told a reporter. "The people are invited to own its stock. No steps will be taken by the management that will not be in compliance with the law and in obedience to the will and best interests of the people. I am happy to say that my life's dream has been realized. The race is surely coming into its own."[133]

Despite Chavers' efforts, it became apparent in late 1921 that the bank would be unable to meet the minimum capital requirements in time to allow for a grand opening that had been promoted for January 1922. Around this time, Rev. John W. Robinson, a member of Douglass' board and whose church may have had funds tied up in the Woodfolk failure and its aftermath, reached out to a Chicago man who was already an established business icon, Anthony Overton.[134]

Anthony Overton was born in March 21, 1865, in Monroe, Louisiana, less than three weeks before the end of the Civil War. His family was part of the early wave of Southerners heading to the Plains in the 1870s, settling in Kansas where he attended school, including studying chemistry at what was then Washburn College in Topeka. Overton had a wide range of experiences within only a few years. He briefly ran a store in Oklahoma and was reportedly involved in establishing a town before returning to Kansas. He moved to Kansas City, in 1898, opened a store and founded the Overton Hygienic Manufacturing Company, perhaps as a successor firm to another business focused on food products.[135] Overton Hygienic initially produced baking powder before expanding into cosmetics and moving to Chicago in 1911.[136, 137] From there, his High Brown cosmetics brand included a face powder that was sold nationwide, competing against the legendary Madam C.J. Walker.

By 1912, Overton's company offered 52 different products, sold primarily by 400 door-to-door agents.[138] Later, in addition to cosmetics, his firm produced and sold shoe polish, hair preparations and flavoring extracts, among other items under various brand names.

In Overton, Robinson found not only a willing bank investor but also a strong proponent of Black banking in particular. Only a few years earlier, Overton had authored an unsigned editorial about the importance of banking for *Half Century*, a monthly publication he established that focused on issues of racial independence.[139, ***] In an article titled "Have You a Bank Account?" Overton wrote about the importance of saving as it relates to a "desire to lift one's head out of the crowd, a desire to stand for something in the world, to be independent, self-reliant, one's own man." Later articles likely authored by Overton but published under the pseudonym McAdoo Baker, focused on a range of financial topics including, notably, borrowing money and the inability of Black borrowers to obtain funds from the city's white banks despite those same banks accepting Black deposits. In addition, he noted that the Black workers were not employed by the banks nor most of the businesses that borrowed from them:

> Negro funds are loaned to white business institutions that likewise would not give employment to one of our race in any capacity. The Negro's money is used to close the door of opportunity in his own face.[140]

Overton agreed to join the bank effort. Although the amount of his investment is unknown, it was substantial enough to make him the institution's chief investor, chairman and president.

With Overton's participation, the bank's board offered Chavers a vice presidency, which he angrily rejected.

"They turned on me," Chavers reportedly said later.[141] "Not one single man spoke up for me. To think I personally selected each one except [Overton] in whom they now place their confidence."

Chavers' anger is understandable, but so is the frustration likely felt by Robinson and

---

*** *Half Century* later became *The Chicago Bee*, a weekly newspaper with a staff that was predominantly female and included, for a time, activist and journalist Ida B. Wells. In addition, the term "Bronzeville" for Chicago's Black South Side neighborhood was believed to be coined by *The Bee*.

the other bank directors. Chavers' original vision was for a bank owned by large number of small investors who all lived in Chicago, paying $130 per share.[142] Even when he was forced to head outside of the city in the search for investors, he still remained well short of his goal. Conversely, Overton brought not only capital, but he also brought a strong reputation that was growing on a national scale. The bank added to a long list of Overton's business interests, including the cosmetics company, Northern Realty Company, Victory Life Insurance and the publications *Half Century* and *Chicago Bee*. He is generally considered the first Black business leader to form a major conglomerate. Eventually, most of the empire operated out of the four-story Overton Hygienic Building at 3618 South State Street, with Overton's offices on the top floor, Overton Hygienic Corporation business operations on the third floor, Victory Insurance Co. on the second and Douglass National Bank and leased space that housed a drug store on the first floor. The *Chicago Bee* operated from the building next door.[143] The Hygienic Building still stands today and is listed on the National Register of Historic Places.

Although Overton may not have provided the banking experience that had been imagined by OCC officials, he had a track record of success. In addition, he was more deeply rooted in Chicago and connected to the city's business community – without question, important relationships for a young bank.

Despite his ouster, Chavers waged war against the bank's leadership for months. Before the end of 1922, he filed a lawsuit claiming the bank was insolvent, that its charter was fraudulently obtained and that the bank was going to be placed at risk for its connection to financing the construction of a building at 36th Street and South State Street to house Overton's various businesses. The case was thrown out of court within a month and the bank passed an OCC review.[144]

After losing the legal fight, Chavers' concern about the potential abuse of bank funds, at Douglass and elsewhere, caused him to turn his attention to creating a plan to protect bank depositors from such a risk.[145] Years before the creation of the Federal Deposit Insurance Corporation (FDIC), the initial "Chavers Plan for Guaranteeing Bank Deposits" became the basis of a 1924 House bill that would have required national banks to hold surety bonds, which would be used to reimburse depositors in the event of a bank failure. Congress, at a time when bank failures were not a concern, had little interest in the proposal. While the bill did not advance, there is some belief that Chavers' proposal was influential in some aspects of the later Banking Act of 1933, which established the FDIC.[†††††]

[†††††] Likely adding to Chavers' pain was the recollection of a 1919 conversation with Binga while the two were on the way to a golf game about possibly joining together to create a bank. The idea never advanced to serious discussion (*The Atlanta Daily World*, May 26, 1932). Chavers would go on to later buy 6,000 acres of land in northern Wisconsin in 1926, where he hoped to establish a camp for Black children living in Chicago as well as a resort. Results were mixed at best before the 1929 stock market crash which effectively wiped him out. The same year, he also apparently suffered an illness, which would linger for years before his death in 1933 at age 56. See: Chavers-Wright, Madrue. *The Guarantee: Chavers, banker, entrepreneur, philanthropist in Chicago's Black Belt of the Twenties.* Wright-Armstead Associates: 1985. *The Pittsburgh Courier*, April 1, 1933.

7.

With the post-war 1920s economic boom in full swing nationwide, the Douglass and Binga banks anchored one of the nation's most vibrant Black communities at the height of what historian Juliet E.K. Walker refers to as a "golden age of Black business."[146] This period, spanning from 1900 to 1930, saw amid a segregated economic landscape the emergence of not only Black capitalists and banks but innumerable Black-owned businesses and associations including the National Negro Business League and groups dedicated to specific business segments including the National Bankers Association, the National Negro Retail Merchants Association and the National Builders Association.

In Chicago, some of the well-known businesses from this era included Your Cab Company, with its 80 maroon-colored taxis rolling down Chicago streets; and The Parker House Sausage Company, founded by Judge H. Parker in 1919 and still in business on South State Street a century later – making it one of the oldest Black-owned firms in the United States.[147] These businesses joined with innumerable barber shops, drug stores, doctors and merchants to fuel a boom in the city's Black business community in the 1920s.[148] In 1923, the listing of Black Chicago businesses ranging from auto repair shops to undertakers filled nearly one-quarter of the Simms Blue Book and National Negro Business Professional Directory. By 1924, 1,400 Black-owned businesses, almost 500 of them retail with the rest in wholesale and, to a lesser degree services, operated in the city with a Black population soaring past 200,000 by the end of the decade.[149, 150]

Perhaps one of the best descriptions of this period comes from the historian Reed. While Reed was discussing Overton's success during this period, the comments are broadly applicable:

> In Dickensian terms, Overton's empire peaked in the decade of the 1920s that represented "the best of all times." Temporally, the decade provided the ideal circumstances for the actualization of the economic component of the Dream of the Black Metropolis. Talent was abundant and competence high. By 1929 [sociologist E. Frederick] Frazier took note of an expanded business spurt in the Black Belt, one that he attributed to the purchasing power of thousands of energized wage earners and consumers who arrived on the wave of the Great Migration.[151]

Overton and Binga, along with Robert S. Abbott, owner and publisher of the nationally renowned "World's Greatest Weekly" *Chicago Defender,* "influenced and directed the affairs of the [Chicago] Black metropolis as no other force."[152] Collectively, they held a vision fostering Black economic independence – a "Black Metropolis" – on the city's South Side. Their efforts included, among other things, support for the idea of "double duty" dollars.[153] The "double duty" concept, initially popularized by academic, activist and author Gordon Blaine Hancock in the early 1900s and remaining popular in some areas into the 1960s, was a clarion call for Black shoppers to patronize Black businesses, thereby creating jobs and fostering additional economic growth.[154]

The trio also formed the Associated Business Clubs (ABC) to promote Black business and entrepreneurship. ABC initiatives included a coupon program created by Binga where – for every dollar spent – shoppers at ABC stores received 3-cent coupons that could be used on future purchases from ABC businesses. By 1925, there were around 1,000 ABC-affiliated merchants.[155]

While the Black Belt was the economic hub and a base, Black residential growth occurred in other areas of the city during this span, including neighborhoods on the city's North and West sides in addition to suburbs to the south. The combined owned real estate of all of these areas was pegged at perhaps more than $400 million in 1930.[156] W.H. Bolton, who completed a research study in 1929, said he believed that Chicago in the 1920s became "one of the great business centers of the ... race, surpassing New York's ... Harlem, which is larger in population."[157]

Harlem, however, had no Black banks at the time. It was not from a lack of effort or need. There were at least two New York attempts – likely more – that did not advance far beyond the initial planning stages before they were disrupted. For example, the white Chelsea Exchange Bank, which had a near monopoly on Harlem's banking business, very likely influenced state officials to a degree that the bank was able to block any new competition. Chelsea, meanwhile, took Black deposits but had little interest in lending money back into the Black community.[158, 159, ‡‡‡‡, §§§§]

‡‡‡‡ The first Black bank in not only Harlem, but all of New York state, was not established until much later with the founding of Freedom National Bank in 1964, chaired by Jackie Robinson, the legendary Brooklyn Dodger who broke baseball's color barrier in 1947.

§§§§ A more detailed exploration of the issues of Black banking and Harlem can be found in Baradaran, Mehrsa. "The Color of Money: Black Banks and the Racial Wealth Gap." The Belknap Press of Harvard University Press. Cambridge, Mass. 2017. The book was an important source of information for this publication.

In Chicago, meanwhile, the burgeoning 1920s economy was reflected in both banks.

Binga State Bank and Douglass National Bank were Black banks of a size not previously seen in the United States. After the national economic downturn of 1920-21, the combined total deposits held by both banks rose six out of seven years from 1922 to 1929 and were essentially flat in the other year. For Douglass, each year was higher than the previous. Lending activity followed a somewhat similar path, although it leveled off around 1927 at Binga.[160]

By the end of the 1920s, just before the nation was thrust into the economic turmoil of the Great Depression, the two banks at the height of their growth held $3 million in total deposits and earning assets. Their combined resources at one point were believed to have accounted for more than one-third of the total resources held by all 21 Black banks in operation in the United States at that time.[161] In summer 1929, Douglass, the larger of the two, touted 35,000 savings accounts and 2,200 commercial accounts with customers in multiple states. Binga, about a year later, had 18,500 accounts, although the vast majority of them were small, holding less than $100.[162]

There was a slight difference in the lending profile of the two institutions. Binga, dating back to its time as a private institution and reflecting its founder's background, was significantly involved in real estate and was "an important factor in the [Black] acquisition of property in Chicago" during the 1920s.[163] Douglass, while also heavily invested in real estate, was also engaged in a significant amount of business lending.[164] Beyond the normal risks presented by both strategies, the racial environment and widespread prejudice created additional tangible financial risk.

For example, in real estate, mortgages in predominately Black Chicago neighborhoods offered the banks little in the way of liquidity. Binga was later accused of leading the bank "somewhat forcefully to invest too much... in real estate loans," which became a significant concern when financial conditions tightened. Many, if not all, of the city's white banks were unwilling to take on the loans Binga State Bank made to Black borrowers. At one point, a Binga official took approximately $200,000 worth of what the bank believed to be its best mortgages – many related to properties along the South State Street business district – to the city's large white banks in search of a buyer and found no takers.**** The big banks said they were "unable to get rid of mortgages on South Side property among white purchasers."[165]

In addition to the same risk of liquidity issues related to its mortgages, commercial

---

**** In modern amounts, the loans would be worth a little more than $3 million.

lending at Overton's bank was also not without its race-related risks even in an area that was a beacon of Black economic strength. Profitability in commercial lending was an issue that faced many Black banks during this era, according to Arnett G. Lindsay, a Black St. Louis banker and research author who visited many banks during this period.[166]

"There are not more than a half dozen banks owned and operated by Negroes, which are actually making even ordinary banking profits by specializing in commercial loans," Lindsay wrote. "The banks serve a useful purpose in promoting thrift and home ownership, but this is not commercial banking in the true sense of the word."

Explained perhaps a bit more clearly: In many communities, while a segregated economy may have created opportunities to serve Black customers who were either barred or unwelcome at other businesses, there could also be an impenetrable ceiling limiting that growth based on the Black population – the same limit that was noted previously in discussing Richmond's Jackson Ward neighborhood around the turn of the century.

Douglass National, in some regards, was in a unique situation in serving a Chicago Black business community with a large population that continued to steadily expand through migration – however, that worked both for and against the bank. Unlike in Greenwood, Jackson Ward and elsewhere, Chicago's expanding Black population fostered interest from white business owners who opened stores in the Black Belt, including chain retailers, that sold to a substantially Black clientele. In most cases, these businesses were largely staffed by an entirely white workforce until some point in the late 1920s when the businesses finally began to hire Black employees.[167] Not only were white businesses competitors, but many of the Black-owned businesses were also paying rent to white landlords.[168]

Of particular concern to both Binga State and Douglass National banks was the direct competition from a number of white-owned banks that developed near the economic heart of the Black Belt. These banks, along with the Loop-based institutions, competed for the deposits that the banks relied on as the source of funds for lending back into the community. By one measure, in the mid-1920s – even though Binga and Douglass were the largest Black banks in the U.S. – combined they may have held perhaps as little as 10 percent of all total bank deposits made by Black Chicagoans.[169]

To encourage a reversal of these numbers, Binga State brought the activist, public speaker and author W.E.B. Du Bois to Chicago in 1927 for a speech on banking.

Du Bois, whose views on the importance of Black economic growth are evident in one of his most well-known observations – "to be a poor man is hard, but to be a poor race in a land of dollars is the very bottom of hardships" – addressed a standing room-only crowd of 3,000 at Wendell Phillips High School.[170, #####]

After talking about the history of banking, Du Bois took on the issue of Black depositors patronizing white banks "where we can have little voice or interest, and no part at all in the industrial process of those institutions, whereas if this money were deposited in our own banks and our forces concentrated as demonstrated by the vast audience present, we could go down to LaSalle Street [the center of Chicago's financial district and its city hall] and gently hint if we wanted a thing, whereas now we must almost throw stones and yell to be heard."[171]

It is reasonable to ask why many Black Chicagoans, particularly after the racial violence of 1919, elected to continue doing business with banks that, in many cases, were blatantly disinterested in using the money to finance the city's Black families, entrepreneurs and businesses. However, in considering the issue, it is also important to acknowledge that a similar question is also relevant today. The nation's Black-owned banks, other minority-owned depository institutions (MDIs) and community banks in general are losing business to large firms often headquartered in distant cities.

In all cases, then and now, there are a number of reasons that can vary by depositor. As it pertains to Chicago through the 1920s, there are a few theories.

The simplest is convenience and proximity, an extremely important issue at a time when mass transit was not yet fully developed. This issue would have been particularly important as the Black population expanded outside the geographic parameters of the Black Belt and the South Side banks were simply not convenient option.

Another potential issue was perceived stability. Prior to the 1919 violence, Binga's then-private bank was the only Black Chicago bank with a history longer than a few months. Over time, as Binga secured a state charter and Douglass followed with the national charter, both banks would have no doubt been viewed as increasingly stable, but even with that, neither bank was established to the degree or scale of the big Loop banks. For example, the founding of the massive Illinois Merchants Trust Company's bank predated the 1871 Chicago fire; and when it merged with Continental National Bank and Trust Company in 1928, it created in Chicago what was touted as a $1 billion bank – then the second-largest

It is believed that this is the same school once attended by Eugene Williams, victim of the 1919 Lake Michigan assault. Williams is believed to have lived in a home, long since leveled, around a block south of the school. Lorezel, Robert. "Searching for Eugene Williams." Chicago. Aug. 1, 2019.

bank in the United States.[172, §§§§§] These large firms would have created, within Chicago, a competitive landscape unique to the city and unlike what was the case in a community like Richmond.

Finally, although there is little question that many of the white-owned banks in Chicago and elsewhere were not willing to extend credit and provide a full range of financial services to Black customers, there were certainly those that did, and some served the community admirably.

Among these was Chicago's Lincoln State Bank. Considered a "white" bank because its founders and leadership were exclusively white until Chicago alderman and former *Chicago Defender* editor Louis B. Anderson joined the bank's board in 1928, Lincoln State had at least 10 Black shareholders at its opening and significant diversity among its employees. In addition, it had the implied safety of a state charter when it opened in 1912 – nearly a decade before Binga obtained such a charter for his bank – and an impeccable standing in the Black Belt.[173, 174, 175]

Lincoln's reputation was a reflection of its founder and president, George F. Liebrandt, who had been a well-respected real estate broker among South Side families before his foray into banking.[176] In 1920, Lincoln State claimed it provided mortgages to more Black families than any other Chicago institution, Black or white.[177] And in 1928, Leibrandt was lauded as someone who had "come to the rescue of hundreds in the renewal of mortgages on homes."[178] One prominent example of its willingness to lend was in financing the launch of Liberty Life Insurance Co., the first Black-owned insurance provider in the North. Liberty not only offered insurance, but it also engaged to some degree in its own mortgage financing for Black homebuyers, fostering additional economic growth.[179]

Like the South Side's Black banks, Lincoln State was also not immune to turmoil during the 1919 violence. In early 1920, the bank endured a significant depositor run with $243,000 withdrawn as it faced both rumors about its financial stability and that it had been involved with a group seeking to bar Black families from buying homes in certain neighborhoods.[180] The bank worked aggressively to discount the rumors and took the additional step of publicly promising depositors who withdrew money during the run that they would continue to earn interest on withdrawn balances if the money was redeposited within a few weeks.[181] This commitment, and the bank's ongoing support of mortgage borrowers, likely

§§§§§ This is the same institution that failed spectacularly in 1984 in what was the largest bank failure in U.S. history until the 2007-08 financial crisis.

resounded strongly with the bank's purported base of 15,000 Black depositors.[182]

8.

Between the dawn of the 20th century and the mid-1920s, both the number of Black banks and their combined total resources trended generally higher, peaking around 1926 at $13 million.[183] Although some of the institutions were short lived, at least 80 Black banks were formed in the United States during this span.[184]

The Great Depression, of course, brought it all to a devastating end.

As some of the nation's white-owned newspapers "talked of unending prosperity," Chicago's Black community was "a barometer sensitive to the coming storm."[185] In 1928, *Chicago Defender* reporters were writing about worsening labor conditions and in January 1929 noted rising unemployment. In March 1929, seven months before the stock market collapse, the paper warned its readers:

> Something is happening in Chicago and it should no longer go unnoticed. During the past three weeks hardly a day has ended that there has not been a report of another firm discharging its employees, many of whom have been faithful workers at these places for years …
> What does this portend?[186]

Black unemployment rates began to climb higher in urban areas early in the Depression with Black workers often the first fired.[187] In Chicago, the damage was especially severe given the local economy's heavy reliance on jobs provided by the hard-hit industrial sector. Although the data from this period is not comprehensive, one survey found more than 40 percent of Chicago's Black males were unemployed in January 1931, and Black unemployment overall was as high as 50 percent in 1933.[188, 189]

The Black Belt banks were among the first to suffer in the downturn. On July 31, 1930, state regulators ordered Binga State Bank to close, setting off a panic at Bronzeville's other banks.

Until the creation of the FDIC in 1933, the risk posed by a loss of confidence in a bank or the entire banking system was a very real concern for both bankers and their customers. While post-1933 depositors can rely on the FDIC to reimburse the losses up to certain amounts, earlier era depositors faced the prospect of getting only a percentage – or worse yet, none – of their money out of a failing bank and only then after a sometimes lengthy liquidation of bank assets.***** To avoid this, during a panic, nervous depositors wanted to be the first in line to withdraw funds at a time when the bank still had cash on hand.

Within days of the Binga failure, withdrawal runs at all of the South Side banks led to the failure of two others while Douglass National and Lincoln State both survived.[190] Depositors who were able to get their money out generally headed to Loop banks to open new accounts there, although Douglass officials later estimated they gained about 500 new depositors in the turmoil.[191]

The Binga collapse was related to, but not wholly the result of, Great Depression turmoil. More than a year earlier, some of the bank's directors had raised concerns about the bank and Binga's leadership in particular, suggesting an apparent circumvention of lending policies and loans related to Binga's personal interests.[192] Then in early 1930, state examiners warned the bank. At the time of failure, examiners found that the bank had inflated the value of its resources, and the receiver leveled accusations of fraud. There was evidence of the potential for a conflict of interest related to more than $300,000 in questionable loans.[193]

Despite these findings, a later review of the failure included in a banking sector analysis found that the primary cause of the Binga State Bank's failure related to the character of the bank's loans and investments. At the time of failure, the loans were almost exclusively to individuals, and around two-thirds of all loans were unsecured.[194] Other Chicago banks, thus, had little appetite taking on these loans or accepting them as collateral.

For a bank heavily invested in real estate, it was a horrible combination of events. Real estate borrowers were unable to make loan payments – a development that not only hurt the bank from a cash flow perspective but also weighed on real estate values, further draining liquidity. Meanwhile, with borrowers unable to pay, savers who had lost their jobs were withdrawing savings to pay the bills.

Prior to the failure, Binga had been attempting to secure a national charter. That effort came to a halt while appeals for assistance and then a possible merger with Douglass and Lincoln that could have united all three under one banner were also abandoned, allegedly due in part to Lincoln officials raising concerns about the value of Binga State Bank paper.[195] Overton offered aid in some form, although Binga was reportedly unwilling to accept

***

***** A handful of individual states at various points did offer forms of deposit insurance.

the terms.[196, ††††††]

The Binga State Bank failure is considered by some to be the first Chicago-area bank collapse of the Great Depression. It was certainly not the last.

Less than a year later, examiners closed Lincoln State Bank – one of a staggering 22 Chicago-area banks shuttered over a single seven-day span in June 1931.[197] The citywide turmoil started amid two separate mergers involving four of the city's five largest banks, which fostered depositor withdrawal runs on some affiliated banks that the public perceived as potentially vulnerable.[198] One assessment at the time was that the turmoil had "elminat[ed] the weak spots" in the city's financial system.[199, 200] That view was far from the mark. More than 150 Chicago-area banks failed in June and July 1932, during one of the most substantial regional banking crises of the Depression era.[#######]

And, in the same way that Black job losses and the Binga failure presaged more widespread damage to come, the failure of Douglass National Bank was among the first events in the 1932 collapse.

Through the second half of 1931 and into 1932, Douglass saw ongoing withdrawals by its depositors, likely related to job losses and families turning to their savings for support. Some savers had no doubt been on edge since the Binga failure. In an effort to calm its customers, Douglass officials hung a sign in the bank's lobby to remind depositors that

†††††† Binga was eventually indicted for incidents relating to his role in attempting to create a nationally chartered bank, some of his dealings related to Binga State Bank and accusations of embezzlement. A protracted legal battle that included a mistrial introduced additional issues including questions about potential attempts to transfer the titles of some property to his wife, who would die in the midst of the turmoil after suffering a cerebral hemorrhage, and even his mental fitness. He was convicted in connection to some of the charges and, after losing numerous appeals, was sentenced to the maximum security Statesville Correctional Center. His conviction was criticized heavily within the Black Belt, where it was seen as yet another attack on one of the nation's most prominent and successful Black men. An ill-fated effort at gaining parole involved the renowned attorney Clarence Darrow and Reverend Mother Katharine Drexel, the founder of the Sisters of the Blessed Sacrament and who was canonized as Saint Katharine Drexel in 2000. At the time of his eventual release after three years in prison, Binga was broke. Reportedly, in 1941 he attended an auction at the former bank headquarters to look on as its remaining assets were sold. A month later, he was pardoned by Illinois Governor Dwight H. Green. Binga was one of 57 Illinois bankers indicted by state officials in 1931. He died essentially penniless in 1950 at age 85. Binga always maintained he was innocent of the charges. For a more detailed examination of Jesse Binga's life, and an important source of information for this publication, see: Hayner, Don. "Binga: The Rise and Fall of Chicago's First Black Banker." Northwestern University Press. Evanston, Ill. 2019.

####### Starting in the fall of 1930 and continuing through early 1933, the United States suffered four major banking panics in addition to numerous localized events such as the one occurring in Chicago.

the bank was nationally chartered and thus a member of the Federal Reserve System and could turn to the Federal Reserve for support if faced with a depositor run. Reportedly, the Federal Reserve loaned $200,000 to Douglass at the time of the Binga failure to protect the bank from a depositor run.[201]

Across a nine-month period, total deposits at Douglass National fell from around $1.5 million to around $400,000 by late May amid ongoing withdrawals. Meanwhile, the value of the bank's securities continued to plummet. On May 20, 1932, the bank's board of directors voted to close the institution. Bank examiners took over the following day.[202, 203]

Douglass National officials contended that the bank was solvent, but it had been unable to gain deposits with an apparent public loss of confidence in the bank dating back to a shakeup in the bank's board that had started in 1930, around the time of the Binga State Bank failure. Overton eventually stepped down from the presidency in February 1932 but remained chairman with some directors accusing him of mismanagement and conflicts of interest related to financing his various businesses.§§§§§§§

He was replaced at the bank's helm by his son-in-law, lawyer Richard Hill Jr.[204] Hill, who refused to accept a salary to reduce operating costs, obtained a loan from the Reconstruction Finance Corporation that appeared to provide some stability, but he was not able to turn the tide of deposit flows in the bank's favor. In what can only be considered a move of extreme desperation, he made a Sunday morning post-sermon plea to the congregation of Bethesda Baptist Church for them to repay a $7,000 real estate loan.

---

§§§§§§§ Overton was accused of multiple questionable moves related to both Douglass National Bank and, especially, Victory Life Insurance Company, ranging from Victory's investments in bank stock through Victory paying rent for space in Overton's building that was well above current market rates. To some, these accusations validated concerns expressed by Chavers at the time he was replaced by Overton when the bank was in its formative stages. Another view of these arrangements is that Overton, as the largest shareholder of both firms, may have viewed himself as the primary decision maker for both. In addition, his accusers had apparently opposed a possible merger involving the insurance company. Overton, unlike Binga, did not face criminal charges, although he did face lawsuits, and Victory Life was suspended from doing business. Eventually, Overton was left with only the businesses where he was the sole owner: Overton Hygienic and *The Bee*. With the insurance company eventually abandoning its lawsuit against Overton and the bank reimbursing depositors, Overton's image improved substantially within the community, although never again reaching its former height. He continued to operate *The Bee* and Overton Hygienic until his death at age 81 in 1946. The paper folded soon after while Overton Hygienic remained a family-owned business until closing in 1983. For more on Overton's life, and an important source for this publication, see: Weems, Robert E., Jr. *The Merchant Prince of Black Chicago: Anthony Overton and the Building of A Financial Empire.* University of Illinois: Urbana, Ill. 2020.

"If your doors must be closed to keep the bank open, the bank must remain open. I have no desire to foreclose on this church, but where the bank and the church are concerned, I have no alternative."

The bank's willingness to lend to the church was most likely because Overton was a member of the congregation. Many of the others who attended the church, however, were not bank customers. Hill noted the lack of Douglass National patronage among the congregation, telling them that he did not want to force Douglass depositors to "suffer because their money has been loaned to people like you." An attempt by the pastor to calm Hill led to an argument about a bank loan to the pastor. The spectacle made headlines and, less than a month later, the bank was closed.[205, 206]

Prior to the failure, and well before Hill's public outburst, Douglass suffered three separate runs that it was able to withstand before it was essentially pushed to the point of collapse.

"Withdrawals by depositors, some based on need because of unemployment and others on account of a lack of confidence in all banks based on the failure of other banks, made providing of the money to meet these withdrawals a problem and the declining value of the bonds the bank had invested in and the slowness of collections on loans made by the bank to our large … organizations added to the burdens," Overton said.[207]

The bank had taken a number of steps in efforts to remain viable, including reducing employee pay, but it was not sufficient. A later analysis found that Douglass' weakness was loans, both real estate and commercial, as well as lending to churches and fraternal societies with illiquid collateral.[208]

Douglass National and Binga State, as the era's two largest Black banks at the heart of a vibrant and growing Black community, no doubt faced extreme pressure both as symbols of Black economic growth and in working to facilitate that growth. The result, as Reed notes in discussing the Douglass National collapse, was that while the bank "did indeed serve the needs of its community … it required questionable business practices to achieve that end. That meant extending loans and mortgages where demands of efficiency within the capitalist system would have denied them. The reality for a community such as … [Chicago] was that banks were meant to process and facilitate the flow of capital to stimulate business and to prosper for the benefit of stockholders and depositors, not benevolently extend credit to [borrowers] who were poor risks."[209]

By some metrics – not merely their size – both Binga State and Douglass National stood above their peers. According to a mid-1930s analysis by Harris, both institutions were generally in line with the overall banking industry in such areas as their ratio of loans and discounts to total deposits – a statement that cannot be made for many of the era's other Black banks. Douglass in particular was more diversified than many Black banks in its securities holdings in comparison to its total loans and discounts. Despite this, the lack of liquidity was still problematic and a weak point for both institutions.[210] While the banks may have been strong in other ways, they still faced the same challenges that caused the failure of many other Black banks at the time: a large amount of real estate loans that were illiquid.

Both failures were major events.

As an unknown author – most likely Overton – wrote in Overton's publication *Half Century* in 1921:

> A bank is the heart of community industrial life. It is the center from which that vital life stream flows, so necessary to the prosperity of a group and the development of that group's industries. No community can progress without a central power plant … Money placed in Colored banks will help the race to finance business and create positions for Colored people.[211]

In addition, the failure left a number of highly skilled workers jobless. For these employees, the idea of finding another position in financial services had to be a particularly daunting task as they faced both overall turmoil in the financial sector and discrimination in hiring for what positions were available.

Finally, both banks had a particularly important symbolic position, not only in Chicago, but also nationally. Cultural "firsts" – as in the first to break through a racial barrier in a particular field or an accomplishment – received widespread notoriety and assured a place in history.

While Douglass National Bank was not the first Black-owned bank to operate under a national charter – an honor which belonged to the First National Bank in Boley – it was the first entity in the United States to issue currency under the signature of a minority.

Those unfamiliar with the history of United States currency may be surprised to learn that to address issues of creating a nationally accepted currency, starting during the Civil War and continuing until 1935, nationally chartered banks were allowed under federal direction to issue bills. The currency was backed by U.S. government securities that nationally chartered banks purchased and deposited with the U.S. Treasury. While it appears First National did not take this step, Douglass National Bank did issue notes, primarily $5 denominations. These bills were printed by the United States Treasury's Bureau of Engraving and Printing before being sent to the issuing bank, where they were then signed by the bank president and cashier before being released at the bank's discretion. Douglass' notes were signed by Overton, a Black man born to enslaved parents in the South in the Civil War's waning days. Some of the notes survive today in the hands of collectors and serve as a powerful symbol and reminder of Black progress in the early years of the 20th century.

Memphis,
Tennessee

I.

In 1968, the fight for economic equality brought Dr. Martin Luther King Jr. to Memphis.

For years, the city's sanitation workers had been engaged in an unsuccessful battle for better working conditions. Black garbage haulers, working under white supervisors in the Delta South, were subject to racism, paid little – many were on welfare or food stamps – lacked job security and received no benefits. It was not unusual for a laborer to work long hours without overtime pay or, conversely, be sent home without notice. Their equipment was often outdated and the garbage trucks poorly maintained.[1]

On Feb. 1, amid a driving rainstorm, a team of five workers took shelter in one of those trucks. The most senior three were able to cram themselves into the cab while Echol Cole and Robert Walker were left to seek shelter riding with the garbage in the back. When an electrical short activated the compactor without warning, both men were crushed to death.

By mid-month, more than 1,200 Black sanitation workers were on strike, a labor action that became a landmark event in America's civil rights history.[*]

The Memphis strike came just as King was in the early stages of a transition with the Southern Christian Leadership Conference (SCLC). The organization that traditionally focused on issues of segregation and social justice became increasingly active on matters of poverty and economic opportunity.

With SCLC's Poor People's Campaign still in its developing stages, King went to Memphis twice in March to support the striking workers – first for a March 18 rally and then 10 days later to lead a march that erupted into a riot after some young marchers used protest signs to shatter store windows. Around 60 people were injured, and one was killed in the violence. A protestor who escaped into the upper floor of a nearby office building recounted the scene unfolding below: "People robbing and looting and carrying away whatever stolen goods could be carried. We saw the police beating walkers and runners as they ran for cover. They beat one young girl so savagely that she crumbled to the sidewalk. Apparently she had talked back."[2]

---

[*] The striking sanitation workers carried signs reading "I AM A MAN," bringing into the Civil Rights Era a phrase that can be traced back to early abolitionist efforts. The phrase was an intended response by Black workers who had been addressed as "boy" by racist bosses. "We wanted some dignity," one sanitation worker later said. "We wanted to be treated like men. We were tired of being treated like boys." Rosenbloom, Joseph. "Redemption: The Untold Story of Martin Luther King Jr.s' Last 31 Hours." Beacon Press. Boston. 2018. p. 15.

State police and the National Guard were brought in to restore order while the city later sought, and obtained, a court injunction blocking King from leading a second march.[3]

The eruption was a blow to King. In the social and political cauldron of 1968, King was already eyed suspiciously by some white Americans who saw little difference between King and some of the nation's proudly militant activists. Now, the practitioner of nonviolent civil disobedience was a key figure in a painful and tragic event – a challenge to not only King's stature but also to the SCLC's ongoing work. As one writer noted, much of King's ability as a civil rights leader hinged on "his personal magnetism ... as he traveled around the country to build support. Without that central pillar of his credibility solidly in place, King acknowledged that the ... [Poor People's] Campaign was 'doomed.'"[4]

King believed that the SCLC's work, in particular a planned Poor People's march in Washington, D.C., could not go forward until he proved he could stage a successful nonviolent event in Memphis.

To address the damage, and hopefully to secure a reversal of the injunction, King's travel schedule was upended. Instead of traveling to Chicago on April 3, as planned under his original itinerary, King returned to Memphis to lead what he hoped would be a peaceful event.

That night, King addressed a group of the striking workers and their allies attending a rally at Mason Temple. His impromptu unscripted remarks, known today as the "I've Been to the Mountaintop" speech, are often noted for the icon's prophetic closing statement on the eve of his assassination:

> Like anybody, I would like to live a long life – longevity has its place. But I'm not concerned about that now. I just want to do God's will. And He's allowed me to go up to the mountain. And I've looked over, and I've seen the Promised Land. I may not get there with you. But I want you to know tonight, that we, as a people, will get to the Promised Land.
>
> And so I'm happy tonight; I'm not worried about anything; I'm not fearing any man. Mine eyes have seen the glory of the coming of the Lord.[†]

The full speech is a travelogue of history with Biblical imagery, a plea for nonviolence and a call for unity in action, not only in protest marches, but also in economic concerns:

† A full text of his remarks is available online through the Martin Luther King Jr. Research and Education Institute at Stanford University: https://kinginstitute.stanford.edu/

boycotting firms that mistreat Black employees while supporting Black-owned businesses – financial services providers in particular:

> We've got to strengthen Black institutions. I call upon you to take your money out of the banks downtown and deposit your money in Tri-State Bank. We want a "bank-in" movement in Memphis. Go by the savings and loan association. I'm not asking you something that we don't do ourselves in SCLC. Judge Hooks and others will tell you that we have an account here in the savings and loan association from the Southern Christian Leadership Conference. We are telling you to follow what we're doing, put your money there. You have six or seven Black insurance companies here in the city of Memphis. Take out your insurance there. We want to have an "insurance-in."‡ Now these are some practical things that we can do. We begin the process of building a greater economic base …

At the time of King's speech, Tri-State was already well known and respected within the civil rights movement. The bank's founders and senior managers in particular were not only leaders in the community and the Delta South region, but they also helped to bring about change nationally as participants in some of the era's most important legal decisions.

Even in establishing the bank they were courageous. The Great Depression had dealt a near fatal blow to the nation's Black banks and marked the beginning of a nearly three-decade span that continued into the early Civil Rights era when few would open – between 1934 and 1961, only five new Black banks were established.[5]

In the midst of this, Tri-State was founded under the leadership of Joseph Edison Walker and his son A. Maceo Walker. Joseph Walker was born in 1880 to sharecropper parents in Tillman, Mississippi, and attended local schools before graduating from Alcorn Agricultural and Mechanical College, now Alcorn State, in 1903. He went to Nashville and did a number of jobs, including carpentry, farm work and summer teaching to finance his education at Meharry Medical College, graduating in 1906. He then returned to Mississippi,

‡ The terms "bank-in" and "insurance-in" may seem unusual to those born after the Civil Rights era. The phrases are a reflection of the numerous "sit-in" non-violent protests. Jesse Jackson, through Operation Breadbasket in Chicago, had been talking about the idea of a "bank-in movement" since the mid-1960s with the focus on asking concerned whites to put money in Black banks, which would, in turn, extend the bank's lending resources. Beltramini, Enrico. "Operation Breadbasket: From Economic Civil Rights to Black Economic Power." Fire!!!, Vol 2., No. 2. 201. pp. 5-47.

setting up a medical practice in the small town of Indianola and inadvertently placing himself on a path that would lead to banking.[6]

While Indianola may have had fewer than 2,000 residents, it was also home to Wayne Cox – then believed to be the richest Black man in the entire Mississippi Delta and founder of the community's Delta Penny Savings Bank.

Wayne Cox and his wife Minnie, both college graduates, had come to the area in the late 1800s, establishing a Black school and investing in cheap real estate they later sold. They were politically active Republicans, and in 1891, Minnie was appointed Indianola postmaster by Republican President Benjamin Harrison, making her almost certainly the first Black woman to hold such a position. In 1897, she was reappointed by President William McKinley and continued to serve under President Theodore Roosevelt. By 1902, racists had begun calls for her ouster. Fearful for her safety, Minnie Cox agreed not to seek a reappointment in 1904, but her promise meant little to those wanting her out, who demanded her resignation by Jan. 1, 1903. In response, Roosevelt stepped in and shut down the Indianola post office, forcing locals to travel to a nearby town to receive their mail for more than a year.[7] The so-called "Indianola Affair" made national news.[8]

The Coxes left town for about a year, making a home in Birmingham, Alabama, before returning to Indianola in early 1904 and founding the Delta Penny Savings Bank in 1905. They followed it with the Mississippi Beneficial Life Insurance Company in 1908. Wayne Cox said the businesses were "monuments of protest to the injustices" that the couple had suffered.[9]

"We had a little post office trouble down there," Cox said during the 1910 National Negro Business League (NNBL) convention in New York City, "and it is my pleasure to tell you that we started a Negro bank with $16,000 subscribed in stock. Now our capital stock is $50,000 and our total resources $165,000. We have today in that town, where a good deal of prejudice exists, the third biggest Negro bank in the world."[10]

Wayne Cox had apparently asked Walker to serve as Delta's president for some time before Walker finally accepted the job in 1913. He also took the helm of the insurance company after Cox's death in 1916.[11]

Walker was credited with growing both businesses.[12] Delta Penny Savings was heavily involved in real estate and business lending, which expanded significantly under his leadership. The nature of financial reporting during this era, and the limited availability of documents, can make it somewhat difficult to fully assess the performance of financial institutions. There is not only a seasonality to business in an agricultural region, but bank deposits at this time could also be particularly transient, especially for depositors of limited funds. However, it is clear that the bank was a significant provider of credit. Lending activity more than doubled during the last four years of Walker's tenure, although deposits appear to have declined, perhaps significantly.[13] If this was a sign of trouble, however, it apparently did not concern state banking officials. Delta Penny Savings was perhaps the only Black bank in the United States at the time where the state guaranteed all deposits. This backing meant that the bank had met certain standards applied by the state after the review of state banking regulators. Regardless of the race of the bank owners, backing by the state was not something that all banks obtained.[14, 15] In addition, at some points, particularly early in its history, the bank had a reputation for being well run and its financials matched other banks operating nearby.[16]

Walker was lauded as a "material benefactor to the farmers of the ... Mississippi Delta region and his name became a synonym for progress and power."[17] As might be expected, local farmers were also engaged in the bank's ownership and oversight. At one point, farmers held 20 of the 23 seats on its board of directors.

"We have built our bank 'on the farm' as it were; we have encouraged our people to buy land, and, unless a man owns his own home or his own farm, why regardless of how much cash notes or gold he has got, we won't accept him for our Board of Directors," Walker said in 1915.[18]

In 1920, Mississippi Beneficial moved its headquarters to Memphis in hopes of expanding the business. Walker moved with the firm, although he maintained his position with the Mississippi bank until 1922. In 1923, with Minnie Cox looking to sell Mississippi Beneficial and the emergence of a leadership battle, he resigned and immediately formed his own firm, the Universal Life Insurance Company.[19, 20] Mississippi Life, meanwhile, soon wound up under the ownership of white-owned Southern Life of Nashville, Tennessee, but it was only a temporary stop. In 1926, Mississippi Life was sold to Walker's Universal Life.[21] Delta Penny Savings, meanwhile, failed in January 1928, the victim of a bank run after the failure of Fraternal and Solvent Savings Bank of Memphis, a bank with which Delta was known to have a close relationship.[22, §]

§ Prior to a 1927 last-ditch merger attempt as both banks struggled to survive, the separate Solvent Savings Bank and Trust and The Fraternal Savings Bank and Trust Company had both been important lenders to Black businesses and entrepreneurs in the Delta South. Nearly 30,000 depositors lost nearly 90 percent of their savings, and innumerable businesses suffered when the bank failed. Source: Biddle-Douglass, Teressa. "Fraternal and Solvent Savings Bank and Trust Co." Tennessee Historical Society. Oct. 8, 2017.

Walker's insurance firm, meanwhile, was booming. Under his leadership, it survived the Great Depression and soon became one of the nation's largest Black-owned businesses. In the post-Depression era, Universal Life helped other struggling insurance providers and rescued Woodmen Union Life Insurance Company of Hot Springs, Arkansas.[23] Walker's stature, meanwhile, rose in tandem with his firm. In 1939, he was elected president of the NNBL.[24]

Walker was known as a decisive if sometimes blunt leader and was a sought-after speaker, often with a message focused on the need for Black business owners to compete and grow aggressively, while also filling a social leadership role.[25]

"We who have achieved some [success] must now begin to look back at our measure of success in the world. It's alright to lead, but the leader must interest himself in the welfare of his followers," he said in his 1941 NNBL convention speech. "We should take time to council with the masses, to explain to them the many new opportunities that are being offered."[26]

In remarks delivered only weeks before the U.S. entered World War II, Walker addressed the issue of defense contractors refusing to hire Black workers.[27] U.S. manufacturers, in some cases reluctantly, had begun transferring out of their core products and into defense goods as early as 1939 with the U.S.'s likely involvement in the war becoming more apparent.[28]

"Do not become corrupt with meanness, poisoned with hatred or inspired with the desire for revenge. Seek your rights, and when necessary and expedient demand them, but above all do not be led astray by temper," he said. "I have been asked several times what we should do when white men publicly acclaim this is a white man's country and each time I have met the query with this answer, 'Just keep on singing "My Country 'tis of Thee."' This is my message to you today, to all Black men over this broad land. Keep singing out of your hearts and out of your souls, 'My Country 'tis of Thee.'"[29]

In addition, Walker also frequently discussed the importance of money management and saving – arguments that appear to have made all but inevitable an eventual return to banking and creating an institution that would "serve as an inspiration to the Negroes of the South as well as give service for the financing of Negro enterprises."[30]

2.

The decision to open a bank was apparently prompted by Walker's son A. Maceo. The younger Walker had been denied a $1,000 loan from a Memphis bank – a bank from which he had previously borrowed a lesser amount and repaid on time.[31]

When Tri-State Bank opened in 1946, it was the first new Black bank in the United States since the mid-1930s and the first Black bank in Memphis since the Fraternal and Solvent failure nearly 20 years earlier. Notably, Tri-State opened near the corner of Beale Street and Fourth Avenue, a location that was previously home to its Memphis predecessor and also believed to have once been the site of W.C. Handy's music publishing business. A historic marker now stands at the location.

"Out of the ashes of the Solvent Savings Bank, [Walker] has written in imperishable ink the story of the Negro's indomitable will to live – to try again and to prove his strength and fortitude," said activist George Lee, during the bank's opening celebration.[32] "Doctor Walker has made every man, woman and child of our race proud."

First day deposits, led by 10-year-old Fayella Johnson who skipped school to be at the front of the line, totaled more than $450,000. Although more than half of the amount came from Walker's insurance business, the bank still attracted a larger number of depositors who trusted the bank with amounts ranging from a few dollars to thousands.[33]

Within the first year, around 1,800 accounts were opened by local and out-of-town depositors including some whites, with nearly $1.5 million in total deposits.[34] Within its first 10 years, the bank claimed it had made more than $10 million in mortgage loans on homes for more than 2,000 Black families.[35]

The bank's name was selected as a reflection of its location in extreme southwestern Tennessee and as an appeal to potential customers living across the nearby state lines – to the west in Arkansas or south in Mississippi.

That accessibility from Mississippi became particularly important in 1955 after white supremacists instituted an "economic freeze" against Black families, workers and businesses in that state. After the 1954 landmark Supreme Court ruling in Brown v. Board of Education found public school segregation unconstitutional, White Citizens Councils developed in the South with an initial goal of maintaining segregation. Within a year there were perhaps as many as 300 councils with a total of more than 60,000 members involved in everything from a private schools movement to other initiatives including the promotion of national and even international networks of supremacist organizations.[36]

While there was no doubt overlap between the councils and other supremacist groups, these councils in general were often made up of individuals who had achieved high social status within the community, either through their business accomplishments or because of their involvement in civic groups. Unlike militant organizations such as the Ku Klux Klan and others that resorted to violence, these councils, starting with what is believed to be the first White Citizens Council meeting – held in Walker's longtime hometown of Indianola, Mississippi, no less – focused on leveraging the authority and clout of their members.[37] This meant actions ranging from white business owners firing Black workers to white bankers cutting off lending to Black borrowers and calling in loans already made, setting the stage for eventual foreclosure. Newspaper accounts from January 1955 detail numerous borrowers who needed to come up with thousands of dollars on short notice or they would lose the collateral of a farm or business.[38]

Emmett Stringer, a National Association for the Advancement of Colored People (NAACP) leader in in Columbus, Mississippi, explained to a reporter how one local business owner in his community learned that he could no longer borrow:

> We had … a merchant who had to give up. A group of white men drove up to his store and told him to get in the car. He did and they took him to his bank and there were the banker, his wholesaler and other people who gave him credit. They told him they would give him no more credit. He had to give up, go bankrupt or get out.[39]

In response, the NAACP and Tri-State coordinated a program seeking deposits from across the United States that Tri-State could use to increase lending specifically to needy borrowers who had been targeted by the white Mississippi banks.[40] By the end of April 1955, organizers said the bank had received around $250,000 in deposits related to the initiative. Dr. T.R.M. Howard, a surgeon and prominent leader in the civil rights fight, however, predicted to the Mississippi Regional Council of Negro Leadership that the program's confirmed success introduced additional risk. The supremacists would not relent in the face of their failed economic initiative.[41]

"We are definitely whipping the economic freeze," he said.[42] "When it develops as a real flop, the next round will be a wave of violence."

In the months that followed, Mississippi racists murdered civil rights leader George W.

Lee, voter registration organizer Lamar Smith, and 14-year-old Emmett Till, whose killing is often viewed as the civil rights movement's galvanizing event, inspiring, among others, Rosa Parks when she refused to relinquish her bus seat to a white man and move to the rear of the vehicle: "I thought of Emmett Till and I couldn't go back."[43, 44]

Tri-State's civil rights activism, meanwhile, would only increase even as the bank's leadership passed to a new generation. A. Maceo Walker, who took the helm at Universal Life, succeeded his father as Tri-State's president after the senior Walker's death in 1958.[45] The bank's CEO title, however, went to Jesse Turner Sr., the bank's cashier since 1949 and a U.S. Army veteran officer who had earned the Gold Star and other honors while serving in Europe during World War II.[46]

The road to Turner's initial involvement in the Memphis bank echoes of the way that Joseph Walker got involved with Wayne Cox's bank in Indianola. In neither case did the protagonist have plans to become a banker.

Turner, after the war, had completed his education, earning a master's in business administration at the University of Chicago and becoming the first Black student to pass the certified public accountant exam in Tennessee. His goal was to establish an accounting business, but the lure of a steady paycheck as the bank's cashier was too powerful to resist, at least in the interim.[47]

At the bank, however, Turner found a home for the rest of his working life, serving until his death in 1989.[48, 49] Across a career that spanned not only the Civil Rights era but was in the same community where some of its most important events unfolded, he was perhaps *the* ideal person for this bank and this place at this time.

For example, as an undergraduate at LeMoyne College, he majored in mathematics. However, according to his college yearbook, Turner's 1941 senior essay was not about cold numbers, but through the lens of "Equality … [and how] the principles of mathematics could be used in social sciences."[50]

His wife later recounted that, before leaving home for work each morning, he would recite from the Declaration of Independence on his way out the door: "We hold these truths to be self-evident, that all men are created equal…"[51]

"The issues of poverty and color, and the injustices that resulted from them pervaded the lives of southern blacks," Turner's wife said after his death.[52] "As Jesse lived daily with one societal wrong after another, he would become consumed with thoughts of justice and equality for all."

To spotlight only two of Turner Sr.'s accomplishments in the fight for civil rights: In 1958, he filed a lawsuit demanding equal access to Memphis Public Library materials, which led to the library's desegregation in 1960.[53] Separately, he filed a lawsuit after twice being refused service in a "white" dining room at a Memphis airport restaurant in 1959, leading to a 1962 U.S. Supreme Court ruling banning the segregation of public facilities at publicly owned airports nationwide.[54]

Turner Sr. was head of the Memphis NAACP branch from 1957 through 1968, including the time of the sanitation workers strike and King's visits to the city. When the March 28, 1968, protest march turned violent, he was in its midst, "seeming taller than usual … using his hands to direct the marchers and shouting as loudly as he could, 'Go back to the church,' … while rock pellets were flying over our heads and glass was crashing at our feet," his wife later recalled.[55]

Throughout the Walker and Turner family eras, bank offices were sometimes used for planning meetings ahead of protests including sit-ins and marches, and the bank also served as a key source of funding. Bank officials would often remain available at night to provide access to bail money for protestors – including, notably, during the sanitation workers' strike.[56, 57]

"Whenever the movement was in a financial pinch, the Walkers were there to bail it out," said Jesse H. Turner Jr., who succeeded his father as bank president in 1990 and led the bank for the next 29 years.[58] "If people needed money or financial advice, they could go to them."

This is, of course, in addition to the business of banking and serving the community.

"Many Black businesses and churches were built because of the institutions he headed," one-time NAACP Executive Secretary Maxine Smith said of Maceo.[59] "[Before the Walkers] many professional Blacks were denied loans for the purposes of keeping neighbors segregated."

Tri-State became known in particular for a willingness to extend credit into redlined neighborhoods, as well as to churches and small businesses that were unable to meet the approval from larger institutions.[60]

During a celebration of the bank's 40th anniversary in 1986, Walker said that his family "decided that Blacks needed a bank if we were going to finance businesses, homes and churches." Turner Sr. then added that four decades later, "the need for making those loans others won't make still exists."[61]

3.

Tri-State was significantly involved in ensuring King's legacy in Memphis. Turner helped to found the Martin Luther King Memphis Memorial Foundation, and the bank was later involved in the deal to acquire the Lorraine Motel facility, the site of King's assassination and now home of the National Civil Rights Museum.[62]

As Baradaran notes in her research, King's legacy has become somewhat diluted in the modern public consciousness when compared against a more comprehensive accounting of his life's work. Those whose familiarity with King encompasses only a few lines and ideals from his epic "I Have a Dream" speech, might be surprised to learn that much of the speech was framed in economic terms. From the steps of the Lincoln Memorial, King said that marchers had come to Washington in August 1963 "to cash a check." America, he said, had not only "defaulted on [a] promissory note" of the unalienable rights of life, liberty and the pursuit of happiness, but it had also "given the Negro people a bad check, a check which has come back marked 'insufficient funds.'"[††]

Economic concerns and the elimination of inequality were central to the fight.

Although the Poor People's Campaign was a still-developing SCLC initiative at the time of King's assassination, economic justice was an issue King recognized as intertwined with the fight for civil rights early on. While the Montgomery Improvement Association (MIA) formed in 1955 for the coordination and organization of the Montgomery bus boycott, its mission quickly expanded.

"It is obvious that our interest in brotherhood extends far beyond the desegregation of the busses," King wrote on the anniversary of the protests.[63] "We are striving for the removal of all barriers that divide and alienate mankind, whether racial, economic or psychological."

Earlier in the year, as a part of the MIA's long-term plan, King had recommended that MIA officials explore establishing a Black-owned bank in Montgomery as a means of "increasing our [Black] economic power."[64] At the time, the idea had already been discussed and received an apparently favorable reception during at least one MIA meeting. In addition, King discussed the proposal during a trip to New York City's Harlem neighborhood to meet with the Committee for Better Human Relations.[65]

---

†† A more detailed and expansive discussion of this relationship and history can be found in Baradaran, Mehrsa. "The Color of Money: Black Banks and the Racial Wealth Gap." The Belknap Press of Harvard University Press. Cambridge, Mass. 2017.

"We have found that in the present situation, many of the Negroes who are active in the protest have been unable to secure loans from the existing banks," King wrote in December 1956.[66]

In addition, there was a separate but related proposal to establish a credit union, an effort that had grown out of "a strong desire among the Negroes to pool their money for great cooperative economic programs," King wrote.[67] "We are anxious to demonstrate that cooperation rather than competition is the way to meet problems."

Despite initial support, both efforts were derailed by regulatory requirements. It appears that the bank initiative was abandoned after it became clear that organizers would not be able to secure the amount of capital necessary to obtain the charter. The credit union proposal apparently made further headway, but it was also eventually abandoned in 1959 when organizers were unable to establish a defined membership for the credit union as required under the far more stringent credit union regulations in place at that time.[68]

Although neither of these efforts made it to fruition, it is difficult – perhaps even unfair – to view either as a "failure." The work necessary to create a Black-owned financial institution amid the turmoil of the 1950s might be somewhat comparable to the challenges facing those who hoped to create a Black bank a century earlier in the years before the Civil War. In the mid-1800s, many who wanted to establish a bank were also key figures in the drive to abolish slavery and heavily involved in the Underground Railroad. During that period, the need for a bank became an understandably secondary priority.[69] Similarly, in the mid-1950s what would become known as the civil rights movement was just beginning and was already faced with growing resistance in response to the 1954 Supreme Court ruling. Although the fight for economic equality was no question of paramount importance, there were other, more pressing matters demanding attention.

Interest in banking, however, soon grew. Between 1962 and 1969, at least 17 Black banks were established in the United States.[70] In each case, it appears that the primary goal was Black economic development with profits a lower consideration.[71] These banks were both an active part of the civil rights movement but also a result of the movement in that they were made viable by other era developments that might be classified within three general areas:[72]

- Litigation, starting with the 1954 Supreme Court ruling in Brown v. Board of Education and encompassing other legal developments, including the Memphis airport lawsuit, that would result in the integration of public schools and public facilities.

- Civil rights activism for economic equality including protests for better jobs and housing with growing Black populations in urban centers as the Great Migration entered its sixth decade.
- Federal legislation, including notably the Civil Rights Act of 1964, which prohibited discrimination on the basis of race, color, religion, sex or national origin, thus outlawing Jim Crow laws; and the Voting Rights Act of 1965, which outlawed discriminatory practices used in some areas that had been designed to limit Black voting, including such things as highly subjective literacy tests.

Beyond these societywide developments, were legislative efforts and government programs designed to improving economic conditions and/or assisting Black financial services providers. These efforts and programs included such things as loan guarantees for Black banks and the Fair Housing Act of 1968, which outlawed redlining. One long-lived program that started around 1970, the Minority Bank Deposit Program (MBDP), created what is essentially a government version of what the NAACP and Tri-State sought to do with their efforts to extend credit into Mississippi: encourage government agencies to deposit some of their money in minority banks as a source of loanable funds. At the surface level, the MBDP appeared to be a good idea, although in practice, critics said it was less than ideal. In the early years, deposits – which were encouraged as opposed to mandated – never reached the lofty goals of program advocates. Meanwhile, some accounts were not static, and their amounts were prone to frequent fluctuations – one example of this was the post office. This created multiple challenges for the banks. One concern was higher servicing costs for the accounts than other deposits, a second was that unstable balances were an unreliable fuel source for funding increased lending. Finally, those banks "lucky" enough to obtain a sizable government agency deposit were required by law to pledge government securities for any balances above $100,000, thus hampering the availability of loanable funds.[73],[##] Some analysis of MBDP over an extended period has suggested it is unclear how much banks might benefit from being part of the program, which continues today.

While government initiatives and the social environment were supportive of the expansion of Black banking, neither should gloss over the fact that the bankers of this era

---

In 2020, approximately 75 banks and credit unions were part of the Minority Bank Deposit Program administered by the Bureau of the Fiscal Service. They fall under various program criteria related to ownership and/or control by minorities and women.

were taking some bold, and high-risk steps. These nascent banks were not only seeking to bring life to a Black banking sector that had been essentially dormant since the 1930s, but many were also opening in neighborhoods where the economic challenges had been growing for even longer, through practices such as redlining and general urban neglect by municipalities.

Andrew Brimmer, the first Black member of the Federal Reserve's Board of Governors, spelled out some of the challenges in a December 1970 paper presented at an annual meeting of the American Finance Association and the American Economics Association.

Brimmer, the son of a Louisiana sharecropper, earned his economics doctorate from Harvard. Before his history-making appointment to the board in 1966 by President Lyndon Johnson, he taught at several universities, spent three years as an economist at the New York Federal Reserve Bank and served as an advisor to the Sudanese government on the establishment of a central bank. For three years, he was deputy assistant secretary for economic affairs at the U.S. Department of Commerce. In 1965, he was named chairman of Tuskegee University's board of directors – a post he would hold for 28 years, making him the longest-serving chair in the school's history. The same year, he was in Los Angeles as part of a federal task force in the aftermath of the Watts rioting and ordered a Census Bureau study that found Watts' Black and Hispanic families suffered falling incomes and rising unemployment in the years before the riots despite improving economic conditions across the rest of the United States.[74]

In his 1970 paper, Brimmer found that Black banks were less profitable than similarly sized peers, with higher costs and lower efficiency. Some of this related to the communities in which they were located where incomes were low and unemployment was high. Another significant challenge for the banks was "a severe shortage of management talent. The reason for this shortage is widely known: … racial discrimination and segregation."[75]

While the banks were important, Brimmer said that overall they were too small, few and inexperienced to "make a major contribution to the financing of economic development in the Black community." Instead, Brimmer was suggesting there may be ways to encourage large, established banks – from regional institutions up through what are known as the "too big to fail" banks in the modern era – to become increasingly invested in Black neighborhoods, particularly with Black businesses, in hopes that they could help in stimulating significant economic growth.

Brimmer, however, did not stop there. He went on to say it was his view that while the Black banks were a source of racial pride, "most … might be viewed primarily as ornaments rather than as vital instruments of economic development.[76]

With that remark, Brimmer inadvertently joined the ranks of innumerable other public officials throughout history who, in discussing a complex problem, saw their analysis lost as the press and public focused on a few poorly chosen words.

Black community bankers and their allies responded swiftly and angrily.

"He's out of his mind," said David Harper, president of Detroit's First Independence National Bank.

"There's so much in his analysis that wasn't fair. What disturbs me most is his basic premise that Black banks must be able to solve all of the community's problems. He's putting too much of a burden on the banks. Sure, they should be instrumental in developing the communities in which they operate, but no bank can service the total needs of all its clients."[77]

Likely compounding the anger was the fact that the nation's Black banks, after a long period of no growth, were on the rise. The 17 Black banks established in the 1960s more than doubled the number in business prior to the decade's beginning. Just as important was the accompanying geographic expansion with new banks opening in locations outside of the South or Midwestern urban centers to places like Seattle, Washington; Portland, Oregon; and Minneapolis, Minnesota.[78]

Of the around 20 Black banks in business at the time of Brimmer's analysis, nearly half had only opened within the previous few years and were still within the period of their development when many banks, regardless of ownership or focus, were not yet profitable. Around a half-dozen had only been open a matter of months. When comparing only the longer-tenured Black banks against their peers, profitability was much more in line with the industry norms.

Edward D. Irons, a former chairman of Howard University's Department of Business Administration and the then-current executive director of the National Bankers Association, said Brimmer's analysis was flawed by its comparison of a large number of nascent Black banks against long-established industry peers.

"Most serious students of banking know that the ... management functions vary markedly between newly chartered banks and mature banks," Irons said.[79]

By failing to make this clear within his remarks, Irons said that Brimmer had created for the public a "dramatically distort[ed]" view of the Black institutions. For example, lost amid Brimmer's overall criticism was his finding that a few of the banks "experienced notable success" in tailoring their lending to local borrowers and a number had "been aggressive lenders in local communities," although perhaps to their own detriment in terms of risk.[80]

In considering overall lending, Black banks were more aggressive real estate lenders than their white-owned peers in loans as a percentage of total assets. Loans to individuals, meanwhile, matched industry levels. Commercial and industrial lending levels were significantly lower at the Black banks versus the rest of the industry, but it is difficult to judge Brimmer's finding in this area without a better understanding of the business environment in which the individual banks were engaged.

Turner, in a 1976 speech to a banking association meeting, talked about the difficulties he faced in his role as a lender in Memphis. Although Tri-State was a prominent bank lauded by many for its willingness to extend credit where others were not, the bank also had its share of critics who felt Turner in particular was still too conservative.

Because minority borrowers found it difficult to borrow elsewhere, Tri-State and other minority banks were "constantly besieged with loan requests," and some of those would-be borrowers presented significant risk. Certainly Tri-State was not alone in facing this challenge nor in suffering the criticism of being overly conservative. Generally, Black banks founded around this time were more conservative than the previous generation, perhaps learning the hard lessons of not only their predecessors, but also the blow dealt to the nation's entire financial system by the Great Depression. As a result, while earlier Black banks may have been more active in mortgages and lending to fraternal societies and churches, the newer banks were lending in these same areas, but they were also investing in government securities and were concerned about crafting more diversified portfolios.[81]

Tri-State, Turner said, certainly understood its obligation to the community "to find the means by which we can make loans," and a percentage of its resources were pledged to not only local lending, but also to what was considered "experimental purposes," including providing financing to some potentially high-risk borrowers. Other allocations, however, were targeted for loan participations involving larger banks as well as some agreements whereby multiple minority banks would combine resources for large-scale lending.[82] One example of the latter: In 1972, Tri-State was one of nine minority-owned banks located across the United States that joined to provide a $1 million line of credit to apparel maker Levi Strauss. Additional similar arrangements were later made with other firms, including a $40 million line of credit for industrial giant General Electric that involved a whopping 53 minority banks.[83]

As far as Brimmer's intended focus – the call for established large banks to lend more freely into neighborhoods of color – were the big banks interested?

Whitney Young Jr., head of the National Urban League and a prominent civil rights leader, wrote that while "many big banks have expanded their role in providing funds to fuel the Black economy" and could probably have a greater impact in Black neighborhoods, "the fact is that it is the nature of such giant financial institutions to place top priority elsewhere."[84]

Young instead urged support for the idea of large businesses and the government to deposit funds in Black banks to provide resources that would foster increased lending. On the corporate side, this was something that was already occurring to some degree and would continue. In 1966, in response to the efforts of SCLC's Operation Breadbasket in Chicago, grocery chain High-Low Foods said it would transfer the store accounts for its locations in predominantly Black neighborhoods to local Black banks. In 1968, automaker Chrysler Corp. announced it would deposit a total of $1.2 million annually in at least three Black banks: Citizens Trust Bank in Atlanta, the Bank of Finance in Los Angeles and a bank then in development in Detroit, First Independence National Bank, which would open in 1970. In 1971, Honeywell deposited a total of $700,000 in 10 Black banks.[85, §§]

In an attempt to build support for what he hoped would be a sizable initiative, Brimmer had inadvertently led many to believe he was rejecting the work being done by many of the Black banks that were doing the core mission of a community bank.[86]

A year after his 1970 remarks, Brimmer did offer a far brighter picture of the nation's Black banks, including data to support the view. Speaking to the press at a 1971 banking convention, he noted that while challenges continued, Black bank deposits were rising faster than the overall banking system, most Black banks were expanding community lending and there were clear signs of progress in the strengthening of capital resources.[87] Notably, the improvement came despite lagging deposits from the government program.[88]

§§ More recently, in 2020, media giant Netflix received substantial attention when it announced plans to deposit around $100 million with Black lenders.

4.

In addition to the rich Memphis banking history, Tennessee is also home to the nation's oldest minority bank of any type and one of four founded in the pre-Depression period that was still in business well into the 21st century: Nashville's Citizens Savings Bank and Trust Company.**

What was originally known as One Cent Savings Bank opened in January 1904. Its founding can be traced to the first Black bank chartered in the United States; Citizens founders said the success of the True Reformers' Bank in Richmond, Virginia, provided them with the inspiration to begin discussions. The momentum from an NNBL meeting in the city likely provided the final boost to see the idea through to fruition.

It was a meeting that was a long time in the making. Nearly a decade before Booker T. Washington founded the NNBL in 1900, he began forming what became a close relationship with Nashville attorney James Carroll Napier. Napier and Nashville publisher Richard Henry Boyd both made presentations at the NNBL's second annual convention held in Chicago in 1901 (as did Overton, the future Chicago banker who was at that time running his business in Kansas City) and were soon in the organization's national leadership ranks. In 1902, Napier founded an NNBL Nashville chapter, and in 1903, the city was home to the NNBL national convention that brought nearly 300 members and 1,000 onlookers in the state capitol building.[89, ††]

Speaking to an audience that included many Northerners, Boyd's opening remarks addressed the city's racial dynamics versus attendees' likely expectations of a trip to the South. In remarks that were at times bitterly sarcastic – as when he noted the city had not yet been "blessed with the Jim Crow streetcar regulations" – he painted a picture of a more forward-thinking community than some Northern visitors might have expected: "You need have no fear while you stay in our midst … your rights will be protected." And also one

---

** Black banks established prior to the Great Depression that were still in business as of June 30, 2020, according to Federal Deposit Insurance Corporation's (FDIC's) list of Minority Depository Institutions (MDIs): Citizens Savings Bank and Trust Company, Nashville, Tennessee; Mechanics & Farmers Bank, Durham, North Carolina; Citizens Trust Bank, Atlanta, Georgia; and Carver State Bank, Savannah, Georgia. In addition, there is one savings and loan: Columbia Savings and Loan Association, Milwaukee, Wisconsin. These institutions accounted for one-quarter of all Black MDIs in business in 2020.

†† Napier became the leader of the NNBL after Washington's death in 1915.

where racism and prejudice were also daily occurrences: "Should you fail to receive services [at a business] ... just walk to the other block for there is a gentleman waiting to serve you."[90]

At the time, Nashville was a city that had not yet discovered its position as the nation's country music capital. Long before the 1925 launching of the WSM radio program Barn Dance, later known as the Grand Ole Opry, Nashville was primarily known for two things: transportation, thanks to early riverboat trade on the Cumberland River and the rail lines into the South; and multiple educational institutions, including Fisk University, the private historically Black university that was established in 1866.[91, ‡‡‡]

Thus Nashville was something of a unique community regarding social conditions and economic opportunity in a state where racial dynamics varied widely depending on where one was standing at the time. In western Tennessee, home to most of Tennessee's Black population, lifestyles were often based in agriculture, with small farms and the racial social environment of the Mississippi Delta region. In the state's eastern regions, meanwhile, Black workers were able to find industrial employment or services sector work. As a result, the racism and prejudice in and around Chattanooga took on a more paternalistic tone – a somewhat nuanced, although not insignificant difference from what occurred in other areas of the state and the South. Nashville, meanwhile, was different. Located in the middle of the state and closer to the Confederacy's northern border than Chattanooga and Memphis, Nashville had more Northern influence including, notably, through the colleges that had Northern support. Thus, while the city had the segregation and discrimination found elsewhere, the environment fostered a business and professional class among the city's more than 30,000 Black residents that was not found in other areas of the state.[92] The environment aligned favorably with the vision espoused by Washington, the NNBL's founder and head, favoring a focus on economic development and opportunity over the political power that had been diminished in Nashville by the time of the convention.

Although Black men in Tennessee gained the right to vote after the Civil War, and a number of Black officials served at the state and local level, in 1889 Tennessee lawmakers instituted so-called "electoral reform," taking a number of steps that disenfranchised Black voters, including the eventual implementation of a poll tax that would remain in place until the 1950s.[93]

---

‡‡‡ Fisk notable alumni include activist and NAACP founder W.E.B. Du Bois, congressman and civil rights leader John Lewis and journalist Ida B. Wells, who was posthumously honored with a Pulitzer Prize citation for her "outstanding and courageous reporting" on lynching in the South in the late 1800s.

While ground was lost politically, there were significant economic gains. At the time of the 1903 convention, the city had a well-developed and burgeoning Black business community, as Boyd explained, and a bank in the developmental stages:

We have in our city, owned and controlled by Negroes, bootblack stands, tonsorial parlors, restaurants and hotels, fruit stands, confectionaries, saloons and dancing halls, lodge rooms and churches, produce and poultry dealers, tailor shops, millinery stores, shirt and pants manufactories, grocery stores, drug stores, furniture dealers, physicians and dentists, school teachers and preachers in numbers like the sands of the sea; last, but best, the religious publications.

Yes, we even have our loafers and gamblers. We have every grade and shape of business and professional men in our city, except dry goods dealers and bankers. We have our bank on Cherry Street that we are now using for headquarters for the league, and everything is in readiness for the transaction of business except the cash and cashier, which we hope in a few days will be put in their places and the wheels of activity started.[94]

Local enthusiasm after the convention appears to have resulted in an increase of civic pride that boosted interest in the bank and, more importantly, generated the necessary startup capital – or "the cash" as Boyd phrased it in his remarks. Three months later, Napier coordinated a meeting with Boyd and a number of the city's other Black business leaders to formerly confirm their investments and the ownership structure.[95] The bank opened the following January with a mission to "encourage frugality and systematic saving among our people, to secure the safe keeping and proper investment of such savings and set in motion business enterprises." One bank official later said "it was not the mission … to make money either for stockholders or the officials. Our officials are paid no lucrative salaries – in fact it is a labor of love."[96] In truth, some bank officials worked on an entirely volunteer basis without pay.

The immediate priority at opening was "first [building] confidence," both in the bank specifically and also in Black-owned businesses in general.[97]

As in many other areas of the South, the failure of the Freedman's Savings and Trust Company had left a lasting impression on Black Tennesseans. Tennessee was home to four Freedman's branch offices. The Nashville and Memphis branches were among the first founded in the United States and larger in deposits than many of the other locations throughout the U.S. Given the branches' prominence the damage suffered by local Black depositors may have been more substantial than what was the case elsewhere.[98]

Perhaps more troubling, although likely unknown to most Tennesseans, it appears that the Freedman's branch offices inadvertently prevented the establishment of at least one Black bank if not more in the state in the immediate aftermath of the war. Tennessee lawmakers approved three limited charters for Black banking operations in the state in 1867 and '68, but none opened for business with the Memphis Freedman's branch office already in operation in 1865 and additional Freedman's branch offices forthcoming.[99] To fully appreciate the significance of this on the community's economic wellbeing, recall that Freedman's did not use what would be considered the traditional banking model in that, rather than lending a percentage of its deposits to borrowers as most banks do, it had no facility for lending, instead investing deposits in securities. Thus Freedman's, unlike a community bank, was not established to use credit as a mechanism for overall economic growth in a community.

This kind of loss – one of opportunities missed – however, was not in the mind of the depositors who were wiped out in the Freedman's failure. Although the event came 30 years before Citizens opened for business, the losses suffered by Freedman's depositors made a generations-spanning impact that some have suggested remained an issue in how Black depositors viewed banks as late as the 1970s.[100] Such suggestions are perhaps at best questionable. As this volume has made clear, there were plenty of other misdeeds involving the provision – or lack thereof – of financial services to the Black community in the years that followed. However, the Freedman's issue was likely keenly felt in Nashville at the time given that, as Boyd explained:

> Some of the elder citizens still living remember and often refer to the lamented calamity of the so-called Freedman's Savings Bank. They have transmitted this lamented tradition to their children. And for years throughout the length and breadth of the state of Tennessee, and many other parts of the South, whenever a Negro banking institution was referred to the cry was always raised by them … "Remember the Freedman's Bank."[101]

Additionally harmful was that Freedman's – despite the fact that it operated under the control of white leadership, including some drawn from the ranks of Wall Street investment firms – was seen by many as a failure *of* the Black community and not a failure *perpetrated upon* the Black community. Sadly, the result of this gross misperception was a loss of trust in not only banking, but Black banks in particular and perhaps even in the potential success of Black-owned businesses.

The Citizens bank, a later biography of one of its founders noted, was hoping to signal to the entire community "a new day; there was a new, confident and successful Black community in Nashville and they could make a go of any enterprise to which they turned their hands. ... These were strong, confident, capable Black men who were determined to create an independent economic entity."[102]

If the goal was building trust, both Boyd and Napier were the ideal individuals to lead the effort.

Boyd came to in Nashville in December 1896, arriving in the city, as he later explained, a stranger "without a dollar ... no credit, nothing but faith in God and the justice of my cause to establish a Negro Baptist publishing house. I was laughed at on every corner."[103] While the portrayal may have been correct in a literal sense, it left out much about Boyd's drive, built over his then 50-plus years of not only surviving, but also thriving, against nearly insurmountable odds.

Boyd was born in 1843 on the Gray family plantation in the east Mississippi county of Noxubee. By the time of the Civil War, Boyd was in Texas. Although many of the accounts published during Boyd's lifetime reported that the Gray family and their slaves relocated to a plantation northwest of Houston when Boyd was a young boy, it appears more likely based on recent research that Boyd was sold to another member of the Gray family, Benoni W. Gray, who lived in Texas.

In Texas, Boyd was forced to work in the cotton fields until Gray and his three sons joined the Confederate army and forced the teenager to accompany them to serve their battlefield needs. After Gray and two of the sons were killed while fighting near Chattanooga, Tennessee in 1863, Boyd brought the badly wounded youngest son back to the family plantation in Texas.[104] Although Gray eventually recovered, it was Boyd who took over management of the cotton plantation. In every practical sense, he had become his master's savior and caretaker to the point of reportedly helping the youngest Gray hide in Mexico when Union forces moved into East Texas.[105]

It was only after the war and gaining freedom that Boyd, by now in his 20s, began learning the alphabet and to read and write. He worked as a laborer, cowboy and cotton trader in Texas. In 1870, he enrolled in Bishop College, a Freedman school in Marshall, Texas, but left after two years because he was unable to afford the tuition. He had been baptized into the Hopewell Baptist Church in Navasota, Texas, and became an ordained minister in 1871. Over the next 25 years he was involved with multiple churches, founding several and helping to organize the Texas Negro Baptist Convention while also serving as a representative to national Baptist conventions.[106]

His move into publishing was the result of an effort by Black Baptists to take greater control of Baptist churches and schools, which created support for a resolution passed at the National Baptist Convention of 1896 in St. Louis recommending the publication of literature penned by Black authors for Black Sunday schools. Boyd was appointed head of a committee to lead the initiative with a goal of beginning publishing on Jan. 1, 1897.[107]

According to a later account by Washington, "At the first meeting of the committee it was found that not one dime had been appropriated for the expenses of this giant undertaking, hence the whole project seemed a joke, and those acquainted with the conditions considered it so."

Two committee members quit almost immediately. Undeterred, Boyd went to Nashville, a hub of religious publishing, to set up shop. After gaining support from the Sunday School Board of the Southern Baptist Convention, he reached an agreement to reprint four periodicals and self-financed the arrangement with the previous publisher. He started in a rented 8-by-10-foot room.[108] Within three years, the National Baptist Publishing Board had expanded its operation, producing nine titles and more than six million copies of *The National Baptist Magazine.* By the time of his death in 1922, the man who had spent much of his life illiterate was the head of one of the largest Black businesses in the United States. The publisher, now known as R.H. Boyd, has been under the leadership of President and CEO LaDonna Boyd since 2017. She is the fifth generation of the Boyd family to lead the company.[109]

Napier, meanwhile, was born most likely on the Nashville area plantation of Dr. Elias W. Napier in 1845, and his family was emancipated in 1848. His father was one of five children born to the plantation owner and James' grandmother Judy who worked as the plantation seamstress.[110]

Napier spent his youth between Ohio and Tennessee where he attended a Black Nashville school his father helped to found until it was forced closed by white militants.[111] Later, he was a student at private Wilberforce University before transferring to Oberlin College. In 1867, he returned to Nashville where he served as a page in the Tennessee State Senate and, a year later, as Davidson County claims commissioner. With urging and assistance from

John Mercer Langston, the first dean of the Howard University School of Law and later congressman, who apparently knew Napier's father, Napier earned his law degree from Howard.[112] In Washington, he worked for the Freedman's Bureau and as a clerk in the U.S. Treasury. Returning to Nashville, he established a law practice, became involved in politics – a path that would lead him to serve on the Nashville City Council from 1878 through 1884 – and began to invest in real estate.

Napier's work in real estate, and his views on home ownership, were comparable to Binga's in Chicago. At the 1901 NNBL national convention, Napier explained his belief that a real estate agent "should place himself where he can render good service in securing [buyers] lands, business houses and good homes – homes with such conveniences as are conducive to good health … and comfort."[113]

Also like Binga, Napier had his own office building in an area that became something of a hub around which other Black-owned businesses developed including restaurants and theaters.[114] The three-story Napier Court at 411 Fourth Avenue was home to Black professional offices including doctors and lawyers and was also where the bank opened for business on Jan. 16, 1904. First day deposits totaled around $6,500.[115, 116]

Although the bank was state chartered, Tennessee, like some other Southern states at the time, did very little in the way of regulation. While bank officials did have to go through a process at least a bit more arduous than painting the word "Bank" on the window and opening the doors, from a regulatory and risk management perspective, there were essentially no rules.[117] This allowed any number of potentially problematic developments including insider lending to bank officials, the ability to make numerous high-risk investments or lending to a point that the bank was unable to meet liquidity considerations in the face of depositor withdrawals. While other banks could, and did, take all kinds of risks – many that would lead to disaster at the time of the Great Depression – Citizens was exceptionally conservative in its activities and regularly promoted the availability of cash to depositors.

"From year to year we have boasted and again repeat that the doors of our institution have not been thrown open a single day for business that we were not prepared to hand to our depositors dollar for dollar for every dollar entrusted to us on demand before the closing of banking hours that day if so required," Boyd said in a 1909 report. It was a comment reflective of remarks that he had made on many such occasions.[118]

While the ability to immediately meet all withdrawal demands may have pleased depositors, it also had an impact on the bank's ability to extend credit by limiting the amount of cash available for investment. This generated at least some amount of criticism. At one point, Napier said he wished that individuals who had been refused loans due to insufficient collateral could understand that his responsibility was first to the bank's depositors and not the would-be borrowers.[119]

Of the two men, Napier had the bigger investment in the bank, both psychologically and financially. While early critics suggested the bank was unlikely to succeed, Boyd said it was Napier, who had been "undaunted in his courage, unfaltering in his faith, unwavering in his determination for the uplift of the financial reputation of his race" in leading the effort.[120] Once the bank was open, Napier took the additional step of pledging his personal fortune to cover all losses if the bank failed.[121] The pledge was likely the result of two events: Napier was in Nashville at the time of the Freedman's failure and witnessed the damage first hand; in addition, he had also likely come out on the losing end of a poorly run Black bank that operated for a few years in Chattanooga in the 1890s.[122]

Although some may have felt the Citizens bank was too tight with credit, it was no question an important source of lending for a burgeoning Black community. In 1907, at the time of a financial crisis and banking panic that was substantial enough to serve as the impetus for creating the Federal Reserve, Citizens reported around $28,000 in loans and discounts, or nearly $800,000 in modern amounts.[123]

"We have been able to make a number of loans that have greatly relieved the wants of our people … saving their property in many instances, and we are determined to go on doing this good work on an ever-increasing scale," Napier said at the time.[124]

Somewhat ironically, it appears Citizens' stability and success may have encouraged the development of a competing Black bank. People's Savings Bank and Trust Company opened in July 1909 at 410 Cedar Street. The bank's founding can be traced back to I.L. Moore, a Nashville dentist who was seeking interest in establishing a real estate and trust business. Although Moore did later become involved in real estate lending, it appears that his early discussions prompted Black business leaders, including some former Citizens directors, to move forward with creating a bank.[125, 126]

According to one history offered by a People's Bank official, "some of the same men who helped to organize the first bank saw that while they had done a good piece of work, they felt that it would be well to have another bank to help care for the needs of our people."[127] These directors –generally younger than their Citizens peers – favored more liberal lending policies to help borrowers "in purchasing homes and embarking in business."[128]

For bank president, People's directors brought in one of the city's most prominent residents, Dr. Robert Fulton Boyd. Dr. Boyd (no relation to Citizens' Richard Boyd), was born in 1855 on a farm near Pulaski, Tennessee. He was separated from his mother when he was still very young after she was apparently sold to another slave owner farther south. After the war, they were reunited and moved to Nashville where he lived as a boy for a few years with Dr. Paul Eve. Eve was a nearly larger-than-life figure. He was a friend of Lafayette, the French hero of the American Revolutionary War, and he served in the Polish military during that country's war of independence, earning Poland's Gold Cross of Honor, the equivalent of the U.S. Congressional Medal of Honor.[129], ***

Dr. Boyd later did farm labor and construction before eventually assisting a Nashville real estate agent to learn the real estate business while apparently also studying. He was a teacher and principal before entering medical school at Central Tennessee College in 1880 at age 25. After graduation, he taught and began practicing medicine in Mississippi. He returned to Tennessee and was involved in both the practice of medicine and education before attending post-graduate medical school in Chicago. In 1887, he turned his entire focus to medicine in Nashville, where he often "went into the alleys, old cellars, dilapidated stables and unhygienic sections of the city" to treat patients.[130] Later, he established a hospital in Nashville and helped to organize the Society of Colored Physicians and Surgeons, which became the National Medical Association.[131] In addition, as noted in his obituary, "between the labors of building up a large and lucrative practice, he devoted much time to enterprises which had for their special mission the uplift of the people."[132]

While Dr. Boyd was charged with leading a bank that sought to grow, and lend, aggressively, achieving the goal was difficult. As had been the case at Citizens, the growth in deposits was slow and, as a result, lending plans were curtailed.[133] For example, when both banks issued annual reports in January 1912, People's $15,400 in loans and discounts was one-half the $30,400 reported by Citizens – the bank seen by some as too conservative with

*** The circumstances of the then-young Boyd's residence with Eve are not clear, nor are Eve's views on race. During the Civil War, Eve treated Confederate soldiers in Nashville before being later made commander and surgeon of Gate City Hospital in Atlanta. Prior to that, he served in the Mexican-American War. Sources: Shelley, Harry S. "The Military Career and Some Urological Works of Paul F. Eve, M.D.," Journal of the Tennessee Medical Association, volume 70, no.4, April, 1977. Available online via the Jean and Alexander Heard Library, Vanderbilt University. https://www.library.vanderbilt.edu/specialcollections/history-of-medicine/exhibits/biopages/peve.php Miller, Benjamin T., James J. Thweatt, Suni K. Geeverghese. "The Surgeon's Duty to Serve: The forgotten life of Paul F. Eve, MD." The American College of Surgeons. 2016. https://www.facs.org/-/media/files/archives/shg-poster/2016/15_eve.ashx.

its lending.[134]

Within a few years, People's changed in significant ways. Dr. Boyd died unexpectedly in July 1912 at age 57.[135] He was succeeded by Dr. J.B. Singleton, a dentist and president of a real estate business, who had also been among the bank's founders.[136] Singleton was well established and respected in the city, but he was unable to achieve the lofty accomplishments of Dr. Boyd. Meanwhile, the bank finally began to step up its lending activity, slightly outpacing Citizens by January 1917.[137] Around this time, the investment portfolios of the two banks began to differ more substantially.

World War I brought a jump in worker wages, dramatically boosting People's total deposits which, along with a post-war issue of capital stock, allowed for an increase in lending, primarily through a number of small loans and short-term real estate borrowing.[138] Conversely, Citizens remained conservative with safe investments and a few large real estate loans.[139, †††]

Although People's was almost certainly the more formidable of the two in facilitating economic growth during the early post-war period, as early as 1924, loan defaults were becoming problematic. In addition, the bank had purchased a number of second mortgages and, as was the case for Chicago's Douglass National Bank, had loans to a number of fraternal organizations and churches with illiquid collateral. People's also had made a number of large loans to the Sunday School Publishing Board of the National Baptist Convention (a competitor of Richard Boyd's publishing operation), which turned out to be insolvent at the time.[140] All of this became too much to withstand amid the economic turmoil at the start of the Great Depression, and the bank failed in 1930.

In the following months, Citizens would see at least two withdrawal runs from depositors. An October 1931 run was averted after Citizens leaders took a step that was not necessarily uncommon at the time – piling stacks of currency in the windows, making them visible to passers-by as an obvious assurance that there was plenty to meet their needs.[141]

Of the two banks, it appears that Citizens was more active in community leadership beyond the provision of financial services.

Almost simultaneous with Boyd's sarcastic comments about segregationist streetcar laws during the 1903 NNBL convention, the matter was becoming a very real concern in the state. That same year, at the encouragement of Tennessee Governor James B. Frazier, the interpretation of existing racist Jim Crow laws was expanded to segregate railroad cars.

††† Citizens officially became "Citizens Savings Bank and Trust" in 1920. Citizens has been used in the text for clarity.

Efforts to overturn the interpretation, including a telegram from Napier to Robert Todd Lincoln asking the Pullman Car Company executive and son of the 16th president to wield his influence in the matter, were unsuccessful.[142]

In 1905, the segregation of mass transit in the state was extended to local municipalities for streetcars "for the comfort and convenience of both classes," with Black riders forced to the back.[143]

As was the case in Richmond and elsewhere, protests soon began with bankers taking a lead role. Boyd and Napier, along with others who were members of the Nashville NNBL chapter, urged operators of freight wagons to begin carrying riders who would have otherwise taken the streetcar. They then set to work establishing Union Transportation Company, with Boyd purchasing a fleet of five steam-powered buses that traveled into predominantly Black neighborhoods in October 1905. When the buses proved incapable of traversing the city's hilly geography, Union traded them in for 14 battery-operated buses that were better suited to the task, but which also required the assumption of around $20,000 in debt, or nearly $600,000 in modern amounts.[144] The bus batteries, however, had to be recharged by the city's electrical utility, which was the same firm that operated the municipal streetcars: the white-owned Nashville Railway and Light Company. After repeated instances of the batteries being damaged by overcharging, Union Transportation Company purchased a dynamo and set up its own recharging operation in the basement of Boyd's publishing house.[145] The problems, however, continued. At least one member of the Nashville City Council urged action to revoke Union's corporate charter while the full council implemented an annual tax on the cars. Eventually the financial burden was simply too steep to continue operations and the buses were parked in the summer of 1906 with the founders taking significant losses in the venture.[146]

One direct outgrowth of the streetcar initiative was that it prompted Boyd to take on an increasingly activist role. Boyd founded *The Nashville Globe* newspaper, which was comparable to Mitchell's *Richmond Planet* with a focus on social activism and economic growth through business development.[147] The paper was particularly supportive of Black banks. It covered regularly – and with apparent fairness – both Citizens and People's. As only one example, on the day the banks' earnings were published on the paper's front page, an editorial column lauded both banks for a strong performance – "our banks have never had a brighter future" – and encouraged deposits in both institutions "where it can and would be used for the benefit of the people" through loans.[148]

Despite Boyd's connection to Washington and the NNBL, the paper, led by Boyd's son Henry, over time took views somewhat more closely aligned with W.E.B. Du Bois' philosophy of political action and activism while sometimes attacking Washington's call for accommodation. The Boyds, and *The Globe*, advocated increased spending on the city's Black public schools, were critical of the aloof white leadership and administration of Fisk University and, along with Napier, were involved in the establishment of Tennessee Agricultural and Industrial School, later Tennessee State University, in 1912.[149]

Finally, one of the Boyds' most touching activist efforts was the establishment of the National Negro Doll Company, which mass produced Black dolls that were not caricatures "of that disgraceful and humiliating type that we have been accustomed to seeing."[150] Orders for the dolls, which ranged from 12 inches to 36 inches in size, came into Nashville from across the United States.

"There is more involved than appears on the surface in encouraging little Negro girls to clasp in their arms pretty copies of themselves. The white race doesn't monopolize all the beauty and lovableness, and it will be a happy day when this is realized," reported *Collier's Weekly.*[151, ####]

Napier, meanwhile, became increasingly active politically, serving on the Tennessee Republican Executive Committee and strengthening his national connections. Notably, beginning in 1908, he served as a trustee of the Anna T. Jeanes Foundation, which funded Black schools in the rural South, joining a board that included Booker T. Washington, Andrew Carnegie, William Howard Taft and others.[152] The role, and the introduction to Taft, was likely key to Taft's decision to appoint Napier as registrar of the United States Treasury in 1911. The Treasury post was one that Napier had sought for some time and contributed to his rejecting an appointment as consul to Bahia, Brazil, by President Theodore Roosevelt in 1908 and an appointment as minister resident and counsel general of Liberia by Taft in 1910. In his Treasury post, Napier was essentially the nation's bookkeeper, leading a

---

The full scope of the various accomplishments and community involvement initiatives of Boyd and his son Henry Allen Boyd, including the founding of the Negro Press Association, are beyond the scope of this work as are some of the details regarding issues of race and the Baptist Church during this period. R.H. Boyd died in 1922. An estimated crowd of 6,000 attended his funeral. Henry Allen Boyd, meanwhile, died in 1959 and the paper ceased publication soon after. A joint biography of both men is one of the longest entries in the following book, which served as an important source for this publication regarding the Boyds and others: Ingham, John N. and Lynne B. Feldman. African-American Business Leaders: A Biographical Dictionary, Greenwood Press: Westport, Conn. (1994).

staff of more than 70 and, among other duties, signing the nation's currency issued between 1911 and 1913.[153] He resigned from the post in protest after President Woodrow Wilson began implementing Jim Crow policies throughout his administration, including requiring Treasury Department workers to use segregated restrooms. Back in Nashville, Napier remained active in civic activities and the bank.[154]

Richard Boyd died in 1922, and his son was named bank president. Napier, meanwhile, died in 1940. At age 94, he was not only among the last of a generation born well before the start of the Civil War, but he was also someone who had made a meaningful difference in Black economic development to a degree that would have been unfathomable when he was a young man. He recounted some of what he had seen during a 1906 speech to students at Tuskegee:

> The Negro started his business having as capital:
> A small amount of money,
> A great abundance of poverty,
> A great lack of credit,
> A great supply of inexperience,
> A great want to education.
> With such a capital to begin business it can easily be seen that progress must necessarily be slow and that success could be attainted only by courage, patience and unrelenting toil.
>
> A true indication of material progress a people is making is the amount of money it handles. Twenty years ago there was not a single Negro bank in this country. The cry then was, get money, save your earnings, open a bank account. Today, the Negro's ambition is not only to open a bank account, but to organize, equip and operate a bank and to persuade others to open the account. And when he goes with his money to invest in stocks, bonds or other securities his color is no disadvantage to him. The broker offers him his best chair. There is no Jim Crow corner provided for him on such occasions.
> Negroes now own and control more than a score of banking institutions. Their deposits amount to hundreds of thousands of dollars and their clearings to millions of dollars annually. Of course, the great volume of the business of these banks comes from the Negroes themselves, but there is a sufficient amount done with the whites to show that in matters of this sort color or race prejudice cuts no figure. As against 22 persons engaged

as bankers and brokers according to the last United States census, we now have that number of banks employing from three to 10 people each. Many of these own the buildings in which they transact their business.

Those of us who realize the possibilities of the Negro people in America are determined never to stop until we shall have won for ourselves and our children an honorable place, until the excellence of all we do and the Christian spirit that inspires it shall banish skepticism as to our future and put down opposition to our efforts to help ourselves and to rise.[155]

Detroit, Michigan

I.

In 2020, a year of uncertainty and events that seemed to grow ever more troubling with each glance at social media – social unrest, a pandemic, a coming election – Kenneth Kelly found hope.

"I will tell you that America has always responded positively when it's been called up and when it's needed. I think this time will be no different than it was in the '60s when we responded with the Voting Rights and Civil Rights Act and the Fair Housing Act," he told a reporter.[1] "That all led to the creation of our business that we're running today."

That business is Detroit's First Independence Bank, the only Black bank in the nation's largest Black majority city. In May 2020, First Independence celebrated the 50-year anniversary of its opening, a founding that came as a direct response to the violence in what is sometimes referred to as the "long, hot summer" of 1967. Nationwide that year, there were more than 140 racial disturbances including both large-scale events as well as smaller but still violent confrontations in major urban centers and smaller communities. The most tragic, and one of the worst in all of U.S. history, erupted in Detroit. One measure of the scope is that the event is sometimes referred to as "The Detroit Rebellion of 1967."[2]

In its aftermath, Detroit citizens "were looking for solutions just as we are today that could demonstrate and provide more inclusion," said Kelly, the bank's CEO and chairman.[3] "A component of that was financial and economic empowerment. The establishment of the bank provided multiple positive outcomes as it relates to the community who had felt excluded."

In the spring and summer of 2020, Black Lives Matter activists were on the streets in Detroit and more than 500 cities after the asphyxiation of George Floyd by a Minneapolis police officer, who kneeled on Floyd's neck while Floyd was being placed under arrest for allegedly using a counterfeit $20 bill. Floyd's killing was not the only one. Protestors in the summer of 2020 also sought justice for Daniel Prude, who died while in police custody in Rochester, New York; Breonna Taylor, who was shot and killed during a botched police raid in Louisville, Kentucky; and Ahmaud Arbery, a jogger who was murdered by white residents of a southeast Georgia community. The summer protests were believed to be the largest in U.S. history according to an analysis of participation estimates.[4]

Although the overwhelming majority of the events were far more peaceful than what occurred in some U.S. cities in the 1950s and '60s, they were not without violence, particularly in the hours after nightfall.[5]

A reporter seeking some historical perspective on the events more than 50 years apart sought out Dan Aldridge, a well-known Detroit civil rights activist and a key figure in the 1967 protests that erupted after decades of economic oppression, institutional racism and segregation.

Sadly, in Aldridge's view, little had changed.

"Basically, we're talking about the same thing [today]," he said.[6] "[But] now we're understanding the broad systemic issue of racism and its connection to other issues."

Kelly said he is "hopeful that we get beyond trying to solve this through episodic solutions and try to figure out how we can do some things that systematically shift the way we think about these problems going forward."[7]

Like many other Black banks throughout history, First Independence is primarily mission driven in its lending with a higher percentage of minority loans than other institutions. However, to fully leverage its ability to serve these borrowers and to achieve broader community economic goals, Kelly says he knows the bank needs support from all segments of society. More long-term deposits, regardless of the source, expand the bank's pool of lendable resources.

There was some indication that 2020's national heightening of social awareness generated interest among a diverse range of depositors that mirrored an increased diversity among the protests when compared against similar events in the Civil Rights era. Many Black banks reported deposit growth in the spring and early summer when protest activity was the most active. It is somewhat difficult, however, to measure the correlation between the deposits and the nation's social landscape. Around this same period, overall banking sector deposits also grew significantly, due in large part to reduced spending as the coronavirus pandemic upended some segments of the U.S. economy. However, some Black banks did substantially outpace the sector's overall growth.[8] Notably, at least a half dozen companies committed to depositing money with Black financial institutions including Netflix, Costco and PayPal.[9]

First Independence also announced an agreement with Bank of America and Comerica in 2020. Under the arrangement, which had been in the works for more than a year, Bank of America took a 5 percent equity stake in First Independence and a handful of other minority-owned institutions. Comerica, meanwhile, deposited $2.5 million in First Independence, part of a broader initiative by that bank.[10]

"The intent is not just to be a bank for only African Americans, but it is to be a bank that really recognizes that we need all segments of society to support a bank like ours, so that we can demonstrate our effectiveness for communities that we have an affinity for, like African Americans," Kelly said.[11] The bank "represents to the community that those who have been disenfranchised have an ability and an ally in reaching their financial goals."

In the summer of 2020, COVID-19 made attaining those goals far more challenging for many small business owners. Black small businesses were hit disproportionately hard, with one study finding their number fell by nearly half within the first months of the pandemic coming to the U.S.[12]

"We have always known that African-American controlled businesses have a higher susceptibility to downturns in the economy. We have seen the data over and over that substantiates that. So what we attempted to do was to try to be a voice of at least echoing these resources as being available for those businesses so the impact is not as difficult for them," Kelly said.[13]

"It's well known that Detroit has a grittiness about it that just continues to fight and fight and fight … And so we represent – just as many Detroiters and those from Southeast Michigan – the fight, the grit to innovate and continue to grow in the midst of facing turmoil and downtrends in the economy."[14]

Perseverance in the face of turmoil is very much in the foundation of Detroit's Black community. Well before the rise of the American auto industry and the jobs that brought migrants from the rural South to the city, Detroit in the years before and during the Civil War was something of a beacon of hope for innumerable fugitive slaves. The city may not have been the promised land, but those seeking freedom could certainly see it from there.

Across the Detroit River lay Canada, making Detroit an oft-used crossing point for thousands traveling north along one of at least seven known Underground Railroad routes culminating at the city.[15] It was both an endpoint of one journey – spent tucked away among a wagon-load of freight, heavily disguised or moving under the cover of night – and the beginning of another as the international border blocked the reach of American slave catchers and bounty hunters.

Before Lincoln's signing of the Emancipation Proclamation, it is believed that perhaps 200 Detroit residents may have been involved in sheltering and assisting fugitives heading to Canada.[16]

Detroit's Black population remained relatively steady after the Civil War until the beginning of the Great Migration and the dawning of mass automobile production – an event that remade both America in general and the city in particular. A *New York Times* reporter described Detroit in the summer of 1919 as "a bonanza town," where one of the biggest concerns was the risk of getting run over by one of the 80,000 automobiles crowding city streets:

> Detroit, the biggest of the Middle Western cities next to Chicago is surely prosperous. It is so rich that you feel it as you walk on the streets. You feel that if Detroit were drinking anything it would be champagne.[17]

In 1914, Ford Motor Company began offering a $5 daily wage to its Detroit area factory workers – then enough to thrust unskilled low-wage workers into the middle class and a powerful enticement to those in the South who might see total earnings of $5 only after a full month of labor.[18] As one autoworker from Tennessee explained it, "We had heard at home that you could make $25 or $30 a week in the factory. I thought I'd be rich. On the farm if you had $5 you'd carry it around for six months. Ten dollars seemed impossible."[19]

Henry Ford's virulent racism – he was a known anti-Semite and Nazi sympathizer who was purportedly admired by Hitler – is difficult to square with Ford Motor Company's role as a major Black employer during this era. Ford Motor Company not only hired substantially more Black workers than its Detroit counterparts, but it also placed those workers in a wider range of jobs. Black workers at Ford Motor Company were in essentially every department of the automaker in the 1920s and '30s, including skilled trades and management, albeit at a lesser degree than their white counterparts.[20] However, despite providing these opportunities to some minority workers, it would be disingenuous to suggest Henry Ford's motivations were entirely pure. The company founder's strategy was to create a paternalistic relationship with much of his work force, the Black workers especially, which might then make them more accepting of future management action. At the very least, the sense of loyalty he built evolved into leverage when autoworkers organized.[21]

It is also important to understand that while Ford did offer a broader scope of employment opportunities to Black workers than any other Detroit manufacturer, for very many of the employees the positions were not necessarily "desirable" jobs. Black workers, regardless of their skill level or rank within the company, were often assigned to a disproportionate degree to areas such as the foundry or other departments where the work was often hot, dirty and potentially dangerous.[22] That said, essentially every Ford job in this era involved long, exhausting workdays.

As one Detroit resident from this period recounted it:

[You] could identify Ford workers on streetcars going home at night. You'd see 20 asleep on the car and everyone would say, "Ford workers." Many times the conductors looked over the car and shook a man to tell him it was his stop. ... Sometimes some people tried to cover it up. They would say it was working in the foundry that made the men sleep. They said it was the fumes. But everybody knew Ford was a man-killing place. That always frightened me.[23]

With the availability of jobs, between 1910 and 1920, Detroit's Black population increased sevenfold – the biggest jump of any of the nation's Northern urban centers at the migration's beginning.

As one man who helped many new arrivals in the city during this period later recalled:

Who were the people who made up this great stream of migration? There were a few individuals, a few families, who were acting on real knowledge of what they wanted and what they hoped to do. But for the most part these were people who were just coming – not knowing what they would do when they got here, having no direction, not knowing where they would sleep, who they were going to see, or who would be interested in them...

These people had heard about Detroit; it was the most publicized city in the U.S. If you lived in the South, and could manage to scrape up the fare, here was an opportunity to better yourself. These were the equivalent of the pioneers who braved the prairies in covered wagons on the European immigrants who took passage in the steerage for a land whose language and customs were unknown to them.[24]

By 1930, a city with fewer than 6,000 Black residents in 1910 was home to more than 120,000 as the Black workforce further swelled amid the same World War I-related immigrant worker shortage that hit Chicago and other major manufacturing and industrial centers.[25] And nearly all of the men found work. More than 90 percent of the city's Black male population was employed in 1920 and nearly 90 percent was employed in 1930 – both figures higher than the employment rate of white men in the city.[26]

As was the case in other cities of the Upper Midwest, the rapid racial diversification of a workforce and a community that had previously been almost exclusively white introduced tension. Until the start of the Great Migration, Detroit had been largely free of the widespread discrimination found elsewhere in the U.S., due likely to the combination of a relatively small minority population and adequate available housing.

To some degree, it appears this continued among workers on the factory floor. While there was no doubt racial tension and some number of workplace incidents – by 1920 the Ku Klux Klan did count some of the city's white factory workers among their members – Black/white violence was not notably higher than intraracial violence during this period. While segregation on some factory floors may have played a role in this dynamic by keeping the races apart, it seems more likely that a plentiful job market that eliminated the risk of someone "taking" an opportunity was a significant contributor.[27]

Whatever degree of agreement existed in the workplace, it was not found at home. Increased migration and a burgeoning housing shortage in the period around World War I fostered increasing segregation and discrimination in the city.[28] Similar to what occurred in Chicago and elsewhere, Black families and men who had come to the city alone or with friends to find work were forced into segregated neighborhoods where they found heavily overcrowded and often substandard living conditions.

"The majority … are living under such crowded conditions that three or four families in an apartment is the rule rather than the exception," read one 1919 report.[29] "Seventy-five percent of the … homes have so many lodgers that they are really hotels. Stables, garages and cellars have been converted into homes… The poolrooms and gambling clubs are beginning to charge for the privilege of sleeping on pool-room tables overnight."

The same year, a visitor from Virginia's Hampton Institute noted that Black families and workers "were lured here by expectation of large wages and when they got here, they were driven down into the disorderly housing district."[30]

At the time, the city's average Black household was home to nine people. While the overcrowding did ease a bit, it was not nearly enough. By 1925, for example, the typical Black household for a Ford factory worker included the wage earner's family and between three and five lodgers.[31]

The result was a housing environment that in many ways mirrored Chicago. Rents in segregated Black neighborhoods became exorbitantly high and Black families financially able to move away from those areas were often met in their new neighborhoods with violence. One event that received substantial attention involved Dr. Ossian Sweet and his family who moved into a white neighborhood, under a police escort, but later found themselves in a home surrounded by an angry mob numbering into the hundreds.[32] With the family essentially trapped as the mob shattered windows, Sweet purportedly grabbed a gun and opened fire. At least one person was killed and another injured.[§] Newspaper accounts indicated it was the third such event in the same number of weeks.[33]

One local resident's recollection suggests that the Sweets' move came just as racial dynamics were taking a dramatic, and downward, turn in the city. Prior to this time, there had been instances of white families taking in Black families who were unable to find homes, but now the environment was changing.[34]

> There had been some mixing of the races in the area for many years. Recently, however, there had been growing signs of trouble … Negro families had lived for years in peace and friendliness with their white neighbors [but] this no longer seemed possible in the changing atmosphere.[35]

Given the potential for violence and rising tensions, even while Black workers at the city's automobile plants may have earned the same wage as their white counterparts, segregation in the city meant that the money did not afford Black workers with similar opportunities to improve their living standards. John C. Dancy, who became leader of the Detroit Urban League in 1918 and held the post for more than four decades, said housing "was the most challenging problem that faced us at that time."

According to Dancy, a typical white family at this time would have spent about $30 a month on housing while a typical Black family would pay somewhere around $50 for often substandard accommodations. In his biography, Dancy recalls one family paying $50 a month for an apartment above a store that the tenants could only reach after climbing a ladder and walking across the roof of a neighboring structure.[36]

§ One reason that the event received significant media attention is that Sweet and others in the house at the time who were charged with murder were represented in court by Clarence Darrow, one of the nation's most well-known attorneys. At the time of the Sweet case, Darrow had just concluded his defense of teacher John Scopes, who had been accused of violating state legislation barring the teaching of evolution in a state-funded Tennessee school. The men in the Sweet case were acquitted.

As a result, many of the families were forced to crowd into Black Bottom, an east-side neighborhood near downtown so-named by early settlers because of its dark marsh bottomland soil; and its neighbor to the northwest, Paradise Valley. Today, after redevelopment initiatives of the mid-20th century and 1960s interstate highway construction, Black Bottom is now the Lafayette Park district while Paradise Valley encompasses Ford Field and Comerica Park as well as neighboring blocks. The region's business main street, is now essentially the route of Interstate 75.

2.

Detroit's Hastings Street was one of the nation's most important and vibrant cultural hubs with regular appearances in its nightspots by renowned jazz, blues and big band performers ranging from Pearl Bailey and Ella Fitzgerald to Duke Ellington and Count Basie.[37] Blues legend John Lee Hooker, who came to Detroit to find work at one of the city's automobile plants, sang about Hastings Street, its clubs and a young man who wanted to be in the midst of it all in his 1948 song "Boogie Chillen." It was one of the first recordings of electric blues to gain prominence and served as an important influence on the soon-to-emerge rock music.

One longtime Detroit resident's description of the area mirrors what others said about The Stroll in Chicago:

> It seemed nothing could keep me from returning to Hastings at night to see cars and traffic moving bumper to bumper both ways up and down the street, to smell food cooking hanging heavy in the air, barbecue chicken, shrimp, pastrami and salami, and the passing scents of perfumed women.[38]

An area that had initially been an enclave for Eastern European immigrants became an economic center of Black-owned businesses in a largely segregated world. Among them were retail stores, hotels and markets, as well as office space for professionals including a number of attorneys and physicians. According to one survey, the city was home to at least 720 Black-owned businesses by 1926.[39]

"The Detroit Black community in its heyday was absolutely fantastic," said Sidney Barthwell Jr., whose father owned a pharmacy chain in the city.[40] "It was better than Harlem."

Despite a vibrant Black business community, Detroit during this period did not become a home for Black banking to the degree that occurred in some other cities. This is likely the result of a number of factors. One thing to keep in mind is that it appears much of Detroit's racial tension and segregation developed in large part after a substantial increase in the city's Black population pressured housing availability. Prior to that, segregation was not widespread in residential areas nor in businesses including those such as bars and restaurants where social interaction was substantial.[41] Some of the city's "white" banks did have Black employees and those institutions, as well as potentially others, did provide some measure of financial services to the Black community, although likely limited in scope.[42]

However, as conditions changed, families and individuals faced strict segregation, and few sources of readily available financing. Dancy and others worked with real estate developers to establish areas where Black families could freely build their own homes, albeit sometimes nowhere near downtown and the Black Bottom community. In Dancy's own words, in some instances it was "far from an ideal solution," because families unable to afford nor finance home construction were in some cases forced to build a floor that they then covered with a tent until they could fund construction. For some period of time, one of these areas was without a connection to a sewer system and the nearest water supply was a quarter-mile trek.[43]

In 1927, a multiracial commission formed by Detroit Mayor John W. Smith in response to racial violence in 1925 included among its numerous recommendations on several topics that the city's banks be "more liberal in their attitude toward Negro loans."[44]

The report, however, did little to improve the availability of financial services.

Barthwell's father, Sidney Barthwell Sr., self-funded the purchase of his first pharmacy – a then failing drug store – out of money he'd saved while working there as an employee.[45] Expanding his successful business, which eventually had 13 locations, however, was an arduous process. In some instances, he had to borrow from multiple "white" banks to fund a single store, despite his business record that, by that time, was well established.[46]

That Barthwell was deemed a poor credit risk on the basis of his race was, tragically, not unusual. As one Black business writer of this period explained, a prospective borrower might "have the necessary collateral, he may be able to obtain the qualified endorsers, he may be able to meet his payments, but because of his general classification, his loan is in many instances not granted."[47]

As a result, Black borrowers in Detroit during this period were often left to turn to private lenders, the less scrupulous of which were loan sharks charging interest rates as high as 50 percent.[48] Their prevalence, and crooked practices, eventually became so widespread that a judge in 1940 suggested to a group of attorneys that they launch a campaign against the firms, some of which advertised their services in the city's newspapers.

"I'm firmly convinced that if these evils could be eliminated it would provide an avenue to escape from the present economic depression," the judge told the Wolverine Bar Association during the group's annual meeting.[49, †]

† The Wolverine Bar Association, formed by and for Detroit's Black attorneys, continues to serve the Detroit community in 2020.

Counter to these lenders, there were a number of efforts to establish businesses, that although they were not banks, were closer to what would be considered mainstream financial services providers.

There were at least two in the 1920s that existed for some period of time. The earliest of these appears to have been D.C. Northcross and Co. Bankers, which is listed in a 1921 business directory.[50]

Dr. David C. Northcross and his wife, Dr. Daisy Northcross, came to Detroit from Montgomery, Alabama, around 1916 after practicing medicine there for a decade and operating a private sanitarium. While there, David was also among the founders of a branch office of Birmingham's Black Alabama Penny Savings Bank, which was one of the nation's first Black banks when it opened in 1890.[51]

For David, the move to Detroit was a return to the Upper Midwest after earning his degree in Illinois and serving an internship at Chicago's Provident Hospital.[52] The couple is best known as the founders of Detroit's Mercy Hospital, an initiative they embarked upon after David was allowed only "visitor" status when attempting to check on a patient at the city's Harper Hospital. Detroit Mercy, which included a nursing school, was Michigan's first Black-owned hospital. After being founded in three rented rooms, Detroit Mercy eventually moved to a three-story building that was among the most prominent in Black Bottom.[53]

In addition to his medical practice and the hospital, Northcross was also a landlord and involved in real estate. His role in these businesses, and his wealth, would have put him in a position similar to Binga in Chicago in terms of real estate dealings and the potential to provide financing.[‡] It appears his bank was only in business for three years.[54]

Shortly after this, the Michigan People's Finance Corp. was established in 1924 – possibly through the reorganization and expansion of a small Detroit-based loan company. Much of the work was done by Douglas Beecher Fullwood, a former accountant at Tuskegee Institute and a University of Chicago graduate who was appointed manager.[55] Within a year of its founding, People's reported assets of around $90,000.[56] In 1926, it consolidated with another firm, Penn Investment, resulting in a larger firm under the People's banner. While finance corporations of this type were generally involved in small loans, People's was able to expand into a full range of lending including commercial, real estate and automobile financing, as well as insurance.

‡ Tragically, Northcross was killed by one of his tenants in 1933 while attempting to collect past-due rent. *The Marshall Evening Chronicle,* Jan. 4, 1933.

It is not possible to gauge People's impact on the community. For a period of time, it operated under the leadership of Dr. A.L. Turner, a physician who had suffered an assault similar to what occurred at the Sweets' home around the same time of that event.[57] John Dancy was also listed as among those involved in the institution. Their involvement suggests a significant interest in home financing. However, the effort is not referenced in a biography Dancy wrote near the end of his life in the mid-1960s, suggesting he had minimal involvement, and/or that the firm accomplished little.[58]

Regardless of whatever financing was made available by People's, the demand was still far greater.

S.R. Williams, a researcher who conducted an economic survey for the National Negro Development Union in 1929 that covered everything from household spending to employment, noted in particular "a great need for a Negro bank. There is a small insurance company, but more are needed. There is need for all sorts of businesses of these types if the city … is to reach the status of … Cleveland, Pittsburgh or Chicago."[59]

Among the financial services initiatives in the years that followed, in 1936 the Fannie B. Peck Credit Union was formed by Peck and her husband, Rev. William H. Peck, pastor of the city's Bethel African Methodist Episcopal (AME) Church.[60] The organization was the result of a discussion in a Sunday school class that Fannie Peck taught where they "discussed … the need of such an organization as a credit union. The young people were quick to see the desirability of the suggested organization to promote thrift, provide loans and give a type of business training not available elsewhere."[61]

Both Pecks were important community leaders after coming to Detroit from Kansas City in 1928.[62] Perhaps more well-known than the credit union was the National Housewives League of America, which grew out of the Detroit Housewives League that Fannie Peck founded in 1930 to encourage Black women to patronize Black businesses. William Peck, meanwhile, founded the Booker T. Washington Trade Association, which had a similar mission.[63]

3.

The Depression dealt a massive blow to Detroit. As devastating as it was for many it was perhaps magnitudes worse for Black workers in Detroit as auto sales slowed to a crawl. With the city's economic engine idled, the ripple effects were felt by workers not only at the auto plants, but also by those working for suppliers and parts manufacturers, and eventually the retail merchants who sold food and other necessities. Some estimates peg Detroit's Black unemployment during this period at as high as 60 percent.

In Detroit, the economic pain of the 1930s, however, came to an abrupt, if not immediate, end with the beginning of World War II. The city's industrialists retooled automotive and other factories for the production of everything from nearly all of the helmets worn by United States Army soldiers to tanks, planes and thousands of vehicles. Detroit was now "the Arsenal of Democracy" in the words of President Franklin D. Roosevelt.[64]

This ramping up of the city's workforce included not only the creation of jobs – by 1943, unemployment in the city numbered little more than a handful of workers – but also a change in workforce composition. Where Ford and a few others had a multiracial workforce in the pre-war era, the 1940s saw additional manufacturers and other firms open doors to not only Black men, but, to a lesser degree, to Black women, who filled jobs previously held by white men.[65] Such moves were not welcome by white laborers who would sometimes take action – events known as "hate strikes" – in response to the hiring or promotion of a Black worker.[66]

This new workforce, the result of a tight job market, as well as labor unions and civil rights initiatives, occurred in conjunction with a more than doubling of the city's Black population between 1940 and 1950 – the largest percentage growth of any major U.S. city during this period outside of California where Black populations had been relatively small.[67] This second wave of the Great Migration, which saw the Black share of the city's population grow from 9.2 percent to 16.2 percent, was not without the pain and violence seen previously, but now on a larger and more frequent scale.[68] The old issues surrounding jobs and housing had become only more pronounced during the Great Depression. One auto industry analysis noted that the industry's Depression slowdown only "intensified the struggle for jobs and produced a fertile field for the sowing of discord. As a result, the [city's Black residents] became a convenient scapegoat for such organizations as the Ku Klux Klan, the Black Legion and other groups that began to flourish after 1931. For several years, Detroit was even a hotbed of pro-Nazi activity."[69] Making this even worse was the arrival of many Southern whites steeped in traditions of discrimination, who also came to the city during this period for war manufacturing jobs.[70]

The resulting confrontations ranged from a number of small clashes and street fights during the 1930s to the 1942 Sojourner Truth Homes riots that began when a white mob created a roadblock to halt the moving vans that Black families were using to move into the public housing development that straddled Black and white neighborhoods. Around 40 individuals were injured as the standoff turned violent, and more than 200 were arrested.[71] The families eventually moved in later under police protection and after federal government involvement.

The following summer, the city suffered a far larger and more violent riot. Like Chicago in 1919, the spark to a long-simmering caldron came on a day when many sought relief from the heat – in this case June 20, 1943, on Detroit's Belle Isle. As beachgoers began to making their way home from the park in the middle of the Detroit River by walking across the crowded Belle Isle Bridge late in the day, a fight – possibly related to an incident that had occurred days earlier – led to large-scale violence that involved hundreds.[72] In the hours that followed, unfounded rumors spread on both sides: that white rioters had thrown a Black woman and her baby from the bridge and that a white woman had been raped near the bridge. Soon, gangs roamed the streets, squaring off with one another. Eventually, 34 were killed – 25 of them Black including 17 shot by police – and some 700 were injured with numerous casualties the result of a gun battle as police surrounded an apartment building.[73]

Dancy's biography, in which he recounts escaping from a white mob chasing his automobile, lists numerous events that occurred in the hours before the violence was finally quelled by the arrival of 6,000 federal troops the following day.[74]

Throughout the day white mobs came in [to the east side] to attack the block between John R. Street and Woodward Avenue. They attempted to set fire to some of the homes. No serious fires resulted, but there was much property damage. Early on the morning of June 21, groups of white men and boys assembled on Woodward Avenue and throughout the day Negroes were attacked, beaten and mauled. At least 43 automobiles driven by Negroes were burned by white hoodlums. This does not include the automobiles that were damaged in other ways. Much criticism was directed against the police department for the ineffective way it handled white mobs on Woodward.

Street cars, buses and public vehicles were stopped or stoned and victims beaten by Negroes or whites, depending on the neighborhood.[75]

It was not lost that, as this battle was waged on the streets of Detroit, Black soldiers were simultaneously overseas in a battle for freedom. Among those pointing to this connection, poet Langston Hughes in his poem "Beaumont to Detroit," which paralleled the Nazis with racial violence in the U.S. occurring in Detroit and the Texas city of Beaumont during this same period. Appearing in *The Detroit Tribune* and elsewhere in the days after the violence, it reads, in part:

You Jim crowed me
Before Hitler rose to power –
And you're still jim crowing me
Right now, this very hour

Yet you say we're fighting
For democracy.
Then why don't democracy
Include me?

I ask you this question
Cause I want to know
How long I got to fight
BOTH HILTER – AND JIM CROW.[76, §§]

Reports issued in the aftermath of the Detroit violence sought to assign responsibility – including a state Fact Finding commission that essentially produced a cover for Detroit police by laying the blame almost exclusively upon the city's "militant" Black population. Others blamed the city's white police force and authorities' handling of the Sojourner Truth standoff. A report by the National Urban League, meanwhile, highlighted the rising frustration in a Black community that faced numerous racial challenges – the most notable among these being the ongoing housing crisis where conditions had only continued to worsen since the

§§ Capitalization is as it was published in *The Detroit Tribune,* July 3, 1943.

World War I era.[77]

In a city with nearly total housing segregation – less than 1 percent of the single-family homes built in the Detroit area during the 1940s were available to Black families because racial covenants barred them from homeownership in the overwhelming majority of neighborhoods – to describe the living conditions that many were forced to suffer under as "substandard" is a disservice of understatement.[78] While around a quarter to one-third of the Detroit area's Black population was able to find homes in enclaves such as those Dancy had worked with developers to establish, the vast majority was still confined to the decaying and grossly overcrowded lower east side of the city.[79] There, some homes were little more than shelters where snow, rain and the bitter Michigan wind slipped through holes in roofs and walls. Those places that offered a covered and enclosed respite from the elements were often grossly overcrowded with sometimes large families cramped into basement utility rooms.[80] Many of the shelters were years old – some with construction predating the Civil War, meaning they were potentially the same structures that had sheltered those fleeing the United States on the Underground Railroad nearly a century earlier. They were breeding grounds for disease, built with aging wood that could ignite with a spark. One survey of the Paradise Valley neighborhood found 3,500 homes where the only toilets were in shacks built above open holes in city sewer lines.[81] These deplorable conditions were faced by families who had come North with a goal of owning a home and land, something that was for all purposes essentially impossible in the South. In both geographies, in addition to the risk of violence, there were also prohibitive economic structures. In the South, it was sharecropping and debt-peonage systems. In Detroit, high-cost housing in a tight market, neighborhoods that were "off limits" to Black families, and unscrupulous and racist real estate agents all presented roadblocks of varying degrees. Because these homes were very nearly the only ones available to Black residents, and because of the excessive costs, families could set aside little – if anything – to save for better accommodations. Underlying all of this was that Detroit's white banks were not a consistent and reliable source of credit for Black homebuyers.[82]

Some lenders did advertise in the city's Black *Detroit Tribune* that they offered credit – one suggested borrowing $100 would cost the borrower "only $7.12" in interest if repaid within six months – but options for the amounts needed to buy a home or finance a business were all but nonexistent.[83] Not unexpectedly, Detroit like Chicago and other urban centers, saw the rise of blockbusters eager to profit financially from racial antagonism and the limited opportunities for housing or funds that were accessible to Black families. It would continue for years.

In the aftermath of the 1943 turmoil and the ongoing problems of housing and access to credit, there were discussions in early 1944 about establishing a Black-owned bank.[84] It appears that the initiative involved a potential reorganization of Victory Loan and Investment Company, a non-bank firm that was incorporated in late 1942 or early 1943. Victory was formed and led by Carlton W. Gaines with involvement from the local Booker T. Washington Trade Association, which served and promoted the city's Black businesses and was a group with which Gaines served in a leadership role. Until Victory's formation, Gaines had been primarily involved in Detroit real estate, but he had a background in finance, establishing and leading the Laborers Penny Loan & Savings Co. in Waycross, Georgia, before moving to the upper Midwest.[85]

The Victory initiative did not advance far, and other Trade Association leaders became involved instead in an initiative that may have been more well-suited to address the issue of housing. That work led to Home Federal Savings and Loan Association, which opened for business in April 1947 with the objectives of "promoting a safe and convenient method for saving and investment and to provide for sound and economical financing of homes."[86]

Much of the work to create the lender was done by Moses Stewart Thompson, founder of Motor City Beverage Company, president of the Trade Association and chairman of the Detroit National Negro Business League.[87, 88] Thompson, whose family came to Detroit from Montgomery, Alabama, when he was a boy, became interested in accounting as a way of understanding why, when it came to the area of Black-owned businesses, "It seemed everything I read was derogatory.

"There was always a Black business, especially banks, going out of business and I wondered why white banks didn't fail."[89]

A year after its founding, Home Federal made headlines when it qualified for mortgages insured by the Federal Housing Administration (FHA), the first minority-owned financial institution in Michigan to earn the designation.[90] Despite the attention, including a press photo of Home Federal President Arthur M. Simmons receiving a certificate from an FHA official, the designation was not a remedy to the housing problem, although federal officials may have tried to present it as such.

Thompson was later among several Black financial services professionals from across the United States involved in a closed-door meeting in Washington where he and others were told by FHA officials that they needed to be doing more to make FHA loans available to minority borrowers. The lenders countered, as might be expected, by noting FHA policies that "largely induced and sanctioned" a segregated housing market — i.e., redlining – blocked the availability of home financing for borrowers in innumerable communities.[91] These restrictions not only hurt would-be buyers, but also crippled the Black banks.

It is impossible to know what Thompson may have said in the Washington, D.C., meeting, although there is little doubt he would have been infuriated. Government redlining maps had effectively deemed only a few pockets of his city – around 20 percent of its total area at the time – as likely to pass even the first step toward qualifying for mortgage financing before a consideration of the would-be borrower's financial history could begin. Huge swaths in the urban core, along with enclaves, were all marked "hazardous" by officials, effectively making them off limits for home financing.* Thompson later wrote to lawmakers urging the approval of the Fair Housing Act which would ban redlining saying the measure was the implementation of actions originally intended to occur a century earlier during Reconstruction. Segregated housing, Thompson wrote, was "the last condition of slavery and colonialism."[92]

One example of the reach of redlining in Detroit:

In the early 1940s, a developer sought to establish a new residential neighborhood for the growing city, but FHA financing was not available because of the proximity to Black-owned properties. To finally appease authorities, and to make FHA financing available, the developer was forced to construct a 6-foot-tall, foot-thick, half-mile-long wall to separate Black families from the planned white subdivision. It became known locally as "the wailing wall."[93]

The Washington FHA meeting was later called into question during Congressional testimony by Clarence Mitchell of the National Association for the Advancement of Colored People (NAACP). Mitchell noted that while the bankers were told the FHA meeting was strictly "off the record," the FHA issued a press release soon after that blamed the Black bankers for the problems of Black borrowers who were unable to obtain FHA financing. Further, the FHA release suggested that some of the banks were charging excessive interest rates.

"The whole purpose of that release is that the colored people weren't doing enough

---

* As noted previously, those with an interest in this issue can access historic Home Owners' Loan Corporation "redlining" maps and some supporting materials that have been digitized through an effort hosted by the University of Richmond in partnership with a number of other universities, individuals and contributors. The maps are available here: https://dsl.richmond.edu/panorama/redlining.

in the way of lending; that somehow this problem of colored people not getting housing could be laid at the door of these colored people [bankers] who only have $180 million in [combined] assets," Mitchell said.

Of that total Mitchell said, about 25 percent was obligated for FHA mortgages. Meanwhile, the nation's largest banks – then with around $55 billion in assets according to Mitchell – were not a part of the D.C. discussion.

"Nobody invited the $55 billion crowd in to find out how more money could be available," Mitchell said in a comment that harkens back to some of Brimmer's views related to the need for increased engagement in minority lending by the nation's large banks. Mitchell, however, also noted there were many other issues that were at play in the Black housing crisis including urban redevelopment initiatives in many cities that were displacing numerous Black families.[94] Setting aside whatever political blame-game federal officials were hoping to play with their meeting and later press release, the significant challenge of access to credit was one of numerous roadblocks – many of them structural – faced by Black homebuyers.

And housing was not the only issue; there was also business development. To those outside of the financial services industry, the distinction between Home Federal and a traditional bank may not be clear. As a savings and loan association during this period, Home Federal focused on home lending that was funded through passbook savings accounts. Checking accounts would not have been available nor would the institution have been in a position to extend business credit such as short-term loans to meet inventory demands in the case of a retail business, for example. From the time of Home Federal's inception there had been talk of it being something of a first step toward becoming a Black bank.[95] However, as late as 1949, Home Federal officials saw the bank idea as still not viable, as explained by Thompson. He did not know whether the Bank could meet the minimum capitalization requirement of around $500,000, nor was he certain about the Black business community's ability to support the institution sufficiently to make the venture profitable.[96]

Although he did not say it, Thompson's opinions about the ability of businesses to support a bank may have reflected the looming and growing threat of urban redevelopment – highway construction in particular – that was just beginning and would soon usher in a nearly mass destruction of Detroit's most important Black neighborhoods. Although the bulk of the work would not ramp up until the 1950s, city officials had been planning for highway construction for some time.[97] Among the projects, the construction of what is now known as the Chrysler Freeway destroyed not only residential areas of Black Bottom, but it also consumed the Hastings Street district. The highway, along with others through the city's core and redevelopment initiatives, leveled thousands of buildings throughout the 1950s and for years to follow.[98]

The destruction, and the urban landscape it would leave behind, seems far removed from the sentiments of some in the city at the time. As the *Detroit Free Press* wrote when expressway construction was moving from the planning to construction phases in the early 1950s:

> [The] projects suggest ultimate changes in community characteristics, the effect of which can only be guessed at. But it is the firm belief of many that the opening of ... expressways will stabilize residential neighborhoods and encourage their improvement, thus checking the flow, to some extent, into the suburbs.

> If these things work out, Detroit can look forward to a bright future as a modern city where, as our slogan proclaims, "Life Is Worth Living."[99]

As freeway construction decimated Detroit's urban neighborhoods, the city's economic engine began to sputter as far as its workers were concerned. For the automakers, the post-World War II era was the beginning of increasing mechanization. Thus, although an American love affair with the car was forming – and interstate construction nationwide portended a future where automobile ownership would become only more extensive – for workers, the outlook was not nearly as bright. Here is one statement that may surprise: In the 1950s, the number of Detroit manufacturing jobs *fell* by almost half. The disappearance of these jobs was caused by multiple periods of significant layoffs amid the closing of some plants (such as the Detroit Packard plant in 1956), coupled with an industrywide rise in mechanization and a move by automakers to use overtime instead of hiring additional workers, which was a practice that had only sporadically been used in the past but would soon become commonplace.[100] The impact of all of this was felt disproportionately by Black workers, as evidenced in the 1960 census, which showed white joblessness at 5.8 percent while Black unemployment was 15.9 percent including nearly 20 percent of the city's Black auto workers – nearly three and a half times the rate of their white auto industry counterparts.[101]

For Black families lured North by the prospect of good-paying jobs, what had been a beacon of hope became instead onrushing headlights carrying a bitter irony that would deal a particularly painful blow. Opportunities for work in auto manufacturing not only began to fall, but the construction of highways on which those cars would travel was also now decimating Black urban neighborhoods in numerous cities including, notably, Detroit. Soon, with expanding automobile use making the idea of a daily commute more viable, conversations would begin about "white flight" out of urban centers and to the suburbs. Although the phrase would become widely used by social commentators for years, in downtown Detroit and elsewhere the phenomena had been going on for decades.

As developers began clearing Detroit's historically Black neighborhoods under the banner of redevelopment, many Black families and businesses moved a few miles to the north where they could find homes. The Virginia Park neighborhood was established in the 1890s as an upper-middle class white enclave. Those living in the neighborhood's turn-of-the-century homes suffered during the Depression, and by the 1940s, the houses were being subdivided into apartments, many of which became for a time a popular housing option for Wayne State students who paid rent to absentee landlords unwilling to invest in maintenance or upkeep.[102] When the leveling of Black Bottom started, Black families replaced the students in the neighborhood.

By the mid-1960s, it was a predominantly Black neighborhood that suffered from gross overcrowding – by some measures about 60,000 people crammed into an area where, on some streets, population density nearly doubled the city average. As had been the case in Black Bottom, the living conditions for many were a near abomination after more than a decade of landlord neglect. A later report found that in the mid 1960s, a quarter of Virginia Park residents lived in structures so substandard that the buildings were at the level of condemnation while another nearly 20 percent lived in housing designated deficient.[103] For example, some landlords subdivided apartments into even smaller units with shared bathrooms. City codes that should have blocked such modifications went unenforced.[104]

By some measures, around 80 percent of the residents were renters, but determining any specific ratio of renters to owners is difficult since some of the individuals considered "owners" were entangled in financing arrangements like those used by blockbusters and other exploitive real estate investors.

As explained by Dr. Karl D. Gregory, an economics professor at Detroit's Wayne State University and an activist involved in numerous initiatives in the late 1960s:

> Some homes that were said to be "owned" were really bought on land contract, since mortgages were hard to get from white-owned banks. Houses bought on land contract

were not really owned. The seller kept the title until the last installment payment was made. Many buyers paid for years but never built up any equity, so that when they missed a few payments, the seller reclaimed the property to repeat the cycle with other prospective purchasers. Please realize the bitterness when one pays for years for a house and then misses a few months and loses the house, particularly after many improvements one has paid for, to see it sold again to another of the exploited.[105]

4.

Between 1964 and 1968, large-scale social unrest erupted in at least 250 American cities in confrontations injuring thousands and killing around 200.[106] Nearly half of these deaths – 83 – came in 1967, including more than 40 in Detroit.

Like the "Red Summer" of 1919, the so-called "hot summer" of 1967 saw large-scale violence in multiple American cities including Newark, New Jersey; Baltimore; Chicago and Atlanta. In Detroit, one of the worst and most violent episodes of social unrest in U.S. history erupted on July 23, 1967, at the corner of Clairmount Avenue and what is now known as Rosa Parks Boulevard, formerly 12th Street.

In the early morning hours, police raided an illegal after-hours club operating out of a second floor apartment above a vacant print shop. There a crowd had gathered to celebrate the homecoming of two Vietnam veterans. Such raids were not particularly uncommon or even unexpected. This particular so-called "blind pig," one of dozens in the city, had been raided twice in the preceding year.[††] This time, however, rather than arresting the organizers or a few individuals, they placed everyone under arrest – a group of about 85. The chaos drew a crowd of onlookers numbering in the hundreds, many kidding their friends about being loaded into police wagons. Soon, however, the environment began to change with rising anger in response to police aggression. A few spectators threw rocks and bottles. Others joined in. By 8 a.m., the crowd numbered into the thousands and a four-day cataclysm that spread across the city had begun.[107]

Authorities marshaled a massive response, which included a combination of more than 17,000 police officers, National Guardsmen and federal troops, and the 82nd and 101st Airborne divisions, with tanks rolling down Detroit city streets. By the end, there were more than 7,000 arrests, hundreds injured and more than 40 killed, including three unarmed teenagers murdered by police at the Algiers Motel, an incident portrayed in the film "Detroit."

More than 2,000 buildings were looted, damaged or destroyed, hundreds of them

††There were allegations among the operators of licensed bars that Detroit police generally resisted raiding the city's various unlicensed "blind pigs" in exchange for bribes. After the riot, there were statements suggesting the owners of the raided blind pig had grown weary of paying off the police who had begun harassing them regularly for about a month ahead of the raid. One of the better and more detailed accounts of the raid and its aftermath can be found here: Fine, Sidney. "Violence in the Model City: The Cavanaugh Administration, Race Relations, and the Detroit Riot of 1967." Michigan State University Press. 2007.

by fire. Many, although certainly not all, were Black-owned businesses including retailers, grocers, pharmacies, gas stations and others that served Virginia Park residents.

A post-riot report in *The Detroit Free Press* described a single block:

Saturday night it held a fruit market, a drugstore, a hardware store, a fish market, a dry goods store, a butcher shop, a party store selling beer and snacks, a currency exchange, a pawnshop, a barber shop a record store and a café.

Sunday afternoon there was nothing left but the … café on the corner.
The rest is a blackened shell and vast pit of twisted wreckage, smoldering figures, and foul, stagnant water seeping higher up the basement walls.[108]

Scars from the violence remain apparent on the city in the form of blocks that are still vacant yet today. Total Detroit business losses were estimated at somewhere near $50 million to as high as $80 million in 1967, although exact figures are difficult to determine because some businesses were underinsured and others had no coverage. In modern amounts, the known loss figures equate to somewhere around $400 million to more than $600 million. The numbers do not include related costs, such as lost wages.

With most small business owners unable to rebuild, the impact of lost jobs and businesses spilled over into neighboring residential areas, which became less attractive without nearby retail, leading to a further decline in property values.[109] According to newspaper accounts, almost immediately blockbusters were already at work in white neighborhoods that were near the violence, attempting to purchase homes at steep discounts.[110]

Although the summer of 1967 was the second largest eruption of civil unrest Detroit suffered in a quarter century, the events of 1943 and the events of 1967 were different in significant ways. In the words of historian Thomas J. Sugrue, "The riot of 1943 came at a time of increasing Black and white competition for jobs and housing; by 1967, discrimination and deindustrialization had ensured that Blacks had lost the competition."[111]

Without question, the forces leading to the events of July 1967 were myriad. A historical marker erected at the site of the initial confrontation on its 50th anniversary spells out the findings of a later government commission as the "frustrations of powerlessness" the result of "poverty, segregation, racism, unemployment … and police actions that enforced a double standard of how people of different races were treated."[112] Trying to determine an exact recipe of which elements contributed more significantly than others is a fools' errand, although issues of economic opportunity flow throughout.

Beyond the substantial Black population effectively forced to live within the cramped parameters of Virginia Park and other constricted urban neighborhoods, Black professionals with well-paying jobs had the financial wherewithal to move to suburban enclaves such as Conant Gardens with its ranch-style homes far from the city's core. Meanwhile, exceptionally wealthy individuals, including boxer Joe Louis and Motown Records founder Berry Gordy, lived in Boston-Edison neighborhood mansions – an area that abuts a section of Virginia Park, but for all practical purposes was a world away.

The 1967 violence fostered the emergence of any number of community-based initiatives and organizations, both formal and informal. They ran the gambit from groups urging a militant and aggressive stance in race-related issues to those that focused their efforts on improving conditions within the community. Among these, was the Inner City Business Improvement Forum (ICBIF).

The ICBIF was established in August 1967 as a nonprofit focused on providing Black inner-city businesses with funding – both grants and loans. Initial financial support came from Detroit's automakers and the phone company Michigan Bell, with the city's banks making available more than $700,000 in Small Business Administration participation loans.[113] One of the things the group sought to address was the racial gap between Detroit's urban population and its business owners. At the time, more than 65 percent of the inner city population was Black, but only 38 percent of the businesses were Black owned.[114] Contributing to this gap was the fact that when Black residents and businesses had been forced out of Black Bottom and Paradise Valley, they moved into areas that already had stores. Thus, in addition to issues of access to credit to finance a new business, many were moving into areas with well-established competition.

Among the ICBIF's founders and early leaders was the economist and activist Gregory. By this time, he had already served as an advisor to President John F. Kennedy and had found himself in the national spotlight on issues of race. In 1962, while a government economist in Washington, D.C., Gregory had attempted to purchase a home in developer William Levitt's whites-only Belair subdivision in Bowie, Maryland. The refusal to sell to Gregory prompted protests, sit-ins and pickets, as well as a number of headlines. Eventually, the developer won out when the FHA was unable to force community integration under the legal parameters in place before the Fair Housing Act of 1968.[115]

Before his work in Washington, Gregory had grown up in Detroit near the Virginia Park neighborhood. As a child, he witnessed the 1943 riot and, nearly a quarter century later, his father's tailor shop was destroyed in the 1967 violence. During that event, Gregory was stopped and held at gunpoint as he tried to help clear the streets amid the National Guard's arrival in the city.[116]

Within two years of its founding, ICBIF had invested in or lent money to 86 Black businesses while assisting with nearly $4 million in the Small Business Administration loans administered through Detroit's banks. The ICBIF proclaimed that the "top priority," however, was to establish a Black bank that would serve as an ongoing source of credit for Black businesses, families and individuals.[117]

"A long discussion was held … and we rightfully came to the conclusion that if you want to have any type of control over your own economic destiny, you should have some control of your financial resources," said Walter McMurtry, a former loan officer at one of the city's largest white banks and who was an integral part of ICBIF's early leadership on the bank initiative.[118, ‡‡] "Therefore, the decision was made to start a Black-owned and controlled bank in the city of Detroit."

While Michigan banks held perhaps as much as $1 billion in savings from Black depositors – much, although not all of it from within Detroit – McMurtry later said that it was "extremely difficult – if not impossible – [for a Black borrower] to get a bank loan to start a new venture."[119]

The state's Black population, he said, was "in a capitalist society, but with very little capital that they control."[120]

Dr. Roberta Hughes Wright, an attorney who became involved in the bank effort, later recalled the environment in Detroit in the 1960s:

"It was difficult for us in many ways. We all just wanted to be able to thrive. Open businesses, buy homes and take care of our families," she said.[121] "We didn't know how to start a bank, but we knew it was what we had to do."

ICBIF formed a committee to explore the bank idea, starting with a feasibility study, which soon led to a stock sale and a bank charter application filing for First Independence National Bank in June 1968, less than a year after the riot. The Comptroller of the Currency

‡‡ Detroit banks hired their first Black employees in non-custodial positions in 1948. McMurtry became the first Black loan officer in the state of Michigan in 1965. *The Detroit Free Press,* March 17, 1986.

granted primary approval in January 1969.[122] The bank opened on May 14, 1970. It was one of the first of more than 30 Black banks that opened in the U.S. in the 1970s. David B. Harper, a senior lending officer with Bank of America in San Francisco, was named president.[123]

At First Independence, the founders' goal was to "serve the financial needs of our community, its businesses and its citizens; no line of financial services is beyond our charter as long as we are serving the financial needs of businesses and families in our community. We will not make profits at the expense of our citizenship responsibilities."[124]

When First Independence opened, Detroit's largest banks were estimated to hold about $800 million in Black depositor accounts, equating to about 9 percent of the city's total bank deposits.[125] While First Independence set out in pursuit of those customers, bank officials secured deposits from the big three automakers.

At the end of its first year, First Independence reported $13.5 million in assets and $12.2 million in deposits – about half the deposits, bank officials said, were held in individual accounts coming from Black depositors. Other First Independence depositors included a number of corporate accounts including the automakers, the city and other firms, as well as churches and some white depositors.

Harper told a reporter that the bank's business strategy was focused on small personal loans, long-term development lending and small business accounts, but that the institution was concerned primarily on addressing the "low levels of expectation in the Black community [about the bank].

"This year we have tried to raise the level of expectation for both the Black and white community. At the same time, we are producing what we can produce. The payoff is that at some point the level of expectation hits the point of action."[126]

One indication of the overall state of minority banks during this period is that while First Independence was not a large bank in industry terms – and it held less than 1 percent of the estimated total Black bank deposits in the city at the time – it was already the third largest of the nation's then-30 minority depository institutions.[127]

The challenge of low expectations in the bank was not unique to Detroit.

For example, in Chicago, Operation Breadbasket worked diligently to generate confidence in that city's Black banks. There, a young Jesse Jackson was heavily involved in encouraging a large percentage of the Black economic base – Black politicians, community leaders, entrepreneurs and business owners – to withdraw funds from the Loop banks and deposit the money with community-based institutions.[128] This was in addition to work that led businesses such as High-Low Foods and others to move their deposits to the institutions.

"[Jackson] called in the Black businesses and he brought in the Black bankers and he said, 'The Black bankers don't know the Black exterminators. The exterminators don't know the Black manufacturers. The Black manufacturers don't know the Black professionals,'" recalled Rev. Willie Barrow, who helped Jackson establish Operation Breadbasket.[129] "There we were, meeting with 200, 300 people every Saturday morning."

One early criticism of Detroit's First Independence, and an issue that received significant media attention, was that the bank was too conservative with its lending, specifically with its extension of credit to Black borrowers.

It is difficult, from a modern perspective, to weigh the validity of this criticism. At the end of 1975, with five years in business, the bank had grown to around $28 million in total deposits, but bank officials said that Black deposits at the time were flat to slightly below 1970 levels.[130] This apparent lack of Black deposit growth is likely reflective of a particularly difficult economy during a time of national "stagflation" with a recession, energy crisis and rising prices. As is so often the case across history, the Black community was hit disproportionately hard by a struggling economy. One survey found 18 percent of Black businesses failed in 1974 versus 1 percent of all businesses nationwide.[131]

It was during this period that Earl Graves, founder and publisher of Black Enterprise, made a statement – perhaps for one of the first times – that has been echoed time and again by cultural observers and commentators during periods of economic difficulty in the United States:

"If in the white community it is a recession, in the Black community it is a depression."[132, §§§]

The uncertain early 1970s economic environment made risk management even more important for First Independence. Bank officials were very open in admitting that sometimes they referred small business borrowers to other Detroit banks, particularly National

§§§ To cite examples from three recessions: Bennett, Lerone, Jr. "White Recession/Black Depression." Ebony Magazine. Aug. 1980. p. 33.
Van Wyke, Jill. "Why is it Tolerated? A White Recession, but a Black Depression." *The Des Moines Register,* June 28, 1992. p.1A
Browne, Michael and Dedrick Asante-Muhammad. *White Recession, Black Depression.* Institute for Policy Studies. Feb. 16, 2009. https://ips-dc.org/white_recession_black_depression/

Bank of Detroit and Detroit Bank and Trust, in those cases where they felt the larger banks were more well-suited to serve the borrower's needs. While this generated some press criticism, First Independence officials believed they had actually helped both institutions expand services to the Black community, including the hiring and promotion of Black bank officers and making loans to those who, only a few years earlier, likely would not have received consideration at the institutions.[133] In terms of lending, First Independence officials also openly admitted that they had no expectation that established Black businesses would forgo existing business relationships and lines of credit they had held for years with other banks.

Despite these challenges and others, a bank that critics labeled "ultra-cautious" and holding too much in government securities, at year-end 1975 had $10.4 million in loans to Black borrowers – or around twice the amount deposited by its Black savers at the time. From a stability perspective – and probably the most important metric for bank leaders who sought its long-term viability – it is noteworthy that First Independence was one of few banks nationally where 1975 loan losses were lower than what was recorded in 1974.[134]

Harper left the bank in 1976 to become president of Gateway National Bank in St. Louis.[135] Founded in 1965, Gateway was the first Black-owned bank in the state of Missouri.[136, **]

** According to a later newspaper account, bank officials said that the bank's origin related at least in part to a protest outside another St. Louis bank in 1963. According to the story, a woman drove by, stopped, rolled down her window and talked with the group, telling them, "If you don't like what's going on, why don't you start your own bank?" *The St. Louis Post Dispatch,* March 24, 1997.

5.

While some local critics continued to view First Independence as too risk-averse in its lending, another analysis suggests the bank was searching for strategy. The conservatism was not consistent, as explained by the *Detroit Free Press:*

> The bank was never able to decide if it was to be a friend to the poor, a risk capitalist or a traditional conservative financial institution. There were elements of all three in its approach. Identity problems arose, and the bank vacillated from being a super-conservative lender – turning away many lucrative deals – to making socially-oriented business decisions.[137]

One later bank official described some of the bank decisions made during this period as following a policy of "if they fall over the doorsill, let's catch them."[138]

In 1978, with unemployment and inflation both climbing, the bank recorded a $1.3 million loss with bad loans and a significant amount of long-term lending backed by short-term deposits – a prescription that has historically led to innumerable bank failures. The near-collapse led to a recapitalization in early 1980 with record producer Don Davis buying a controlling interest in the bank with 51 percent of the stock.[139] This was not only an ownership change, but it was also a major structural change for the institution.

Since the bank's founding, its ownership had been composed by design of a large number of small shareholders – more than 2,000 by the late 1970s. In the initial materials promoting the bank idea, the ICBIF explicitly touted the idea of a "community owned institution."[140] At the time that Davis bought his shares, the bank's 18-member board combined to hold only about 9 percent of its outstanding shares. Bank President William Bailey, who had succeeded Harper after he left the bank, owned only 100 shares.[141]

"I saw a couple years ago that the bank had some financial problems, and I always felt some compassion for that bank in particular because it's a community bank," Davis said. "About a month and a half ago, I saw the circular that they were trying to raise some cash, so I thought it was time for me to get in and help the bank in any way possible."

Davis started his working life playing guitar in Detroit nightclubs and as a studio musician in the city in the 1950s. Notably, given the turn his adult life would take, what might be considered his big break as a musician involved playing on the Barrett Strong hit, "Money (That's What I Want)" released by Tamla, the record label that would soon be known as Motown. Davis played on, wrote and produced numerous recordings with Motown, Memphis' Stax Records and other labels before purchasing Detroit's United Sound Systems Recording Studios in the 1970s. He started building new studios, and artists continued to keep them full.[142] By the end of the decade, United Sound Systems was one of the nation's top recording studios for artists including Aretha Franklin, Albert King, Marilyn McCoo and a long list of others.[143] Davis said that after George Clinton's Parliament-Funkadelic basically ran him out of the studio while recording, "I knew I needed to go someplace else and that's when I started in other areas ... That's when I got involved with the banking business."[144]

Ironically, the same bank he invested in had shunned him years earlier when he was seeking financing to buy the studio.[145]

With the First Independence stock purchase, Davis became the bank's chairman, Bailey resigned and the economist Gregory took over as president on an interim basis. For Gregory, although his tenure was only temporary, it was also the realization of childhood aspirations. Growing up, he had wanted to become involved with banking, but when he graduated college in 1955, banks were not hiring Black college graduates. Instead, he joined the military and after that earned masters and doctorate degrees, becoming an economist.[146]

Davis later said it took him about six years to transition from someone who had built a life and career relying on creative skills to develop the analytical skills of a banker. Eventually, he said he discovered that both sides could coexist.[147] While Davis was developing his analytical skills, Charles Allen, the chief administrative officer for United National Bank in Washington, D.C., began regularly traveling to Detroit on weekends to help Davis, Gregory and other First Independence officials work through problem loans. Soon, it became clear to Davis that Allen should serve as bank president. Allen was not convinced.

"I turned him down four times …," he said.[148] "But Don Davis can be very persuasive."

When Allen became bank president, the bank was failing and operating under restrictions put in place by the Comptroller of the Currency. He curbed lending, called in overdue loans, sold some real estate holdings, cut costs and began trying to secure major corporate accounts.[149]

"He let it be known, 'I'm inheriting a bank that's in trouble and I'm going to do what's necessary,'" McMurtry told a reporter.[150] "He stood by his convictions. The best report card he could ever have is the 1981 results."

That year, the first year under Allen, the bank recorded a net income of $404,000, the best performance in its 11-year history with about $43 million in assets.[151] During his seven-year tenure, bank assets more than doubled to $87 million, making it the nation's sixth-largest minority-owned bank. The bank gained a national reputation for providing low-cost financial services, some of it through storefront check-cashing businesses called Money Stores, which the bank began to open in inner-city Detroit in 1987.[152, †††]

In an exploration of banking, particularly community banks and their traditional role in providing financial services, the Money Store concept may be a somewhat divisive topic. The Money Stores were not akin to payday lenders, nor were they banks. They could not take deposits and they did not loan money. Their business model, based on a program pioneered by a Philadelphia bank in 1978, was tightly focused on low-margin services: they cashed checks for non-bank customers with a fee of 1 percent to 2 percent depending on the amount, handled money orders, forwarded utility payments, offered Western Union services and rented mailboxes.[‡‡‡] The Money Store development came after a roughly three-year period when 25 percent of the bank branches within Detroit's city limits had been shuttered by their parent banks – in some instances prompting customer pickets outside bank offices.[153] Banks blamed the closings on deregulation, which eliminated the cap on interest rates paid to depositors. Without the lid, banks began offering higher interest rates to attract deposits, thereby compressing margins. The end result was a closure of branches in areas where deposit activity was viewed as lackluster or weak in comparison to the branch's operating costs. In some instances, the closures were in suburban areas where planned growth – and where some banks had raced to open offices in trailers while facilities were under construction – did not develop as expected. Many of the closures, however, were in poor areas of the inner city.[154]

As bank branches closed, urban check-cashing businesses and small retailers – notably so-called "party stores," the neighborhood convenience stores selling beer, liquor and cigarettes – began cashing checks for individuals without bank accounts. And they charged exorbitant fees to do it: often around 20 percent.[155]

††† The business should not be confused with mortgage lender The Money Store, which is a New Jersey-based mortgage lender.
‡‡‡ Later, the stores accepted payments of fines and penalties for some traffic violations. *Detroit Free Press,* June 14, 1988.

Because First Independence was a small bank, opening multiple branches and offering a full menu of banking services at each location – in areas where other, large banks had decided such operations were not viable – was too costly of a proposition. In introducing the Money Store, Allen said the purpose was "to make it real tough for people to gouge our community," while allowing the bank to "move closer to the community we serve."[156] That said, it seems somewhat unlikely that Money Store customers would have been aware of the connection between the check-cashing business and First Independence. Since regulators strictly prohibited First Independence solicitation or promotion within Money Store locations, customers may have only learned of the connection if they read the business pages or happened to catch a story on the local news.[157]

While the concept received a lot of attention, and bankers from other cities reached out to First Independence to discuss creating similar entities, the Money Store did not prove feasible. With the slim check-cashing margins, the business struggled to remain profitable, and the idea was soon abandoned.[158, 159]

Making things potentially more challenging for the bank, Allen decided to move on. There is no indication that his 1988 departure was in any way related to the unsuccessful Money Store initiative but instead his own desire for a career change. He became an advisor to government regulators during the savings and loan crisis and became involved in finding buyers for real estate seized by the federal government from bankrupt institutions. He later expanded into a number of other business ventures.[160]

First Independence suffered. In the years that followed Allen's departure, profits evaporated, nonperforming loans rose well above the national average and the bank went through a revolving door of presidents – three different presidents in a three-year span at one point. There were also several legal issues and accusations ranging from the handling of safety deposit boxes through a federal investigation of fictitious loans in the mid-1990s.[161, §§§]

At a community bank, these events can have a sometimes painful impact on the community by impairing access to credit. One car dealer who had a decade-long relationship with First Independence talked with a reporter about having to abandon the bank because it had become unable to meet his credit needs. While the dealer was able to gain financing through a different and larger bank, it is likely that such an option was not available to others who had obtained credit from First Independence.[162]

§§§ The bank blamed the loans on two employees, who circumvented internal controls. See *Detroit Free Press*, July 30, 1996.

Meanwhile, as First Independence struggled in the early 1990s, the Detroit metro area gained a second Black-owned bank. In 1990, the failing River Rouge Savings Bank, established nearly a century earlier in 1906, was recapitalized with around 60 percent of its shares acquired by cable television executive William T. Johnson and Kenneth Hylton, an attorney and civil rights activist who had been involved in the founding of First Independence.[**]

Hylton's interest in banking stemmed from a tragic experience while he was a college student in Alabama in the 1940s when he helped a family take their sick child to a local hospital. The child had pneumonia and needed an oxygen tent; but the hospital demanded a deposit, and the family didn't have money. The child died.[163]

Johnson, who also had a law degree, was the first Black man in the United States to own a cable television franchise when he acquired the Columbus, Ohio, system in 1977. He soon followed that deal with franchises in other U.S. cities. When cable boomed in the 1980s, he sold two of four franchises he had at the time, with the profits eventually going into buying the bank.[164]

The bank was rebranded OmniBank to separate it from its failed predecessor, with Johnson soon chairing its board of directors and implementing an aggressive growth strategy.[†††] Although the bank turned barely profitable in 1990, its profits (albeit small) increased in the following years. However, nonperforming loans remained high.[165]

From a business perspective, the bank was in a very literal difficult place to build a banking business. River Rouge, Detroit's neighbor to the south along the Detroit River, covers an area of about 3 square miles, but much of the land – perhaps a third – is home to heavy industry, including the Zug Island steel mill. The city formed in 1922 to block annexation by Detroit, and it hit its population peak at around 20,000 residents in 1950. By 1990, the community was about half that size with no indication the decline was ending. When several homes had to be leveled for a construction project, Johnson offered the homeowners guaranteed mortgages if they would stay in River Rouge. No one took him up

---

[**] Notably, in 1960 River Rogue Savings Bank was the target of protestors for refusing to integrate its hiring. In 1961, the Michigan Fair Employment Practices Commission found the bank guilty of discrimination and ordered the immediate hiring of teller Loy A. Cohen. The bank refused, prompting an extended legal battle. *The Detroit Tribune*. Jan. 16, 1960, and *The* (Benton Harbor) *News-Palladium*, May 3, 1961. *The Detroit Free Press*, July 14, 1962.

[†††] The name created any number of difficulties and often confusion in media accounts. While "Omnibank" appears in Federal Deposit Insurance Corporation (FDIC) records and was the name of the bank, the holding company was "Omnibanc." The names were often published with unconventional capitalizations, as are used here.

on the offer, because none of them wanted to stay.[166]

Johnson's strategy, perhaps out of a degree of necessity, was to grow through aggressive branching and acquisitions. While OmniBanc did open a handful of other locations, its most serious acquisition target – Chicago bank holding company Indecorp, owner of two banks in that city, Bank of Chicago and Drexel National Bank – failed to materialize.#### Johnson, meanwhile, said that the OmniBanc was still interested in finding a Chicago acquisition target while continuing to expand the branch footprint, at one point discussing with a reporter his vision of an eventual branch in Johannesburg, South Africa, that would serve Americans overseas while acting as a trade office for the State of Michigan.[167]

Meanwhile, OmniBanc struggled.

A summer 1995 newspaper profile of Davis and Johnson showed OmniBanc was barely profitable.[168] In 1996, the bank reported a loss of $667,000 with a $3.3 million loss in 1997 caused by a number of loan failures, primarily to small businesses, and a check scheme that was perpetrated against the bank by a local supermarket.[169]

Regulators were becoming increasingly concerned about OmniBanc's financial conditions in early 1998. OmniBanc was small with around $40 million in deposits, but it held some relatively large deposits from area municipalities, churches, community organizations and the local school district. Combined, those accounts were $17 million above federal insurance limits.[170] A failure would place those funds in jeopardy.

As a result, the bank was ordered to increase its capital and to hire permanent management – Johnson and Hylton had been splitting the president and CEO duties on an interim basis for months amid leadership turnover. While bank officials struggled to meet the demand for additional capital, both the City of River Rogue and the school district made significant withdrawals from their accounts. Bank regulators, fearing a bank run, seized OmniBanc in April 1998 and it was sold to Chicago-based Shorebank, a white-owned bank holding company whose South Shore Bank had been lauded for minority lending in Chicago.[171]

At the time of the failure, OmniBanc was working toward an acquisition by Black-owned Boston Bank of Commerce, but that deal still had far to go and regulators decided

---

As regulators were conducting the merger review, interest rates rose, causing a decline in the value of Indecorp's substantial bond holdings. By the time the deal gained regulatory approval, OmniBanc wanted to rework the merger terms, saying its initial offer was too high given the bond portfolio's now-reduced value. OmniBanc tried to negotiate a lower price, although how much lower is not clear – anywhere from one-third to two-thirds below the initial offer according to various sources. Regardless, there was no agreement, and Indecorp was eventually acquired by Shorebank, the holding company for Chicago's South Shore Bank.

they could not wait to see whether an agreement would be reached.

"I had to make a very difficult decision," Michigan's financial institutions commissioner said.[172] "My concerns were [that] the cities and community groups were very, very close to losing substantial money."

6.

Around the time that OmniBanc was starting its decline, First Independence was recovering from its late 1980s and early 1990s turmoil. After terminating Bank President Richard Shealey, Don Davis stepped in as an interim president in early 1996 and returned the bank to profitability with tightened controls and the hiring of a former Comptroller of the Currency regulator as senior auditor.[173]

That the bank survived the 2007-08 housing bubble collapse and the ensuing financial crisis was no small accomplishment. With minority communities hit hard, minority banks also suffered disproportionately. In comparison to nonminority peers, minority-owned depository institutions had a higher ratio of nonperforming loans, a lower share of core deposits and higher expenses relative to income.[174] In total, more than 500 banks of all types failed between 2007 and 2014, the last year of double-digit failures, with almost 300 of those failures coming in 2009-10.[175] Across that time period, the number of Black banks in the United States was cut nearly in half, falling from 44 in 2006 to 25 in 2015. On a percentage basis, it was the most severe decline in any of the minority depository institution designations tracked by the Federal Deposit Insurance Corporation (FDIC) and outpaced the overall decline in the number of community banks in the United States.[§§§]

Among the crisis-related failures was Detroit's Home Federal Savings Bank in 2009 – the Black-owned institution that was established as Home Federal Savings and Loan almost 60 years earlier in 1947, but had been struggling since before the financial crisis.[176] Home Federal's retail deposits were acquired by the New Orleans-based Black-owned Liberty Bank, and the Detroit locations reopened under Liberty Bank and Trust Company ownership.[177]

First Independence did report losses during the period, but it appears that most of the impact on the bank was the result of overall economic and financial sector turmoil. The bank's core lending around this time was not primarily mortgages but instead was focused on small businesses, personal loans, churches and some large corporate lending.[178] After the crisis, however, the bank's strategy expanded to focus on mortgages for moderately priced homes with the bank acquiring the mortgage business of a failed Michigan bank.[179] From a financial perspective, this activity presented an opportunity with potentially limited

---

§§§ Number of FDIC-insured minority-owned depository institutions (MDIs), year-end totals, 2006/2015, by minority status: Black 44/25; Hispanic 48/41; Asian or Pacific Islander 81/79; Native American 20/18. Source: FDIC data.

downside risk. Around that time, the average sale price for a nonforeclosed home within Detroit's city limits was around $15,000 versus nearly $86,000 in areas outside the Detroit city limits – both figures well below the national average of more than $170,000.[180]

As the bank was moving back toward stability and making plans for the post-crisis era, the man who saved the bank in 1980 was lost when Davis died after a brief illness on June 5, 2014. His majority ownership position went to his widow, Kiko Davis, as trustee of the Donald Davis Living Trust. Kiko Davis, who also established a foundation named for her husband to assist underserved communities and who had a background in real estate, did not, however, step into the chairman's role.[181] The position was instead filled by others until Kenneth Kelly was appointed chairman and CEO in 2017.

Kelly is somewhat like Don Davis in that he had a successful career outside of financial services before banking. He came to Detroit from the South, where he'd held positions in the utility business at Alabama Power, Georgia Power and Southern Power. He'd received numerous honors for his community leadership in both Birmingham and Atlanta, and, among other initiatives, he established an endowment for minority students living in his hometown of Eufaula, Alabama, to study engineering at Auburn University, his alma mater.[182]

Among his banking-related activities, he's served as chairman of the National Bankers Association, following in the footsteps of Allen, who also had a senior position with the trade group for America's minority bankers when he was First Independence's CEO. Kelly has also served as an American Bankers Association board member and a member of the Federal Reserve Bank of Chicago's Community Depository Institutions Advisory Council, among other roles.

In 2019, Kelly testified during a House Financial Services Committee subcommittee hearing on the decline of minority depository institutions and the impact it was having on America's underserved communities.

In his comments, he explained the difficulties First Independence faced as an example of the issues facing many of the nation's minority-owned depository institutions (MDIs): The bank is relatively small with limited resources to cover compliance costs; it is mission driven and focused on low- and moderate-income communities, which can be costlier to serve; the business model can often be at odds with the views of bank examiners who may be unfamiliar with the institution; the investor community may not see value in the bank's mission.

"These are all challenges, in addition to the normal marketplace challenges that every financial institution faces, and yet, First Independence remains – like so many MDIs

– the bank of first and last resort for the communities we serve."[183]

A few months later, he talked with a reporter for a story on the bank's 50th anniversary. At a time when civil unrest in many cities seemed to parallel Detroit at the time of the bank's creation, the questions focused on what can a Black bank do, and how much can it do in Detroit when it is a single, relatively small institution.

Kelly said:

You know, there's only approximately 20 African American-controlled banks in the country. And in many ways we find ourselves competing with banks of scale and size that just make it not economical to compete on a dollar-for-dollar basis. But it also shows a lack of distribution, the economic injustice in ways that kind of permeate across America, just as we saw with health care during COVID-19. African American homeownership is the lowest it's been since they started measuring it in 1970, as of last year, the 2018 year … So those are all items that I think are symptomatic … of the underlying economic inequality in the country.[184]

Whether you look at when we started the Federal Reserve in 1913 to today, you can see how banks have played a part in economic growth and economic vitality. So, banks play a vital role in communities being redeveloped, they play a vital role in job creation, which basically translates into social justice.[185]

In Your Hands

I.

In 2016, Michael Render became one of the nation's most well-known activists for Black banking.

That summer, demonstrators took to the streets in nearly 100 American cities after the police killing of Black men, including two on succeeding July days: Alton Sterling, 37, shot at point-blank range by officers as they pinned him to the ground outside a convenience store in Baton Rouge, Louisiana, on July 5; and Philando Castile, 32, shot in his car while reaching for a driver's license he was asked to retrieve during a traffic stop along the side of the road near Minneapolis, Minnesota, on July 6. On July 7, a protest against police brutality turned violent in Dallas when a gunman opened fire, killing five police officers. And on July 8, the MTV and BET television networks scrapped their usual programing to jointly host town hall discussion on the violence.

Render called in.

"We cannot go out in the street and start bombing, shooting and killing," he told viewers.[1] "I encourage none of us to engage in acts of violence that will cause more peril to our community and others that look like us. I encourage us to take our warfare to financial institutions."

By this point, Render was already an established voice on the issues of police violence and social unrest, coming onto the mainstream media stage after appearing on CNN in 2014 to discuss the police killing of Michael Brown in Ferguson, Missouri. In 2016, however, he combined issues of social justice with economic equality. His "warfare" against financial institutions was a plea for 1 million people to deposit $100 each in Black-owned banks or credit unions that would, in turn, lend to Black individuals, families and business-es – a hoped-for $100 million step toward economic equality. This was the beginning of what became the #BankBlack movement, an online social media tag that reached a broad audience – and, bankers said, increased deposits at several banks including in Render's home-town of Atlanta where the Black-owned Citizens Trust Bank received more than 8,000 account applications in a matter of days.[2,] [*] It was in part a response to the power of Render's celebrity as a rap artist under the name Killer Mike.[3]

Those quick to dismiss Render's credibility on the complexities of social justice and economic equality because of his celebrity or his stage name ("I 'kill' microphones, and I

---

* "#BankBlack" has been trademarked by OneUnited Bank. Fortune. Sept. 21, 2020.

trust that people are intelligent enough to get it.") do so at their own peril.[4] As one writer described him: "Killer Mike contains multitudes, but if you had to boil him down, you'd get a concerned citizen who just happens to be a rapper."[5]

Born in 1975 to a teenage mother, Render was raised until his teen years primarily by his grandparents in Atlanta's historic Collier Heights – an upscale Black subdivision featuring large lots with ranch and split-level homes along winding streets. Created in the Jim Crow era as urban redevelopment and interstate construction remade swaths of Atlanta, Collier Heights residents were a "who's who of Black Atlanta," including Rev. Ralph Abernathy, Martin Luther King Sr. and a long list of others.[6] As one account suggested, it was a place where neighbors might spend one night together at the local PTA meeting and the next organizing a protest.[7] The activists included Render's grandmother who protested with King and was a member of both the National Association for the Advancement of Colored People (NAACP) and the Southern Christian Leadership Conference (SCLC).[8]

She also educated her grandson about the world.

"My grandmother marched me into a Black bank at about five years old. She opened up a bank account for me," Render said.[9] "My grandmother walked me into a mayor's office meeting … and other meetings because she thought it was imperative that I understood from a very young child how to control your economics and how to control your community."

Already a celebrity, business owner, activist, husband and father, in 2020 Render added to his long list of responsibilities. He joined television executive and entrepreneur Ryan Glover, and civil rights icon and former Atlanta Mayor Andrew Young to begin founding Greenwood, a financial services provider focused on serving the nation's Black and Hispanic communities with an entirely digital structure, operating through a website and a mobile app. Their hope is is to attract individuals and families who are currently reliant on providers of alternative financial services (AFS), particularly check-cashing services.[10] The fees charged by these firms can be substantial. While the cost can vary based on a number of factors including the frequency of use and local regulations, one estimate places the amount of money lost to AFS fees at $40,000 across the course of a career.[11] A 2019 Federal Reserve report pegged total U.S. payday loan fees at as much as $9 billion annually – the figure including only loans and not other types of AFS charges such as financing costs from rent-to-own stores, pawnshops or check-cashing fees.[12]

As created, Greenwood is not a bank. It offers individual saving and spending accounts, peer-to-peer transfers, ATM access and, with automatic paycheck deposits, two-day early access to pay. It does not, however, offer lending or business accounts and as an entity does not provide depositors with the protection of FDIC deposit insurance, although it is partnering with FDIC-insured institutions in which it will place the deposits.

"What [Greenwood is] on a very basic level … is an alternative to check cashing places, and an alternative to predatory banking," Render said.[13] "And the next level after that is for people who are small business owners, medium business owners, or people who may not be in traditional businesses like tech and things to have a bank that's willing to … risk it with you. So they're going to be capital lenders as well. And what we grow into, only the imagination can conceive of, but I'd like to see us grow into one of the more competitive banks in the market …. Less check cashing places and more of our bank right here in my hand"[14]

Historical explorations are often endeavors of hope. While an understanding of past events can provide important perspective on the environment we find today, often incumbent within the search is a hope that previous experiences will offer some hint of path forward in the face of modern-day challenges. Here, in pursuit of fostering economic equality and based on relevant history, we will consider three areas that are often discussed for their potential to affect change in the modern-day environment. They are institution size and the ability of banks to expand economic opportunity on a large scale; proximity in financial services access; and the role and future of Black community banks.

In considering first the significance of a bank's size, it must be said that it is in no way correct to assume that a larger bank is somehow a "better" institution – the importance of community institutions will be discussed in short order – but larger banks may be able to offer a wider range of services on more competitive terms than a smaller institution. And, of course, there is the matter of being able to serve as an economic catalyst for change on a large scale where bank size is an implicit function.

In this regard, two established banks announced plans in 2020 to create the largest Black bank in U.S. history and the first to achieve $1 billion in assets: the merger of Los Angeles' Broadway Federal Bank, a Black bank with a history dating back to the mid-1940s, and Washington, D.C.'s City First Bank, a non-MDI (minority-owned depository institution) Community Development Financial Institution (CDFI) founded in the 1990s. Banks with the CDFI designation, which Broadway Federal also had, must do at least 60 percent of their lending in low-to-moderate income communities.

Under the combination, the merger of equals placed ownership under Broadway Financial Corp. Brian Argrett, CEO of City First since 2011, was picked to lead the merged bank, which plans to focus on lending for housing, small businesses and nonprofits.[15]

"We have all seen the compounding impacts from centuries of racial inequities in this country – social unrest, higher unemployment, poverty. Economic injustice is at the root of racial injustice," Argrett told a reporter around the time of the announcement.[16] "That's why the work of MDIs and [CDFIs] are more important than ever – they are squarely focused on these inequities like getting capital to those who truly need it.

"We'll be able to increase the amounts of capital we can offer and offer more systemic solutions. This is about creating a national platform where we can scale our solutions to help with these problems."

Argrett is another among those who come to banking from another career. In his case, private equity and, before that, as an attorney working on real estate transactions. In his own words, he reached a turning point when violence erupted in Los Angeles after the acquittal of four L.A. police officers who, in 1992, violently beat Rodney King at the end of a car chase through the city. In a time before cell phones, the assault on King drew widespread attention across the United States because a bystander happened to catch it on video. After the court's decision, a riot erupted lasting days that resulted in more than 50 deaths, 2,000 injuries, 6,000 arrests and destroyed more than $1 billion in property.[17]

"The fourth day of the 1992 Los Angeles riots, I saw firsthand the frustration built on the economic situations that the communities were facing, such as lack of jobs and lack of improvement. As an African American, I could identify a lot about what the community was feeling," he said in a 2011 interview.[18] "The unrest was pivotal in refocusing me on the community. I started thinking about what I could do to help. A year later, I went into private equity because I felt like I could make a difference by creating opportunity. At the private-equity firm, we were financing entrepreneurs to help them grow their business, particularly in underserved communities."

While the establishment of a Black bank with more than $1 billion in assets passes a history-making threshold, it is not a finish line. The bank is still far smaller than the nation's largest banks. At the time of the announcement, there were more than 700 banks in the United States with more than $1 billion in assets, with the largest banks measuring their assets in hundreds of billions.[19]

Beyond the size of the Broadway Federal/City First merger, the deal is also noteworthy in that this merger of equals is a combination of a Black MDI with a non-MDI bank. This raises a question of racial dynamics that is often a part of "Black bank" discussions: Is majority Black ownership necessary for a bank serving the Black community?

For much of American history, the answer to that question was very much "yes." Strictly enforced segregation left Black depositors and would-be borrowers cut off from America's mainstream financial system in all but a relative few instances. While desegregation was a long overdue step and expanded economic opportunities, it did not eliminate racism nor the challenges facing bank customers.

More recently, in the summer of 2020, with much of the nation focused on a raging pandemic and an increasingly heated presidential race, many Americans may have overlooked news stories about another trending social media hashtag related to Black access to financial services: #BankingWhileBlack. Unlike Render's social media campaign to encourage the support of Black financial institutions, this hashtag was about experiences of overt racism suffered by Black bank customers, sometimes doing something as mundane as trying to cash a check when they faced fraud accusations and, in some instances, the arrival of police after a bank manager's call to 911.[†]

These incidents are without question troubling. However, from the perspective of economic opportunity, more damaging is the data on lending. Overall, Black credit applications are denied at a higher rate than those from white or Hispanic borrowers with the discrepancies between Black and white credit applicants rising with income levels. At income levels below $40,000, a Black borrower is about 1.5 times as likely to be rejected as a white applicant, but that gap grows to nearly 2.5 times at income levels between $40,000 and $100,000 and 2.7 times at incomes above $100,000.[20] Additional data looking at specific types of credit shows that lenders reject Black mortgage applications at a higher rate than they do those from white borrowers.[21] Black small business owners, meanwhile, have been found to have their loan requests rejected at higher rates than their white peers, and those who do receive loans may be less likely to receive the full amount sought.[22]

Beyond the impact on individual potential borrowers, Gregory, the Detroit economist, talked in 2015 about his concerns related to banking and the flow of capital in that city. According to Gregory, while non-MDI banks happily accepted deposits from a range of

† Stories on this issue include *The San Jose Mercury News,* May 17, 2019, but became more widespread with wire service coverage of the issue and television reports including CNN. July 2, 2020; *The New York Times,* June 18, 2020.

savers, the reinvestment into Detroit – i.e., bank loans – by some of the banks were "largely to provide funds for white-owned businesses. Loan rejection rates for Black businesses were very high."[23]

When his accusation was vigorously contested by the city's large banks, Gregory noted a massive, multiday series of articles published by the *Detroit Free Press* in 1988 that found, among other things, that Detroit area banks and savings institutions made loans to white middle class neighborhoods at three times the rate of what they did in similar Black neighborhoods.[24] The number was supported by a separate analysis of race and Detroit savings and loan mortgage application rejections conducted around this same point in the late 1980s.[25] Regardless of how the environment may have changed – or not – between 1988 and 2015 or later, at least at the time of the *Free Press* survey, there was a particularly insidious application of financial services access that was fostering, even if unintentionally, economic development in one segment of the population at the expense of another. Sadly, such disinvestment is in no way unique to Detroit.[26]

"The huge siphoning of the deposits from local Black and white communities went to financially empower others," Gregory said.[27] "This drainage of purchasing power from the Black and lower income community is exactly the opposite of the view held by some whites – that view holds that funds from outstate are drained into poor Detroit Black areas and squandered there. The truth is greatly different and complex."

Conversely, in terms of lending, when it comes to minority bank ownership, the data shows that MDIs do in fact serve a substantially higher share of minority mortgage borrowers than their non-MDI peers and originate a greater share of Small Business Administration-guaranteed small business loans to borrowers in low-to-moderate income census tracts with higher shares of minority residents.[28]

These findings suggest that significant minority ownership remains an important factor in bringing credit to minority communities, particularly where income levels are low to moderate. This, of course, presents additional challenges as the community bank business model is based on taking a community's combined financial resources – its savings – and turning it into loans that foster economic opportunity within that same community. That is not possible to any great degree when the savings are small and prone to significant withdrawal activity. The one-time Detroit banker Charles Allen remarked after he left First Independence that this was one of his frustrations in Detroit. While he saw economic potential, there was very much a relationship between the lack of overall economic progress and the bank's condition because it was reliant on small depositors and thus the bank's somewhat constrained ability to fuel that progress with the extension of credit – the bank needed more dollars from sources outside the community.[29]

In her study of the wealth gap and Black banks, the author Baradaran's conclusion discusses this "fundamental misunderstanding of what banks do."

"The Black community needs banks to grow and prosper, but the banks cannot achieve that growth and prosperity alone," she wrote.[30] "Self-help microfinance cannot overcome macro inequality and systemic racism."

As this history illustrates, public interest in Black banking has been the highest at times of social unrest. Such events have prompted the founding of banks and also an increase in Black bank deposits by nontraditional Black bank depositors through government programs, corporate initiatives and individuals. Such developments are important, but for banks to serve as consistent catalysts of growth, particularly in low-income minority communities, these deposits must also flow consistently into the banks from multiple nontraditional sources and not just in reaction to social developments.

This issue, of course, has been an ongoing challenge for Black bankers and has proven difficult to solve and sometimes generated criticism of bankers from all sides, as has been made clear with some experiences in Detroit, which may provide a beneficial example for further discussion.

In 2013, the city of Detroit filed the largest municipal bankruptcy in the nation's history. To echo an observation made by others, the city spent decades on the rise – reaching very near if not *the* pinnacle of American manufacturing and economic muscle – only to find itself mired for a nearly equal amount of time in a decline with the loss of jobs, population and opportunity.[31] Even its post-bankruptcy life, which initially appeared bright – perhaps even more so than many expected – was clouded over by uncertainty, like much of the United States and world amid the COVID-19 pandemic.[32] How this will turn out is, and may remain for some time, one of the many unknowns of the pandemic era.

It might be easy to consider the city's economic and social arc to be somewhat unusual among American urban centers. But while the scope and breadth of the issues that Detroit faced during its decline were more extreme than what occurred in other American cities, its experiences were not solely Detroit's. The same things happened in most other major urban centers. Strict residential segregation including informal pacts and sanctioned redlining, white flight and large-scale urban redevelopment of predominantly Black residential and commercial areas and minority job losses are a part of the history of every American city of any significant size.

In the discussions that led to the creation of First Independence, those in the Inner City Business Improvement Forum believed very strongly that "Detroit needed to have a bank which hopefully would take deposits from Blacks *and* whites in Detroit and elsewhere but which would be more open to making loans to African American and white households and businesses doing business in Detroit."[33]

The need for a broad customer base beyond the low-to-moderate income segment of the minority population made creating the bank something of a leap of faith by its founders in hoping that high-income and affluent individuals of all races, as well as established businesses, would use the bank as they would any other financial institution and not as a one-off repository for excess funds in times of social awareness. This need became abundantly clear when First Independence officials soon came under heavy criticism for not bringing dramatic and immediate economic growth to the city's low-income population. *Detroit Free Press* business columnist Allan Sloan posed a question: "What real purpose does the bank serve?"

Harper, then the bank president, pointed out that "the decision to put a bank here came ahead of the demand for loans." That demand, he and others hoped, would come over time, but it would be a slow process if the bank's financial base was limited to low-income depositors and hopeful entrepreneurs.[34]

Along these same lines, and around this same time, the separate Independence Bank in Chicago also came under fire for focusing too extensively on corporate accounts versus local families and small businesses. There, the bank co-founder and CEO explained that, "You have to build a base before you can provide adequate financing. Our priority has been to assist Black businesses.[35]

"Our goal has to be success in the mainstream of banking if we are to help anybody."[36]

Proximity of financial services access, both bank and non-bank, relates to one of the most lasting legacies of America's generations of segregation and racism.

While the complexion of many modern-day urban neighborhoods may be changing through forces of development and gentrification, the imprint left by more than a century of strict segregation and redlining remains firmly implanted in the geography of many cities.[37] Boundary lines first drawn on Home Owners Loan Corporation (HOLC) "redlining" maps in the 1930s still demarcate areas of racial segregation in the 21st century, sometimes very abruptly.[38]

Thus, today a business, should it desire, can make decisions to target or avoid specific neighborhoods based on easily accessible demographic characteristics with relative ease.

While firms would no doubt react strongly against the accusation that they might seek to exploit (or avoid) a particular customer base along racial lines, data and research suggest otherwise. For example, research conducted after the collapse of the mortgage market found that high-cost subprime lenders were far more aggressive in minority communities than they were elsewhere, resulting in Black homeowners in some areas being 105 percent more likely to receive a high-cost mortgage than a similar white home buyer after controlling for risk factors including credit score and debt-to-income ratios.[39]

In addition, as it pertains to access to financial services, research supports what is already known to the attentive residents of most American cities: AFS providers are more common in neighborhoods with larger populations of color, including Black and Latino; those with lower incomes; and those with higher numbers of immigrants. Additionally, traditional bank branches are less common in areas with large populations of color. Black neighborhoods in particular are more likely than white neighborhoods to have *no* financial services providers at all.[40]

Such racial discrepancies are not purely a function of local income levels. Even in neighborhoods with higher incomes, those with a predominantly Black population are more likely to have an AFS provider than a white neighborhood with the same income levels.[41] The implicit racism aside, does the location of these businesses have a tangible economic impact on families? Research suggests it does. At least one study has found that residents of higher income neighborhoods are more likely to use an AFS provider than might otherwise be the case when those providers are located nearby.[42] Although some might find a willingness to use a more costly option puzzling, others have suggested it is a situation similar to someone who struggles to eat healthy foods because they live in a neighborhood filled with fast food joints while the grocery is located across town.[43] Proximity matters. Compounding this is the oft-discussed distrust of banks within the Black community – a suspicion traced back to the Freedman's failure and certainly reaffirmed in numerous ways throughout history to the modern day including the structural segregation of redlining through current-day loan rejection rates and the #BankingWhileBlack incidents that are detailed on social media.[44]

"In the African American community, they don't see the big banks as being for them," said Sidney King, CEO of the Mobile, Alabama, Black-owned Commonwealth Bank.[45]

"You go back over the years, grandparents didn't have banking relationships, parents in many instances didn't have banking relationships. So a lot of people don't feel comfortable going to those institutions."

Something that may be relevant here is First Independence's experience with its Money Store initiative in the late 1980s. While the subsidiary may have been intended to provide services primarily to low-income individuals, Bank President Allen said when the business started, the transaction amounts were "substantially larger" than any of the bank's pre-launch projections. In addition, the money-order business also exceeded anticipated volumes.[46] These two unexpected developments, which would have upended the Money Store business model, likely had a significant role in the Money Store's inability to capsize the AFS business model.

Are low-cost digital alternatives and phone applications a viable option to compete against, and defeat, local AFS providers? So far, it is not clear. Certainly, readily available online access can be an issue in low-income households. Meanwhile, the idea of using financial services via the internet is not unique to the Greenwood initiative. Online banking developed in rudimentary forms early in the dot-com era and has continued to evolve with technology and the use of phone-based applications. Through these systems, it is certainly possible to open a bank account and conduct banking business without ever entering the bank or even the city in which it is based. Boston-based OneUnited Bank, the nation's largest Black bank in its number of depositors, aggressively promotes online banking for customers nationwide, although its actual physical branch locations are limited to the Los Angeles, Boston and Miami metropolitan areas.[47, ‡]

In considering the question of online banking, there is no question that visits to bank branches in the United States have declined. However, branch location remains an important consideration for many in the selection of a financial institution.[48] In small business lending, while nonlocal lenders have taken on an increasing role in providing credit, local bank branches still continue to be the primary loan source.[49] Here, of course, there is a relationship to the potential use of soft information in lending, where there are multiple studies supporting the importance of physical banks or branches versus the potential of an online model.

One study that may be particularly relevant regarding neighborhoods with large minority populations, as well as those with large immigrant or ethnic populations, examined lending practices and "cultural proximity." The study, which focused on the financial system in

‡ One discussion on the various other participants seeking to disrupt the AFS sector can be found in Rosen, Ellen. "Trying to Correct Banking's Racial Imbalance." *The New York Times,* June 30, 2020.

India, found that when borrowers and lenders shared common background and cultures it produced a win-win result: Lenders were more willing to lend more money on less collateral than what was the case when there was not such commonality, while the loans also performed better with fewer late payments and defaults.[50], §

Separate research analyzing small business and mortgage lending has found that bank branch closings can have a significant and sustained impact on lending – small business credit in particular. Overall, after a branch closure there is a heavy concentration of lending declines within low-income and high-minority census tracts of the branch's former business area. In these locations, soft information may be particularly important in credit decisions, especially in the case of small businesses. Thus, the study states that, while there may be a wide range of credit options in the U.S. financial system, "there are some markets and some segments of the population for whom local credit markets still play an important role in determining local credit access."[51], **

Community banks, as history makes clear, play an invaluable and essential role in their communities. Research on the loss of local access caused by bank or branch closure confirms that there is significant value in local banking. In addition, the findings from the study of cultural proximity and lending in India – and certainly the racial disparity in U.S. loan rejections – make clear that close associations between lender and borrower are beneficial for both parties and, as a result, can foster meaningful economic development. Recent academic studies, of course, serve to reaffirm the experiences of Black banks and the historical emergence of economic enclaves in places like Boley, Oklahoma; Richmond, Virginia; and Chicago, Illinois. Similarly, the absence of such Banks may have increased the difficulties faced by some during times of challenge, such as Detroit after World War II.

Beyond the provision of financial services, the banks often helped to meet important community responsibilities. Bank officials, particularly those at the helm of Black banks,

§ Of particular interest: In India, which was the focus of the study, bank managers regularly rotate, and the changes in lending occurred almost immediately. Overall, loan amounts increased 6.5 percent, the number of loan recipients grew 5.7 percent and the likelihood of an applicant getting any amount of credit rose 2.5 percent. Fisman, Raymond. Daniel Paravisini and Vikrant Vig. "Cultural Proximity and Loan Outcomes." The American Economic Review. Feb. 2017. Vol. 107, No. 2. Pp. 457-492. Fleisher, Chris.

** Another challenge facing the online financial services model is digital access, which may not be readily available for some with low-to-moderate income levels.

have throughout history served as community leaders with an impact, influence and reach that extends well beyond the parameters of the bank's customer base. Historically, many of the nation's most important Black bankers have viewed their work not as a financial opportunity, but as a catalyst for community improvement.

History is filled with innumerable examples of this. While the story of Richmond's Maggie Walker is perhaps the most well known of the early Black bankers – and her former Richmond, Virginia, home welcomes visitors today as a National Historic Site – many others are equally inspirational in work both as bankers and community leaders. They include John Mitchell Jr. and his dangerous fight to expose racial violence in the South; Thomas Haynes, who all but singlehandedly created Boley, Oklahoma, and founded its bank; Roger Woodfolk and R.W. Hunter, extending credit – much to their own detriment – during the Chicago riots; and Jesse Turner's work in the fight for civil rights from his Memphis bank.

Arguably, however, the most important work in the role of financial catalyst is achieved serving a single customer – borrower or saver – at a time. The same is true for even large community banks – if they are community-based lenders that provide credit to their communities.

Against the headwinds of Detroit's large banks in the 1980s, Allen talked about how smaller banks were still extremely important to serve "the small under-capitalized businesspeople we see. That's the strength of this bank."[52]

In a separate interview, Allen provided an example of what that means – and even the sometimes unusual form that assistance may take:

If we can't finance a deal for someone, we'll do what we can to get that person financing.

I'm talking about things like a 28-year-old man who couldn't get anyone to lend him money for a pizza restaurant. We're working with him. Who knows what that business may turn into.[53]

Today's Challenges, Yesterday's Lessons

Esther L. George

PRESIDENT *and* CHIEF EXECUTIVE OFFICER

FEDERAL RESERVE BANK *of* KANSAS CITY

Inequity in access to financial services is a problem that should concern us all. An inclusive financial system benefits our nation's economy and its prosperity: as more individuals prosper, so does the country as a whole.

Overall, about 80 percent of the households in the United States are considered fully banked, however, there is significant disparity along racial lines. For example nearly half of Black households in the United States are either unbanked or what is known as "under-banked." Often, an underbanked household is one where they have a checking account, but rely on alternative financial services providers (AFSPs) such as check cashing services or auto title lenders, which may change high rates of interest, to meet some financial needs.[1] As a result, AFSPs are more likely to be located in areas where Black residents make up a large percentage of the population.[2] Meanwhile, bank branch penetration in majority-minority communities, including Black, Hispanic and Native American neighborhoods, trails the national average.[*]

Black-owned banks were our nation's first minority depository institutions (MDIs) predating the first Asian American, Hispanic American and Native American banks by decades. Their decline, meanwhile, has been more precipitous than what has occurred among each of the other MDI designations and across the banking sector overall.

With this volume, we hope to contribute in a meaningful way to understanding the implications of fewer Black-owned community banks and the resultant challenges to economic opportunity. In this way, we also are trying to foster a dialogue focused on achieving improved outcomes.

As the history highlighted here makes apparent, a discussion about banking and financial services within communities of color encompasses any number of relevant issues. Some are along racial lines such as an understandable skepticism towards financial services firms. Other issues are inherent characteristics of the banking industry, such as the challenges small banks face in competing with the scale and scope advantages afforded larger banks and a regulatory framework that can be burdensome.

Despite these challenges and others, we know that there are a number of people and institutions doing important and beneficial work in extending credit. Community banks,

---

[*] According to a 2016 study on Bank Branch Penetration published by Magnify Money by Lending Tree, minority-majority counties had approximately 27 bank branches per 100,000 population. The figure was around 75 percent of the national average. There were approximately 41 branches per 100,000 population in majority white counties. https://www.magnifymoney.com/mmassets/uploads/2016/02/mm_branch_presentation_V4.pdf

of course, play an important role here, but they are certainly not alone. There has been increasing interest in recent years related to non-bank lending within minority communities through Community Development Financial Institutions (CDFIs) of various types, in addition to private equity and angel investors.[3] While this work has found success in some communities, those engaged in these efforts tell us that there is more demand for credit than there is available supply. There is no question among any who have given this issue serious consideration that more must be done.

In early summer 2021, while work on this volume was well underway, two of America's most recognized and established Black-owned financial institutions announced a merger agreement.

Memphis' Tri-State Bank, a bank featured prominently in this publication and pictured on its cover, was being acquired by New Orleans' Liberty Bank & Trust Co. Liberty, founded in 1972, received national attention, and was featured in multiple articles in *The New York Times,* as it took exceptional measures to serve its customers after Hurricane Katrina decimated both the community and the bank's offices in 2005.

This merger of two historically significant Black banks is the result of challenges that have become all too familiar among America's community banks in recent decades.

The chairman of the Tri-State's board of directors told a reporter that developments in the regulatory and credit environment put the bank in the position of either growing substantially to achieve the benefits and economies of scale or securing a buyer.[4] Media accounts talked about the bank struggling in recent years, a reduction in lending and a loss of depositors to larger institutions.

These issues are not unique to Tri-State. Since the mid-1980s, the United States has seen a declining number of community banks and a growing consolidation of industry assets within the nation's largest banking organizations. This trend has been encouraged by a relaxation of interstate banking restrictions, regulatory changes and court decisions. Because of this, we have seen two very different types of institutions emerge. The larger banks utilize a business model whereby a significant portion of their income can be drawn from noninterest sources. Community banks, meanwhile, are focused on traditional banking services to generate income. The good news for community banks is that this strategy may produce less earnings volatility than what we see in the big banks, but it has also resulted in a generally lower rate of return than their larger competitors across the past 20 years.[5] As a result, while we can and should explore the ways of encouraging minority bank ownership, challenges to the business model exist in today's landscape.

To what extent can a historical review such as this one point to success and inform change where needed?

One of the features of many banks within this historical review, is that of a "relationship banker," a traditional role of a community banker. While all banks seek to foster a strong connection with their customers, relationship banking's strength comes from the community banker's ability to foster a long-term and mutually-beneficial relationship at the local level whereby the bank utilizes what would be considered soft information in lending decisions.

These are things that cannot be quantified for the metrics of standard risk analysis. For example, a relationship lender's personal knowledge of the borrower might mean that someone who has lost a source of income could still obtain credit based on the banker's own risk assessment of the individual.[†] This type of lending can be difficult to document to the satisfaction of current regulatory standards.

In considering this issue, it is important to recognize that the needs of the low- to moderate-income community differ from the type of credit needed by businesses or home buyers. In particular small dollar loans to meet basic needs such as paying utility bills and buying groceries in times of financial difficulty can offer a bridge of stability. This was a role filled by many of the banks within this historical volume and something that modern-day community bankers understand as well. However, we know that within many communities this demand for credit falls to the province of AFSPs, which operate in some regions with few consumer protections and typically charge much higher rates of interest. When annualized rates are more than 100 percent, which is sometimes the case, even very small amounts of borrowing introduce the risk of a debilitating debt spiral for the borrowers. It is significant to note here that in 2020, as the U.S. economy struggled under the weight of the pandemic and many workers were unable to earn income needed to pay their bills, some of these lenders reported record-high profits.[6]

In recent years, some states have shown an increased understanding of the risks presented to borrowers by AFSPs and have implemented increased consumer protections along with more stringent regulations around non-bank firms, although there is still room for improvement in some areas.

---

† A more detailed discussion of this, including a list of sources documenting the role of "soft" information in community bank lending can be found in Hauner, Matt. Brent Lytle, Chis Summers, Stephanie Ziadah. *Community Banks' Ongoing Role in the U.S. Economy.* Federal Reserve Bank of Kansas City. June 2021.

Technology has shown some potential to address issues hampering the availability of credit to some borrowers. Some online and application-based fintech firms are bringing data into their small business lending decisions that was not previously available to lenders – for example, sales data from marketplace platforms and even information from social media. Such data is being analyzed with proprietary algorithms and, in some cases, it is resulting in not only lending, but a process that is potentially quicker and more efficient for the borrower than what is the case with a traditional bank where there may be significant fixed costs or other challenges.[7] Bankers and regulators are taking steps to understand such innovations and determine their suitability for not only business lending, but to see if similar tools might be applicable to consumer loans.[8]

While technological innovation may offer potential for the future, CDFIs have been providing credit for more than a generation. Some histories trace the roots of these community-based lenders to the earliest MDIs that focused on underserved areas up through community development corporations in the 1960s and non-profit loan funds in the 1980s. More recently, during the Covid pandemic, CDFIs received significant attention as they filled a critical role in helping small businesses access Paycheck Protection Plan (PPP) funds.

CDFIs are mission-driven lenders of federal dollars and private funds within low- and moderate-income communities. They operate in various forms, including banks, credit unions and venture capital funds. The majority of CDFIs, however, are loan funds organized as non-profits. Because of this structure, loan fund CDFIs can operate with more lending flexibility than a regulated bank. They are nondepository institutions and thus generally not under banking regulations. Although they are subject to state laws, they operate under covenants with their funding sources, for example, philanthropies.[9]

While their numbers have grown, in 2021 the United States had around 1,200 CDFIs certified by the United States Treasury, up from fewer than 1,000 five years earlier, there is no question that they face challenges.[10] Most are small and want to offer additional products but may lack in sufficient staffing, expertise or capital.[11] Scaling remains a significant challenge as does sustainability, although partnerships may offer some potential in addressing these issues.[12, 13]

Seeking ways to emulate the successful practices utilized by the banks reviewed within this volume is a worthy endeavor, but it is at least equally important that we highlight the motivation of the people involved in many of these early initiatives. Within this history you will find very few individuals who were motivated to become engaged in providing financial services out of a desire to increase their own wealth or in pursuit of substantial profits. Some came into banking with significant resources gained through other successful endeavors and businesses, but the decision to engage in banking was driven in very many cases by a recognition that the community was being restrained and unnecessarily challenged by an inability to access mainstream financial services. Many placed themselves and their families at significant physical risk in times of increased racial tension as they worked to serve their communities.

Conversely, in recent years, we've seen the growth of our nation's largest banks and, in the minds of many, the profession of "banker" has become something of a caricature of the Wall Street baron. This image does not reflect the engaged, local community bankers that I have known who work in the service of their communities. We need to find ways to bring into banking more of those individuals who are motivated by the opportunity to engage in meeting this market need. The current social environment and heightened attention to these needs provide an opportunity to act. The summer of 2020 saw increasing support for moving money into Black-owned financial institutions. This focus on doing business with local, community-based institutions, has the potential to yield significant results within communities of all types.

Hand in hand with this, of course, is the need for an expanded focus on bringing increased diversity to the financial system. Minority bank ownership has historically made a difference in minority communities while increased diversity at all levels of any commercial bank is important in attracting a diverse customer base and expanding access to credit. All of us can act with intention to bring diverse talent to the business of banking.

Improved access to financial services will not solve every problem in underserved communities, but it can serve as a catalyst to a better future. Whether investing in education, purchasing a home, or starting a business, the ability to borrow money can be a key step in building financial security.

My colleagues and I at the Kansas City Fed do not pretend to have the answers. We do find in our historical exploration in this volume and the previously published *"Let Us Put Our Money Together: The Founding of America's First Black Banks,"* the potential to consider avenues that have value and merit further study and research. We invite you to be part of this exploration.

Endnotes

....

FOREWORD
1.   *The Houston Post,* Sept. 9, 1906.

RICHMOND, VIRGINIA
1.   *The New York Times,* Aug. 18, 2015.
2.   Kashian, Russell D., Richard McGregory and Derrek Grunfelder McCrank. "Whom do Black-Owned Banks Serve?" *Communities & Banking,* Federal Reserve Bank of Boston, May 28, 2014.
3.   One national study of this issue that incorporates multiple additional references: Prager, Robin A. "Determinants of the Locations of Payday Lenders, Pawnshops and Check-Cashing Outlets." Board of Governors of the Federal Reserve System. June 2009.
4.   "Report on the Economic Well-Being of U.S. Households in 2019." Board of Governors of the Federal Reserve System. May 2020.
5.   This event occurred on Feb. 5, 2020 while the author and Alden McDonald were being driven to the Federal Reserve Bank of Richmond for a luncheon and panel discussion on the issues facing the nation's African American banks.
6.   Edwards, Ana. and Phil Wilayto. "The Significance of Richmond's Shockoe Bottom: Why it's the Wrong Place for a Baseball Stadium." *African Diaspora Archaeology Newsletter.* Vol 15, Issue 1. Spring 2015.
7.   "Mortgage exec gives struggling bank a digital makeover." *American Banker.* Sept. 10, 2018.
8.   "Virginia's Payday and Title Lending Markets Among the Nation's Riskiest." The Pew Charitable Trusts. Oct. 2019.
9.   Ibid.
10. Virginia Corporation Commission data, Feb. 12, 2020.
11. Todd, Tim. *Let Us Put Our Money Together: The Founding of America's First Black Banks.* Federal Reserve Bank of Kansas City: Kansas City, Mo., 2019.
12. *The Richmond Planet,* Nov 13, 1897.
13. Todd.
14. Burrell, William Patrick. *Twenty-Five Years History of the Grand Fountain of the United Order of True Reformers, 1881-1905,* Grand Fountain of the United Order of True Reformers: Richmond, Va. 1909.
15. Todd.
16. Burrell.
17. *The Richmond Planet,* July 30, 1898.
18. Lamb, Daniel Smith. "Howard University Medical Department: A Historical, Biographical and Statistical Souvenir." R. Beresford: Washington, D.C. 1900. p. 220.
19. *The Colored American* (Washington, D.C.), May 7, 1904.

20. Mitchell, Susan. Essay on Dr. Richard Fillmore Tancil published by the Friends of East End Cemetery. https://eastendcemeteryrva.com/person/dr-richard-fillmore-tancil/ Note: Mitchell is the great-granddaughter-in-law of Richard Fillmore Tancil.

21. *The Richmond Planet,* May 28, 1898.

22. Ibid.

23. Ibid.

24. Ibid.

25. *The Richmond Planet,* July 3, 1897.

26. Richings, G.F. *Evidences of Progress Among Colored People.* Twelfth Edition. Geo. S. Ferguson Co.: Philadelphia, 1905. pp. 490-491.

27. Washington, Booker T. *The Story of the Negro: The Rise of the Race from Slavery, Volume II.* Doubleday, Page & Co. 1909.

28. See advertisement in *The Richmond Planet,* Jan. 6, 1900 as well as numerous other editions.

29. McCrery, Anne, Errol Somay and the Dictionary of Virginia Biography. "John Mitchell Jr. (1863–1929)." *Encyclopedia Virginia.* Virginia Humanities, May 6, 2019. Web. 4 Mar. 2020.

30. *The Richmond Planet,* July 22, 1899.

31. Lucey, Donna M. "Brother from the Richmond Planet." *Humanities. The Magazine for the National Endowment for the Humanities.* July/August 2010. Vol. 31, No. 4.

32. Lucey.

33. Wolfe, Brendan. "The Fighting Editor." Interview with Kimberly Wilson, great-great niece of John Mitchell Jr. *Encyclopedia Virginia.* Virginia Humanities, April 26, 2019. Web. 20, Feb. 2020.

34. *The New York World,* Feb. 22, 1887. As appearing in Penn, Irvine Garland. *The Afro-American Press and its Editors.* Willey & Co. Publishers: Springfield, Mass. 1891.

35. Harris, Abram L. *The Negro as Capitalist: A Study of Banking and Business Among American Negroes,* The American Academy of Political and Social Science: Philadelphia, Pa., 1936, p. 75.

36. *The Pittsburgh Courier,* April 8, 1911.

37. *The Washington Post,* Sept. 6, 1890.

38. Ingham, John N. and Lynne B. Feldman. *African-American Business Leaders: A Biographical Dictionary,* Greenwood Press: Westport, Conn. (1994), pp. 460-461.

39. Ingham and Feldman, p 462 and Harris, p. 79.

40. *The New York Times,* Sept. 17, 1904.

41. Ibid.

42. Burned District in Richmond. *Encyclopedia Virginia.* Virginia Humanities. Library of Virginia. https://www.encyclopediavirginia.org/slide_player?mets_filename=sld1190mets.xml

43. Chesson, Michael B. *Richmond After the War, 1865-1890.* Virginia State Library: Richmond, Va. 1981.

44. Logan, Tevon D. "Do Black Politicians Matter? Evidence from Reconstruction." *The Journal of Economic History,* Vol. 80, No. 1 (March 2020).

45. Randolph, Lewis A. and Gayle T. Tate. *Rights for a Season: The Politics of Race, Class and Gender in Richmond, Virginia.* University of Tennessee Press: Knoxville, Tenn. 2003. pp. 89-90.

46. Chesson, p. 182.

47. Wilkins, Joe B., Jr. *The Participation of the Richmond Negro in Politics.* University of Richmond: Richmond, Va. Aug. 1972.

48. Chesson.

49. *The Richmond Planet,* June 6, 1896 and *The Norfolk Landmark,* May 13, 1896.

50. *The Richmond Planet,* June 6, 1896.

51. Bowen, Dawn S. "The Transformation of Richmond's Historic African American Commercial Corridor." *Southern Geographer.* Vol. XXXXIII, No. 2. Nov. 2003. pp. 260-278.

52. McCrery, Somay and the Dictionary of Virginia Biography.

53. *The New York Times,* Sept. 17, 1904.

54. McCrery, Somay and the Dictionary of Virginia Biography.

55. Edwards, Kathy, Esme Howard, and Toni Prawl. *Monument Avenue: History and Architecture.* U.S. Department of the Interior: National Park Service. 1992.

56. Bowen.

57. Comments about splitting Jackson Ward's large African American population for political reasons and the idea that this move could be used in other cities can be found in *Report of the Proceedings and Debates of the Constitutional Convention: State of Virginia. Vol. II.* The Heritage Press Inc.: Richmond, Va. 1906.

58. Du Bois, W.E. Burghardt. *The Souls of Black Folk.* Seventh Edition. A.C. McClurg & Co.: Chicago. 1907. p. 177.

59. *Northwestern Christian Advocate,* Sept. 28, 1904.

60. Bowen.

61. Ibid.

62. National Register of Historic Places Inventory – Nomination Form. *Jackson Ward Historic District.* United States Department of the Interior.

63. Meier, August and Elliott Rudwick. "The Boycott Movement Against Jim Crow Streetcars in the South, 1900-1906." *The Journal of American History,* Vol. 55, No. 4 (March 1969) pp. 756 775.

64. Meier and Rudwick.

65. *The Richmond Planet,* April 23, 1904.

66. *The Richmond Planet,* April 9, 1904.

67. Meier and Rudwick.

68. *The Richmond Planet,* July 23, 1904.

69. *The Richmond Dispatch,* Aug. 27, 1902.

70. Burrell, W.P. "History of the Business of Colored Richmond," *Voice of the Negro,* Aug. 1904, pp. 317-322 as appearing in Lynch, Hollis R., *The Black Urban Condition.* Thomas Y. Crowell Co.: New York, N.Y. 1973.

71. *The Negro in Business.* Edited by W.E.B. Du Bois. Atlanta, Ga. 1899.

72. Bowen.

73. Harris.

74. Walker, Juliet E.K. *The History of Black Business in America: Capitalism, Race, Entrepreneurship.* Twayne Publishers: New York, N.Y., 1998. p. 182.

75. Walker.

76. Jackson, Giles B. and D. Webster Davis. *The Industrial History of the Negro Race of the United States.* Negro Educational Association: Richmond, Va. 1911. Copyright 1908. Giles B. Jackson.

77. Jackson and Davis, p. 90.

78. Harris, p. 101.

79. Jackson and Davis, p. 90.

80. Harris, p. 65.

81. *The Richmond Times.* Sept. 6, 1893.

82. Harris. pp. 78-79.

83. *The Times.* Aug. 26, 1902.

BOLEY, OKLAHOMA

1. Prince, Richard. "April 4, 1968, as Told by Black Reporters." *The Root.* April 4, 2018. https://journalisms.theroot.com/april-4-1968-as-told-by-black-reporters-1824321852

2. Interview with Hollie West. Robert C. Maynard Institute for Journalism Education. African American Museum and Library at Oakland. 2001. The full interview is available at: https://californiarevealed.org/islandora/object/cavpp%3A14818

3. *The Washington Post,* Feb. 9, 1975.

4. A portion of this quote has been widely used in numerous publications. The extended version used here is from "Testimony of Henry Adams regarding the Negro Exodus." From Herbert Aptheker, editor, *A Documentary History of the Negro People in the United States,* (New York, 1951), p. 715. It can be found online at the Gilder Lehrman Center for the Study of Slavery, Resistance, and Abolition at: https://glc.yale.edu/testimony-henry-adams-regarding-negro-exodus

5. *The Washington Post,* Feb. 9, 1975.

6. More details on the Nebraska settlements can be found at: https://journalstar.com/news/local/-blacks-in-nebraska-timeline/article_3f0c8ee2-2bc1-57d6-93f5-7c7e51e9fb4a.html

7. O'Dell, Larry. "All-Black Towns," T*he Encyclopedia of Oklahoma History and Culture.* Oklahoma Historical Society, 2009.

8. Oklahoma Historical Society: https://www.okhistory.org/research/airemoval

9. Museum of the Cherokee Indian. https://www.cherokeemuseum.org/archives/era/trail-of-tears?gclid=EAIaIQobChMI2rG1hMjC6AIV0f_jBx1jMQ6mEAAYASAAEgI2wfD_BwE

10. For more on the history of slavery and Native American tribes in Oklahoma, see: Barbara Krauthamer, "Slavery," The Encyclopedia of Oklahoma History and Culture, https://www.okhistory.org/publications/enc/entry.php?entry=SL003

11. Gallay, Alan. *Indian Slavery in Colonial America.* University of Nebraska: Lincoln, Neb. 2009.

12. Doran, Michael F. "Negro Slaves and the Five Civilized Tribes." *Annals of the Association of American Geographers,* Vol. 68, No. 3. (Sept. 1978). pp. 335-350.

13. One discussion of this appears in Smith, Ryan, P. "How Native American Slaveholders Complicate the Trail of Tears Narrative." Smithsonianmag.com. March 6, 2018.

14. The low estimate is based on Doran. The high estimate is drawn from the Oklahoma Historical Society, which estimates slaves accounted for 14 percent of an overall population of 1,000. https://www.okhistory.org/publications/enc/entry.php?entryname=CIVIL%20WAR%20ERA

15. Grinde Jr, Donald A. and Quintard Taylor. Red vs. Black Conflict and Accommodation in the Post-Civil War Indian Territory, 1865 – 1907. *American Indian Quarterly*, Vol. 8, No. 3., (summer 1984) pp. 211-229.

16. Stuckey, Melissa N. "Boley, Indian Territory: Exercising Freedom in the All-Black Town." The *Journal of African American History*, Vol. 102, No. 4. (Fall 2017). pp. 492-516. For more on the discussion of slave society versus society with slaves, see Berlin, Ira. *Many Thousands Gone: The First Two Centuries of Slvery in North America.* The Belknap Press of Harvard University Press: Cambridge, Mass. 1998.

17. Grinde and Taylor.

18. Oklahoma Historical Society. https://www.okhistory.org/publications/enc/entry.php?entry=RE001

19. Grinde and Taylor.

20. Ibid.

21. Oklahoma Railway Museum. https://www.oklahomarailwaymuseum.org/about-us/brief-oklahoma-rail-history/

22. Oklahoma Historical Society. https://www.okhistory.org/publications/enc/entry.php?-entry=AL011

23. Higgins, Billy D. "Negro Thought and the Exodus of 1879." *Phylon*, Vol. 32, No. 1 (Q1 1971) pp. 39-52.

24. Butler, John Sibley. *Entrepreneurship and Self-Help among Black Americans.* Revised Edition. State University of New York Press: Albany, N.Y. 2005. pp. 133.

25. Dann, Martin. "From Sodom to the Promised Land: E.P. McCabe and the Movement for Oklahoma Colonization." *The Kansas Historical Quarterly.* Autumn 1974 (Vol. XL, No. 3) pp. 370-378.

26. *The Boston Post,* Feb. 1, 1879.

27. Douglass, Frederick. *The Life and Times of Frederick Douglass.* Park Publishing Co. Hartford, Conn. 1881. p. 441.

28. Data analysis in Painter, Nell Irvin. *Exodusters: Black Migration to Kansas after Reconstruction.* W.W.Norton & Co. 1992. pp. 146-147.

29. Oklahoma Historical Society. https://www.okhistory.org/publications/enc/entry.php?entry=MC006

30. Bell. John Daniel. *Boley: A Study of a Negro City.* University of Kansas: Lawrence, Kan. 1928.

31. *The Macon* (Ga.) *Telegraph.* July 8, 1889, and Littlefield, Daniel F., Jr., and Lonnie E. Underhill. "Black Dreams and 'Free' Homes: The Oklahoma Territory, 1891-1894." *Phylon,* Vol. 34, No. 4 (Q4 1973) pp. 342-357.

32. Oklahoma Historical Society. https://www.okhistory.org/publications/enc/entry.php?entry=MC006

33. Ibid.

34. Hill, Mozell C. "The All Negro Communities of Oklahoma: The Natural History of a Social Movement: Part I." *The Journal of Negro History.* Vol 31, No. 3 (Jul 1946), pp. 254-268.

35. Ibid.

36. Stuckey.

37.   Bell.

38.   *The Weekly Progress,* Dec. 22, 1910.

39.   Bell.

40.   Hamilton, Kenneth Marvin. "Townsite Speculation and the Origin of Boley, Oklahoma." *Chronicles of Oklahoma,* Volume LV, Number I, Spring 1977.

41.   Ibid.

42.   Oklahoma Historical Society https://www.okhistory.org/publications/enc/entry.php?entry=WE010

43.   Bell.

44.   *The Weekly Progress,* Dec. 22, 1910.

45.   Stuckey.

46.   Ibid.

47.   National Register of Historic Places Inventory – Nomination Form. Boley, Oklahoma Historic District.

48.   *The Weekly Progress,* March 9, 1905.

49.   Washington, Booker T. "Boley, a Negro Town in the West." *The Outlook,* Jan. 4, 1908. Vol. 88, No. 1.

50.   McMahan, Hazel Ruby. *Stories of Early Oklahoma – A collection of interesting facts, biographical sketches and stories relating to the history of Oklahoma.* Oklahoma Society. Daughters of the American Revolution: 1945.

51.   Bell.

52.   *The Weekly Progress,* March 9, 1905.

53.   Oklahoma Historical Society. https://www.okhistory.org/publications/enc/entry.php?entry=BO008

54.   *The Boley News,* Jan. 25, 1918.

55.   Washington.

56.   Stuckey.

57.   Texas State Historical Association. https://tshaonline.org/handbook/online/articles/fta79

58.   *The Topeka Plaindealer,* April 7, 1916.

59.   Stuckey.

60.   *The Parsons* (Kan.) *Daily Eclipse,* Feb. 20, 1913.

61.   Bell.

62.   *The Weekly Progress,* Dec. 15, 1910.

63.   Bell.

64.   McMahan.

65.   *The Weekly Progress,* Dec. 22, 1910.

66.   Nichols, J.L. and William H. Crogman. *Progress of a Race.* J.L. Nichols and Co.: Naperville, Ill.

67.   Moss, Gary. "Mrs. McClinton did not study black history – she lived it." *University Gazette,* Feb. 27, 2015. University of North Carolina at Chapel Hill.

68.   *The Weekly Progress,* Dec. 3, 1915.

69.   *The Weekly Progress,* March 17, 1910.

70.   *The Okfuskee County News,* Nov. 10, 1921.

71.   Stuckey.

72. Oklahoma Historical Society. https://www.okhistory.org/publications/enc/entry.php?entry=BO008

73. *The Weekly Progress.* Nov. 24, 1910.

74. *The Topeka Plaindealer.* May 7, 1915.

75. Ibid.

76. Oral History Interview with Henrietta Hicks. Interview conducted by Lynne Simpson and Tanya Finchum. April 6, 2012. *Spotlighting Oklahoma, Oral History Project.* Oklahoma State University. https://dc.library.okstate.edu/digital/collection/Spot/id/478

77. Washington.

78. Walker, p. 175.

79. *The New York Times,* April 11, 1922.

80. *The Washington Post,* Feb. 9, 1975.

81. Thirteenth Census of the United States Taken in the Year 1910. Vol. VII. Agriculture 1909 and 1910. Department of Commerce. Bureau of the Census. 1913.

82. Oklahoma Historical Society. https://www.okhistory.org/publications/enc/entry.php?entry=FA019

83. *Monthly Crop Reporter,* U.S. Bureau of Crop Estimates. April 1921. Vol. 7. No. 4.

84. *The Topeka Plaindealer.* March 6, 1925.

85. Iles, R. Edgar. "Boley (An Exclusively Negro Town in Oklahoma)." *Opportunity: Journal of Negro Life,* Aug. 1925.

86. Nichols, J.L. and William H. Crogman. *Progress of a Race.* J.L. Nichols and Co. Naperville, Ill.

87. *The Washington Post,* Aug. 21, 1973.

88. Accounts of this and other incidents can be found in Littlefield, Daniel F., Jr., and Lonnie E. Underhill. "Black Dreams and 'Free' Homes: The Oklahoma Territory, 1891-1894." *Phylon,* Vol. 34, No. 4 (Q4 1973) pp. 342-357.

89. National Register of Historic Places Inventory – Nomination Form. Boley, Oklahoma Historic District.

90. *The Oklahoman* published a list in its Feb. 13, 2005 edition.

91. Parsons (Kan.) *Daily Eclipse,* Feb. 20, 1913.

92. Bell.

93. *The Washington Post,* Nov. 24, 1932.

94. *The Washington Post,* Feb. 9, 1975.

95. Wills, Shomari. "Black Fortunes: The Story of the First Six African Americans Who Escaped Slavery and Became Millionaires."*Amistad.* New York, N.Y. 2019.

96. Ibid.

97. Ibid.

98. Ellsworth, Scott. *Death in a Promised Land.* Louisiana State University Press: Baton Rouge, La., 1982.

99. *The New York Times.* Dec. 19, 1999

100. Ibid.

101. Madigan, Tim. *The Burning: Massacre, Destruction and the Tulsa Race Riot.* St. Martin's Griffin. New York, N.Y. 2001.

102. Harris.

103. Hammond, Bray. *Banks and Politics in America from the Revolution to the Civil War.* Princeton University Press: Princeton, N.J., 1957, p. 69.

104. *The Tulsa Star,* Jan. 9, 1915.

105. See *The Tulsa Star,* Jan. 17, 1914 and June 24, 1920, among others.

106. Wills.

107. Madigan.

108. *The Topeka Plaindealer,* May 12, 1913.

109. Interview with Kristi Williams, vice chair of the Tulsa African American Affairs Commission published https://www.history.com/news/black-wall-street-tulsa-race-massacre

110. *The Tulsa Star,* Jan. 24, 1914.

111. Notable Kentucky African American Database. University of Kentucky Libraries. https://nkaa.uky.edu/nkaa/items/show/865

112. Krehbiel, Randy. *Tulsa, 1921: Reporting a Massacre.* University of Oklahoma Press: Norman, Okla. 2019.

113. *The Tulsa Star,* April 3, 1915.

114. *The Iola* (Kan.) *Daily Index,* Dec. 1, 1908.

115. The results of his suit are unknown. *The Coffeyville* (Kan.) *Daily Journal,* May 4, 1910.

116. Christian, Charles M. Black Saga: The African American Experience, a Chronology. Civitas/Counterpoint: Washington D.C. 1995/1999.

117. Oklahoma Historical Society. https://www.okhistory.org/publications/enc/entry.php?entry=TU013

118. *Chicago Defender,* June 11, 1921.

119. Wells, Ida B. *Southern Horrors: Lynch Law in All its Phases.* 1892.

120. Williamson, Joel. "Wounds Not Scars: Lynching, the National Conscience and the American Historian." The Journal of American History. Vol. 83, No. 4 (March 1997) pp. 1221-1235.

121. White, Walter. "The Eruption of Tulsa." *Nation.* June 29, 1921.

122. Ibid.

123. *The New York Times,* Dec. 19, 1999.

124. Franklin, B.C. *The Tulsa Race Riot and Three of its Victims.* Collection of the Smithsonian National Museum of African American History and Culture. Gift from Tulsa Friends and John W. and Karen R. Franklin.

125. Tulsa Historical Society and Museum. https://www.tulsahistory.org/exhibit/1921-tulsa-race-massacre/

126. Oklahoma Historical Society. https://www.okhistory.org/publications/enc/entry.php?entry=TU013

127. Madigan.

128. *The New York Times,* Dec. 19, 1999.

129. Ibid.

130. Ibid.

131. *The Chicago Defender,* Nov. 5, 1921.

CHICAGO, ILLINOIS

1. Paddon. Anna R. and Sally Turner. "African Americans and the World's Columbian Exposition." *Illinois Historical Journal,* Vol. 88, No. 1. (Spring 1995) pp. 19-36.

2. Ballard, Barbara J. "A People Without a Nation." *Chicago History.* Summer 1999. pp. 27-43. And *The Chicago Daily Tribune.* Sept. 24, 1893.

3. Drake, St. Clair and Horace Cayton. *Black Metropolis: A Study of Negro Life in a Northern City. Revised and Enlarged Edition.* University of Chicago Press: Chicago, Ill. 1993.

4. Paddon and Turner.

5. *Chicago Daily Tribune,* Aug. 21, 1893.

6. Blight, David W. *Frederick Douglass: Prophet of Freedom.* Simon and Schuster, New York, N.Y. 2018.

7. Blight.

8. *Chicago Tribune,* Aug. 26, 1893.

9. *Chicago Tribune,* Aug. 25, 1893.

10. Cohn, Raymond L. *Immigration to the United States.* EH.Net Encyclopedia, edited by Robert Whaples. Revised August 2, 2017. URL http://eh.net/encyclopedia/immigration-to-the-united-states/

11. *The New York Times,* July 2, 1917.

12. *The Chicago Defender,* Jan. 15, 1916.

13. Williams, Fannie Barrier. "Social Bonds of the 'Black Belt' of Chicago." *The Negro in the Cities of the North.* Charities Publication Committee: New York, N.Y., 1905, pp. 40-43 as appearing in Lynch, Hollis R., *The Black Urban Condition.* Thomas Y. Crowell Co. New York. 1973.

14. Miller, Donald L. *City of the Century: The Epic of Chicago and the Making of America.* Touchstone: New York, N.Y., 1997.

15. Moberg, David. "Work." *Encyclopedia of Chicago.* Chicago History Museum, The Newberry Library and Northwestern University. http://www.encyclopedia.chicagohistory.org/

16. Street, Paul. "The Logic and Limits of 'Plant Loyalty': Black Workers, White Labor, and Corporate Racial Paternalism in Chicago's Stockyards, 1916-1940." *Journal of Social History,* Vol. 29, No. 3 (Spring 1996) pp. 659-681.

17. Herbst, Alma. *The Negro in the Slaughtering and Meat-Packing Industry in Chicago.* Houghton Mifflin Co. Boston, Mass. 1932. p. 4.

18. Canaan, Gareth. "Part of the Loaf: Economic Conditions of Chicago's African-American Working Class During the 1920s." *Journal of Social History,* Volume 35, Number 1, Fall 2001. pp. 147-174.

19. Hautzinger, Daniel. *How World War I Transformed Chicago.* WTTW. April 10, 2017. https://interactive.wttw.com/playlist/2017/04/07/how-world-war-i-transformed-chicago

20. *The Chicago Defender,* April 22, 1916.

21. This comment is attributed to jazz musician Eddie Condon. Kenny, William Howland. *Chicago Jazz: A Cultural History 1904-1930.* Oxford University Press: New York. 1993. p. 14.

22. Hughes, Langston. *The Big Sea: An Autobiography.* Alfred A. Knopf, Inc.: New York, N.Y. 1940.

23. *Chicago Tribune,* July 28, 1919.

24. Ibid.

25. Text from the Provident Hospital annual report is from Drake and Cayton.

26. Hayner, Don. *Binga: The Rise and Fall of Chicago's First Black Banker.* Northwestern University Press: Evanston, Ill. 2019. pp. 134-138.

27. *The Chicago Defender,* Oct. 19, 1918.

28. *The Chicago Defender,* Aug. 9, 1919.

29. *The Chicago Defender,* June, 14, 1919.

30. *The Chicago Defender,* Aug. 9, 1919.

31. *The Chicago Defender,* Nov. 1, 1919.

32. *The Chicago Defender,* April. 13, 1918.

33. Ibid.

34. *The Chicago Defender,* Nov. 2, 1918.

35. Advertisement. *The Chicago Defender,* Sept. 27, 1917.

36. *The Broad Ax,* Oct. 18, 1919.

37. *The Negro in Chicago: A Study of Race Relations and a Race Riot.* Chicago Commission on Race Relations: University of Chicago Press. Chicago, Ill. 1922. p. 131.

38. *The Chicago Defender,* June 14, 1919.

39. *The Chicago Defender,* July 12, 1919.

40. *The Broad Ax,* Nov. 29, 1919.

41. Reed. Christopher Robert. *Knock at the Door of Opportunity: Black Migration to Chicago, 1900-1919.* Southern Illinois University Press: Carbondale, Ill. 2014.

42. *The Chicago Defender,* July 10, 1920.

43. Reed.

44. *Negro Education: A Study of the Private and Higher Schools for the Colored People in the United States.* U.S. Department of the Interior, Bureau of Education. 1917.

45. *The Chicago Defender,* June 14, 1913.

46. *The Chicago Defender,* Nov. 1, 1919.

47. *The Dayton Herald,* Jan. 31, 1911.

48. *The New York Age,* Dec. 14 ,1911 and *The Washington Bee,* Jan. 4, 1908.

49. *The Chicago Defender,* April 1, 1933.

50. Reed, Christopher Robert. *The Rise of Chicago's Black Metropolis 1920-1929.* University of Illinois Press: 2011. pp. 88-89.

51. Weems, Robert E., Jr. *The Merchant Prince of Black Chicago: Anthony Overton and the Building of A Financial Empire.* University of Illinois: Urbana, Ill. 2020.

52. The quote appears in Reed, *The Rise of Chicago's Black Metropolis 1920-1929,* but is drawn from the relatively obscure Chavers-Wright, Madrue, T*he Guarantee: Chavers, banker, entrepreneur, philanthropist in Chicago's Black Belt of the Twenties.* Wright-Armstead Associates: 1985. Chavers-Wright who was Chavers' daughter, notes in her book that some parts of the work are fictionalized but based on actual events.

53. Reed. *The Rise of Chicago's Black Metropolis 1920-1929.*

54. Hayner, p. 2.

55. Hayner.

56. Landon, Fred. "The Negro Migration to Canada after the Passing of the Fugitive Slave Act." *The Journal of Negro History,* Jan. 1920. Vol. 5, No. 1. (Jan. 1920) pp. 22-36.

57. *The Broad Ax,* Jan. 1, 1910.

58. Hayner, p. 2.

59. *The Broad Ax,* Jan. 1, 1910.

60. *The Chicago Daily Tribune,* May 8, 1927.

61. Hayner.

62. *The Chicago Daily Tribune,* May 8, 1927.

63. Hayner.

64. Gibson, Campbell, and Kay Jung. *Historical Census on Population Totals by Race, 1790 to 1990, and by Hispanic Origin, 1970 to 1990 for Large Cities and Other Urban Places in the United States,* U.S. Census Bureau. Washington, D.C., February 2005.

65. Hayner.

66. Washington, Booker T. *The Story of the Negro: Volume II.* Doubleday, Page & Co.: New York. 1909.

67. *The Broad Ax.* Dec. 21, 1907.

68. Hayner.

69. Baradaran, Mehrsa. *The Color of Money: Black Banks and the Racial Wealth Gap.* The Belknap Press of Harvard University Press: Cambridge, Mass. 2017.

70. *The Chicago Daily Tribune,* Nov. 23, 1912.

71. Bogart, Ernest Ludlow and John Mabry Matthews. *The Modern Commonwealth, 1893-1918.* Illinois Centennial Commission: Springfield, Ill. 1920.

72. Bogart, Ernest Ludlow and Thompson, Charles Manfred. *The Industrial State: 1870-1893.* A.C. McClurg & Co., Chicago, Ill. 1922.

73. Bogart and Matthews. *The Modern Commonwealth, 1893-1918.* pp. 411-417.

74. Weems, Robert E., Jr., and Jason Chambers. *Building the Black Metropolis: African American Entrepreneurship in Chicago.* University of Illinois: 2017. pp. 411-417.

75. Hayner, p. 64.

76. *The Broad Ax,* Jan. 1, 1910.

77. *The Chicago Defender,* March 7, 1914.

78. *The Chicago Daily Tribune,* Nov. 23, 1919. This statement is attributed to "The Commercial Chronicle."

79. Hayner.

80. *The Chicago Daily Tribune,* May 3, 1915.

81. Sandburg, Carl. *The Chicago Race Riots.* Harcourt, Brace and Howe: New York, N.Y. 1919. pp. 14-15.

82. *The Chicago Daily Tribune,* May 2, 1915.

83. *The Chicago Defender,* May 8, 1915.

84. *The Chicago Daily Tribune,* May 2, 1915.

85. Ibid.

86. *The Chicago Daily Tribune,* May 3, 1915.

87. *The Chicago Defender,* May 18, 1919.

88. Sandburg, p 15.

89. Rothstein, Richard. *The Color of Law: A Forgotten History of How our Government Segregated America.* W.W. Norton & Co.: New York, N.Y. 2017.

90. Hirsch, Arnold R. *Blockbusting*. The Electronic Encyclopedia of Chicago. Chicago Historical Society. 2005.

91. Rothstein.

92. *Negro Housing: Report of the Committee on Negro Housing*. The President's Conference on Home Building and Home Ownership. National Capital Press, Inc., Washington, D.C. 1932.

93. Ibid.

94. Brooks, Richard R.W. and Carol M. Rose. *Saving the Neighborhood: Racially Restrictive Covenants, Law, and Social Norms*. Harvard University Press. Cambridge, Mass. 2013. pp. 89-91.

95. Ibid.

96. Ibid.

97. A detailed examination of the issue can be found in Rothstein.

98. Ibid.

99. Rothstein. See also: *A 'Forgotten History" of How the U.S. Government Segregated America*. NPR. May 3, 2017. https://www.npr.org/2017/05/03/526655831/a-forgotten-history-of-how-the-u-s-government-segregated-america

100. Much has been written about this including, Perry, Andre M. and Davis Harshbarger. *America's Formerly Redlined Neighborhoods Have Changed, and So Must Solutions to Rectify Them*. The Brookings Institution. Oct. 14, 2019. https://www.brookings.edu/research/americas-formerly-redlines-areas-changed-so-must-solutions/

101. Wilson, Bev. "Urban Heat Management and the Legacy of Redlining." *Journal of the American Planning Association,* May 22, 2020. In addition, an examination of this issue in Richmond, Va. was published by *The New York Times* on Aug. 24, 2020.

102. Sandburg, p. 41.

103. *Chicago Tribune,* May 8, 1927.

104. Hayner, p. 138.

105. Rothstein, p. 144.

106. Hayner.

107. *Chicago Tribune,* Aug. 26, 1921.

108. Chicago Commission on Race Relations. T*he Negro in Chicago: A Study of Race Relations and a Race Riot*. University of Chicago Press: Chicago, Ill. 1922. p. 131

109. Hayner.

110. Tuttle, William M. *Race Riot: Chicago in the Red Summer of 1919*. University of Illinois Press: Urbana and Chicago, Ill. 1970. p. 54.

111. Krugler, David F. *1919: The Year of Racial Violence*. Cambridge University Press: New York, N.Y. 2015.

112. *The Chicago Daily Tribune,* Aug. 1, 1919.

113. *Chicago Tribune.* June 4, 1921.

114. Chicago Commission on Race Relations. p. 227-228.

115. Ibid.

116. Ibid.

117.   Ibid, p. 230.

118.   Ibid, p. 228

119.   Ibid.

120.   Ibid, p. 221.

121.   Ibid.

122.   *The Crisis,* Vol. 21, No. 3. Jan. 1921. p. 102.

123.   Hines, George W. *Negro Banking Institutions in the United States.* Howard University: Washington, D.C. 1924. p. 13.

124.   Ibid.

125.   Baradaran, pp. 93-95.

126.   *Chicago Tribune,* Dec. 30, 1920.

127.   *The Chicago Defender,* April 24, 1920.

128.   *The Chicago Defender,* Jan. 8, 1921.

129.   *Chicago Tribune,* May 8, 1927.

130.   Weems.

131.   *The Chicago Defender,* Dec. 10, 1921.

132.   Weems.

133.   Quote likely from *The Chicago Daily News* as reprinted by *The Negro Star,* Aug. 12, 1921.

134.   Weems.

135.   *Proceedings of the National Negro Business League. Its First Meeting Held in Boston, Mass. Aug. 23 and 24, 1900.* National Negro Business League.

136.   *The Pittsburgh Courier,* Aug. 10, 1929.

137.   Uncredited Anthony Overton biography. *The Journal of Negro History.* Vol. 32, No. 3, July 1947. pp. 394-396.

138.   Ingham and Feldman.

139.   Ibid.

140.   Weems, pp. 69-73.

141.   Reed. *The Rise of Chicago's Black Metropolis 1920-1929.* p. 91.

142.   *The Broad Ax,* Sept. 3, 1921.

143.   Reed. *The Rise of Chicago's Black Metropolis 1920-1929.* p. 72.

144.   Weems.

145.   Weems, Robert E., Jr., and Jason Chambers. *Building the Black Metropolis: African American Entrepreneurship in Chicago.* University of Illinois. 2017. pp. 411-417.

146.   Walker, p. 183.

147.   Reed. T*he Rise of Chicago's Black Metropolis 1920-1929.*

148.   Ibid. p. 76.

149.   Drake and Cayton.

150.   Gibson and Jung.

151.   Reed. *The Rise of Chicago's Black Metropolis 1920-1929.* p. 73.

152.   Ibid, p. 72.

153. The phrase "Black Metropolis" is sometimes used to discuss the creation of such a community, but is notably the title of Drake and Cayton.

154. Gavins, R. Gordon Blaine Hancock. Encyclopedia Virginia. Retrieved from http://www.EncyclopediaVirginia.org/Hancock_Gordon_Blaine_1884-1970

155. Hayner, pp. 134-138.

156. *The Chicago Defender,* May 3, 1930

157. This quote appears in *The Chicago Defender,* May 3, 1930 and is attributed to W.H. Bolton. However, this same statement also appeared in a piece written by Carroll Binder in a 1927 *Chicago Daily News* article entitled "Chicago and the New Negro." It is not known whether Bolton used Binder's work as a source for his analysis.

158. Baradaran. pp. 75-77.

159. *The Wall Street Journal,* April 20, 1964.

160. Harris.

161. Ibid.

162. *The Chicago Daily Tribune,* Oct. 11, 1931.

163. Lindsay, Arnett G. "The Negro in Banking." *The Journal of Negro History,* April 1929. p. 192.

164. Ibid.

165. *The New York Amsterdam News,* Aug. 6, 1930.

166. Lindsay, pp. 156-201.

167. Reed. *The Rise of Chicago's Black Metropolis 1920-1929.* p. 142.

168. Ibid, p 78.

169. Ibid. p. 76.

170. Du Bois, p. 8.

171. *The Chicago Defender,* March 5, 1927.

172. *The New York Times,* Sept. 8, 1928.

173. *The Chicago Defender,* May 18, 1912.

174. *The Broad Axe,* May 6, 1922.

175. *The Pittsburgh Courier,* Jan. 21, 1928.

176. *The Broad Axe,* Nov. 6, 1909.

177. *The Chicago Defender,* Feb. 21, 1920.

178. *Pittsburgh Courier,* Jan. 21, 1928. The article, with a Chicago dateline, likely originated with a Chicago publication that was reprinted in Pittsburgh.

179. Ingham and Feldman, p. 199.

180: Chicago Commission on Race Relations. p. 576.

181. *The Chicago Defender,* Feb. 21 and 28, 1920.

182. Reed. *The Rise of Chicago's Black Metropolis 1920-1929.* p. 84.

183. Harris, pp 49, 193-195.

184. Harris, Appendix. 2.

185. St. Clair and Cayton. p. 83.

186. *The Chicago Defender,* March 16, 1929.

187. Sundstrom, William A. Last Hired. First Fired? Unemployment and Urban Black Workers During the Great Depression. *The Journal of Economic History.* Vol 52, No. 2 (Jun., 1992).

188. *The Forgotten Tenth: An Analysis of Unemployment Among Negroes in the United States and Its Social Costs.* National Urban League. 1933.

189. Deutsch, Tracey. "Great Depression." The Electronic Encyclopedia of Chicago. Chicago Historical Society. 2005.

190. *The Chicago Defender,* Aug. 9, 1930.

191. *The New York Amsterdam News,* Aug. 13, 1930.

192. *The New York Amsterdam News,* Aug. 6, 1930.

193. Harris, p. 161.

194. Harris, pp. 153-160.

195. *The Chicago Defender,* Aug. 9, 1930.

196. *The New York Amsterdam News,* Aug. 6, 1930.

197. *The Wall Street Journal,* June 11, 1931.

198. *The New York Times,* June 10, 1931.

199. Esbitt, Milton. "Bank Portfolios and Bank Failures During the Great Depression: Chicago." *The Journal of Economic History.* Jun 1986. pp. 455-462.

200. *The New York Times,* June 14, 1931.

201. Weems. *The Merchant Prince of Black Chicago: Anthony Overton and the Building of a Financial Empire.*

202. *The Chicago Defender,* May 28, 1932.

203. *The Pittsburgh Courier,* May 28, 1932.

204. *The Chicago Defender,* May 28, 1932.

205. Weems. *The Merchant Prince of Black Chicago: Anthony Overton and the Building of a Financial Empire.*

206. *The Chicago Defender.* April 30, 1932.

207. *The Pittsburgh Courier.* May 28, 1932.

208. Harris, pp. 144-153.

209. Reed. *The Rise of Chicago's Black Metropolis 1920-1929.* p. 91-92.

210. Harris.

211. *The Half Century Magazine,* July – Aug. 1922.

MEMPHIS, TENNESSEE

1. Rosenbloom, Joseph. *Redemption: The Untold Story of Martin Luther King Jr.'s Last 31 Hours.* Beacon Press: Boston. 2018. *Memphis Sanitation Workers' Strike.* The Martin Luther King, Jr., Research and Education Institute. Stanford University.

2. Turner, Allegra W. *Except by Grace: The Life of Jesse Turner.* Four-G Publishers: Jonesboro, Ark. 2004. p. 94.

3. https://www.nps.gov/places/tennessee-the-lorraine-hotel-memphis.htm

4. Rosenbloom.

5. Ammons, Lila. "The Evolution of Black-Owned Banks in the United States Between the 1880s and 1990s," *Journal of Black Studies,* Vol. 26, No. 4 (March 1996), pp.467-489.

6. Ingham and Feldman, pp. 655-670.

7. *Minnie M. Cox: A Postmaster's Story.* Smithsonian National Postal Museum. https://postalmuseum.si.edu/research-articles/the-history-and-experience-of-african-americans-in-america%E2%80%99s-postal-service/minnie

8. Garrett-Scott. Shennette. *Minnie Geddings Cox and the Indianola Affair, 1902-1904.* Mississippi Historical Society. March 2018.

9. Garrett-Scott. Shennette. "To Do a Work that Would Be Very Far Reaching: Minnie Geddings Cox, the Mississippi Life Insurance Company, and the Challenges of Black Women's Business Leadership in the Early Twentieth Century Untied States." Enterprise & Society. Vol. 17, Issue 3. Sept. 2016. pp. 473-514.

10. *Report of the Eleventh Annual Convention of the National Negro Business League.* A.M.E. Sunday School Union: Nashville, Tenn. 1911.

11. *The Pittsburgh Courier,* March 23, 1929.

12. *Who's Who in Colored America: A Biographical Dictionary of Notable Living Persons of African Descent in America.* Sixth Edition. Thomas Yenser Editor and Publisher, Brooklyn, N.Y. 1942.

13. Data from bank reports published in various editions of *The Enterprise-Tocsin* between 1918 and 1922.

14. Ingham and Feldman, pp. 655-670.

15. *National Negro Business League Annual Report of the Sixteenth Session and the Fifteenth Anniversary Convention.* African M.E. Sunday School Union. Nashville, Tenn. 1915. pp. 192-195.

16. Garett-Scott, Shennette. *Minnie Cox Geddings.* Mississippi Encyclopedia. Center for the Study of Southern Culture. April 13, 2018. https://mississippiencyclopedia.org/entries/minnie-geddings-cox/

17. *The Pittsburg Courier,* May 18, 1929.

18. *National Negro Business League Annual Report of the Sixteenth Session and the Fifteenth Anniversary Convention.*

19. *Who's Who in Colored America: A Biographical Dictionary of Notable Living Persons of African Descent in America.* Sixth Edition. Thomas Yenser Editor and Publisher, Brooklyn, N.Y. 1942.

20. Garrett-Scott. Shennette. "To Do a Work that Would Be Very Far Reaching: Minnie Geddings Cox, the Mississippi Life Insurance Company, and the Challenges of Black Women's Business Leadership in the Early Twentieth Century United States."

21. More detail on the complex history of Mississippi Life can be found in Ingham and Feldman, pp. 655-670.

22. *The Enterprise-Tocsin,* Jan. 5, 1928.

23. *The Atlanta Daily World,* Dec. 13, 1946 Ingham and Feldman, pp. 655-670. New York Amsterdam News, Sept. 7, 1946.

24.	*Who's Who in Colored America: A Biographical Dictionary of Notable Living Persons of African Descent in America.*

25.	*The Atlanta Daily World,* June 6, 1938 and April 2, 1940.

26.	*The Atlanta Daily World,* Aug. 29, 1941.

27.	Christian, p. 361.

28.	Tassava, Christopher. The American Economy during World War II. *EH.Net Encyclopedia,* edited by Robert Whaples. February 10, 2008. URL http://eh.net/encyclopedia/the-american-economy-during-world-war-ii/

29.	*The Atlanta Daily World,* Aug. 29, 1941.

30.	*The Chicago Defender,* Dec. 28, 1946.

31.	Turner, Allegra W. *Except by Grace: The Life of Jesse Turner.* Four-G Publishers: Jonesboro, Ark. 2004. p. 208.

32.	*The Atlanta Daily World,* Dec. 20, 1946.

33.	*The Atlanta Daily World,* Dec. 20, 1946.

34.	*The Pittsburgh Courier,* Jan. 17, 1948.

35.	Tri-State Bank of Memphis. https://www.tristatebank.com/history-information/

36.	*The Pittsburgh Courier,* Jan. 7, 1956.

37.	Rolph, Stephanie R. Ph.D. "The Citizens' Council." *Mississippi History Now.* The Mississippi Historical Society. Oct. 2019. http://www.mshistorynow.mdah.ms.gov/articles/427/the-citizens-council

38.	*The Chicago Defender,* Jan. 8, 1955.

39.	*The Pittsburgh Courier,* Jan. 7, 1956.

40.	*The Atlanta Daily World,* Feb. 1, 1955.

41.	*The Daily Advertiser.* May 1, 1955.

42.	Ibid.

43.	Library of Congress. https://www.loc.gov/exhibitions/rosa-parks-in-her-own-words/about-this-exhibition/the-bus-boycott/emmett-till-with-his-mother/

44.	Beito, Linda Royster and David T. Beito. Emmett Till, a New Investigation, and T.R.M. Howard. *Independent Institute.* Aug. 13, 2018.https://www.independent.org/news/article.asp?id=10472

45.	Ingham and Feldman, p. 662.

46.	Turner.

47.	Ibid. p. 206.

48.	Frank, Ed. "Tri-State Bank." *Tennessee Encyclopedia.* Tennessee Historical Society. March 1, 2018. https://tennesseeencyclopedia.net/entries/tri-state-bank/

49.	*The Civil Rights Era Begins in Memphis.* The Benjamin L. Hooks Institute for Social Change. The University of Memphis. https://www.memphis.edu/benhooks/mapping-civil-rights/civil-rights-begins.php

50.	Turner, p. 23.

51.	Ibid. p. 39.

52.	Ibid. p. 29.

53. Dowdy. G. Wayne. *Hidden History of Memphis.* Memphis Public Libraries. https://www.memphislibrary.org/digmemphis/libraryhistory/

54. *The New York Times,* March 27, 1962.

55. Turner, p. 95.

56. Frank.

57. Turner.

58. Ingham and Feldman, p. 665.

59. Turner, p. 208.

60. Ibid. p. 212.

61. Ibid. p. 211.

62. Lautherbach. Preston. "The Crucible: The National Civil Rights Museum." *Memphis City Magazine.* Jan. 20, 2020.

63. King, Martin Luther, Jr. *We Are Still Walking.* New York, N.Y., Dec. 1956.

64. King, Martin Luther, Jr. *Recommendations to the MIA Executive Board.* May 24, 1956. The Martin Luther King, Jr., Research and Education Institute. Stanford University.

65. Various documents. The Martin Luther King, Jr., Research and Education Institute. Stanford University.

66. King, *We Are Still Walking.*

67. Ibid.

68. King, *Recommendations to the MIA Executive Board,* Footnote 1.

69. See: Todd.

70. Ammons.

71. Brimmer. Andrew F. *The Black Banks: An Assessment of Performance and Prospects.* Presented before a joint session of the 1970 annual meetings of The American Finance Association and The American Economic Association. Detroit, Mich. Dec. 28, 1970.

72. These ideas are drawn from Ammons and other sources.

73. Baradaran, pp. 185, 202-203.

74. *The New York Times,* Oct. 12, 2012. *The Washington Post,* March 9, 1966. Andrew F. Brimmer. *Federal Reserve History.* Board of Governors of the Federal Reserve System. https://www.federalreservehistory.org/people/andrew-f-brimmer

75. Brimmer.

76. Ibid.

77. This quote is combined from *The New York Times,* Dec. 29, 1970 and *The Chicago Daily Defender,* Dec. 31, 1970.

78. Ammons.

79. *The Washington Post,* Jan. 17, 1971.

80. Brimmer.

81. Ammons.

82. Turner, pp. 217-218.

83. *The Wall Street Journal,* March 29, 1972. *The New York Amsterdam News,* April 20, 1991.

84.   *The New York Amsterdam News,* Feb. 6, 1971.

85.   *The Washington Post.* Nov. 26, 1966 and Dec. 5, 1968. *The Chicago Daily Defender* June 12, 1971.

86.   Brown, Daniel. Spotlight *On Community Bank Lending.* U.S. Small Business Administration Office of Advocacy. Sept. 2019.

87.   Brimmer, Andrew F. *Recent Trends in Black Banking. Statement by Andrew F. Brimmer at a Press Conference Held on the Occasion of the 1971 Convention of the National Bankers Association.* Washington, D.C.. Oct. 6, 1971.

88.   Some additional insight on this can be found in Lash, Nicholas A. "Asymmetries in US Banking: The Role of Black-owned Banks." *Global Divergence in Trade, Money and Policy.* 2006.

89.   *The Hartford Courant,* Aug. 20, 1903.

90.   · *The Nashville Banner,* Aug. 19, 1903.

91.   Paine, Ophelia. *Nashville.* Tennessee Encyclopedia. Tennessee Historical Society. March 1, 2018. https://tennesseeencyclopedia.net/entries/nashville-metropolitan-nashville-davidson-county/

92.   Analysis of the Tennessee social environment in the early 1900s drawn from Lamon, Lester C. *Black Tennesseans, 1900-1930.* University of Tennessee Press: Knoxville. Tenn. 1977.

93.   Lester, Connie E. *Disenfranchising Laws.* Tennessee Encyclopedia. Tennessee Historical Society. Oct. 8, 2017. http://tennesseeencyclopedia.net/entries/disfranchising-laws/

94.   *The Nashville Banner,* Aug. 19, 1903.

95.   *The Nashville Globe,* March, 17, 1911.

96.   *The Nashville Globe,* Jan. 22, 1909.

97.   Ingham and Feldman, p. 48/.

98.   Fleming. Walter J. *The Freedman's Savings Bank: A Chapter in Economic History.* The University of North Carolina Press. Chapel Hill, N.C. 1927.

99.   Lamon, p. 183.

100. Baradaran, p. 31.

101. Lamon, p. 184.

102. Ingham and Feldman, p. 103.

103. *Report of the Second Annual Convention of the National Negro Business League.* 1901. pp. 31-32.

104. Thompson, Nolan. *Boyd, Richard Henry.* Handbook of Texas Online, accessed October 27, 2020, https://www.tshaonline.org/handbook/entries/boyd-richard-henry. Published by the Texas State Historical Association.

105. Early, Joe, Jr. "Richard Henry Boyd: Shaper of Black Baptist Identity." *Baptist History and Heritage.* Vol. 42, No. 3. Fall-Summer 2007.

106. Ibid.

107. Washington, Booker T. *The Negro In Business.* Hartel, Jenkins & Co., 1907. pp. 186-189.

108. Ibid.

109. R.H. Boyd Publishing Corp. https://www.rhboyd.com/history

110. Ingham and Feldman, p. 483.

111. Ingham and Feldman, p. 483-484. Clark, Herbert. "James C. Napier." *Tennessee Encyclopedia.* Tennessee Historical Society. Oct. 8, 2017. https://tennesseeencyclopedia.net/entries/james-c-napier/

112. Ingham and Feldman, p. 484.

113. *Report of the Second Annual Convention of the National Negro Business League.* 1901. pp. 42-43.

114. Ingham and Feldman, p. 486.

115. Lamon, p. 185.

116. Washington. *The Negro In Business.*

117. Lamon, p. 184.

118. *The Nashville Globe,* Jan. 22, 1909.

119. Ibid.

120. *The Nashville Globe,* March, 17, 1911.

121. Ingham and Feldman, p. 103 among other sources. Napier made this statement in multiple newspaper articles.

122. Ingham and Feldman, p. 103.

123. *The Nashville Globe,* Jan. 3, 1908.

124. *Report of the Seventh Annual Convention of the National Negro Business League.* 1907 pp. 347-348.

125. *The Nashville Globe,* Aug. 6, 1909 and March 22, 1918.

126. *The Nashville Globe,* Aug. 6, 1909.

127. *The Nashville Globe,* Jan. 12, 1917.

128. *The Nashville Globe,* Aug. 6, 1909.

129. Miller, Benjamin T., James J. Thweatt, Suni K. Geeverghese. *The Surgeon's Duty to Serve: The forgotten life of Paul F. Eve, MD.* The American College of Surgeons. 2016. https://www.facs.org/-/media/files/archives/shg-poster/2016/15_eve.ashx

130. Haley, James T. *Afro-American Encyclopedia; or the Thoughts, Doings and Sayings of the Race.* Haley & Florida: Nashville, Tenn. 1895. pp. 59-62.

131. Lovett, Bobby L. and Linda T. Wynn. *Profiles of African Americans in Tennessee.* The Annual Local Conference on Afro-American Culture and History. Nashville, Tenn. 1996.

132. *The Nashville Globe,* July 26, 1912.

133. Lamon, p. 187.

134. *The Nashville Globe,* Jan. 12, 1912.

135. *The Nashville Globe,* July 26, 1912.

136. *The Nashville Globe,* Aug. 23, 1912.

137. *The Nashville Globe,* Jan. 12, 1917 and Jan. 19, 1917.

138. Wynn, Linda T. *People's Savings Bank and Trust Company.* Leaders of Afro-American Nashville. Nashville Conference on Afro-American Culture and History. Department of History. Tennessee State University. 1999.

139. Lamon.

140. Ibid.

141. *Black Enterprise,* June 1980. p. 191.

142. Lamon, pp. 6-7.

143. *The Nashville Banner,* June 24, 1905.

144. Ingham and Feldman, p. 106-107. Lamon, pp. 31-33.

145. Lamon, p. 34.

146. Ibid. p. 35.

147. Ingham and Feldman, p. 107.

148. *The Nashville Globe,* Jan. 12, 1912.

149. Ingham and Feldman, p. 109.

150. *The Nashville Globe,* Aug. 28, 1908.

151. Collier's quote as appearing in Ingham and Feldman, p. 108.

152. *The Hartford Courant,* March 2, 1908.

153. Ingham and Feldman, p. 489.

154. Ibid. p. 489.

155. *The Tuskegee Student.* Tuskegee Institute. Alabama. April 28, 1906.

DETROIT, MICHIGAN

1. *Crain's Detroit Business,* July 12, 2020. Quotes throughout this section intermingle comments that Kelly made to both *Crain's* and *Detroit Free Press,* June 21, 2020 for Q&A articles that covered the same series of topics including the bank's 50th anniversary, racial unrest and the COVID-19 pandemic.

2. "Uprising of 1967." *Encyclopedia of Detroit.* Detroit Historical Society. https://detroithistorical. org/learn/encyclopedia-of-detroit/uprising-1967

3. *Detroit Free Press,* June 21, 2020.

4. *The New York Times,* July 3, 2020.

5. Kishi, Roudabeh and Sam Jones. *Demonstrations & Political Violence in America.* Armed Conflict Location and Event Data Project. 2020. https://acleddata.com/2020/09/03/demonstrations-political-violence-in-america-new-data-for-summer-2020/

6. *Detroit Free Press,* June 14, 2020.

7. *Crain's Detroit Business,* July 13, 2020.

8. Author analysis of FDIC data. Dec. 11, 2020.

9. Wieczner, Jen. "Making Black banks matter." *Fortune.* Sept. 21, 2020.

10. *Crain's Detroit Business,* Aug. 14, 2020.

11. *Crain's Detroit Business,* July 12, 2020.

12. Mills, Claire Kramer. *Double Jeopardy: Covid-19's Concentrated Health and Wealth Effects in Black Communities.* Federal Reserve Bank of New York. August 2020. The noted decline in businesses is for the February-April 2020 period only.

13. *Detroit Free Press,* June 21, 2020.

14. Ibid.

15. *Encyclopedia of Detroit.* Detroit Historical Society. 2020.

16. Siebert, William. "The Underground Railroad in Michigan." *Detroit Historical Monthly,* Vol 1, No. 1 (March 1923).

17. *The New York Times,* Dec. 14, 1919.

18. Boyd, Herb. *Black Detroit: A People's History of Self-Determination.* Harper Collins: New York, N.Y., 2017.

19. Peterson, Joyce Shaw. "Black Automobile Workers in Detroit, 1910-1930." *The Journal of Negro History*, Vol. 64, No. 3 (summer 1979), pp. 177-190.

20. "Mr. Ford, Blacks and the UAW." *The Detroit News.* Jan. 30, 2000.

21. Brueggemann, John. "The Power and Collapse of Paternalism: The Ford Motor Company and Black Workers, 1937-1941," *Social Problems,* Vol. 47, No. 2. (May 2000), pp. 22-240.

22. Bailer, Lloyd H. "The Negro Automobile Worker." *Journal of Political Economy,* Oct. 1943. Vol. 51, No. 5. (Oct. 1943), pp. 415-428.

23. Maloney, Thomas N. and Warren C. Whatley. "Making the Effort: The Contours of Racial Discrimination in Detroit's Labor Markets, 1920-1940." *The Journal of Economic History,* Vol. 55, No. 3 (Sept. 1995), pp. 465-493.

24. Dancy, John C. *Sand Against the Wind: The Memoirs of John C. Dancy.* Wayne State University Press: Detroit, Mich. 1966. Copyright 1966 by Detroit Urban League. Detroit, Mich. pp. 55-56.

25. U.S. Census Bureau data.

26. Maloney and Whatley.

27. Peterson.

28. Ibid.

29. Ibid.

30. *Detroit Free Press,* March 12, 1917.

31. Peterson.

32. In addition to newspaper accounts, one of the most detailed accountings of the events surrounding the Sweets can be found in Dancy.

33. *The Pittsburgh Courier,* July 18, 1925.

34. Dancy, p. 54.

35. Ibid., p. 22.

36. Ibid., pp. 56-57.

37. "Black Bottom Neighborhood." *Encyclopedia of Detroit.* Detroit Historical Society. 2020.

38. Quote by Dr. Jiam DesJardin from *The Detroit Metro Times,* Dec. 14, 2011.

39. *Detroit Free Press,* Dec. 5, 1980.

40. *Detroit Free Press,* Dec. 15, 2013.

41. Peterson.

42. Dancy.

43. Ibid., p. 57.

44. *Detroit Free Press,* Mar. 6, 1927.

45. *Detroit Free Press,* Dec. 5, 1980. Gann, Brian. "Sidney Barthwell (1906-2005)." Retrieved from https://www.blackpast.org/african-american-history/barthwell-sidney-1906-2005/

46. Gann, B. (2011, June 18) Sidney Barthwell (1906-2005). Retrieved from https://www.blackpast.org/african-american-history/barthwell-sidney-1906-2005/

47. *The Pittsburgh Courier,* Oct. 20, 1928.

48. *Detroit Free Press,* Dec. 5, 1980.

49. *The Detroit Tribune,* Feb. 3, 1940.

50. Work, Monroe N. *Negro Year Book: An Encyclopedia of the Negro, 1921-1922.* Negro Year Book Co: Tuskegee Institute, Alabama. 1922.

51. *The Birmingham Age-Herald.* Feb. 18, 1910. For more on the Alabama Penny Savings Bank see Todd.

52. *The Chicago Defender,* Feb. 23, 1918. *The Detroit Tribune,* Jan. 14, 1956.

53. Thompson, W. Arthur and Robert Greenridge. "The Negro in Medicine in Detroit." *The Journal of the National Medical Association,* Nov. 1963. *The Chicago Defender,* Feb. 23, 1918.

54. Clarke, Geoffrey P. *Essays in North American Economic History. A dissertation submitted to the School of Graduate Studies, Rutgers, the State University of New Jersey. In partial fulfillment of the requirements for the degree of Doctor of Philosophy.* Graduate Program in Economics. Rutgers University. 2019.

55. *The Pittsburgh Courier,* Jan 21, 1933.

56. *The Pittsburgh Courier,* Jan. 31, 1925.

57. *Detroit Free Press,* March 29, 2004. Boyd. Lindsay. Dancy, p. 23.

58. *Michigan Manufacturer and Financial Record,* Vol. 32 (July-Dec. 1923) p. 28. *Who's Who in Colored America: A Biographical Dictionary of Notable Living Persons of African Descent in America.* Sixth Edition. Thomas Yenser Editor and Publisher, Brooklyn, N.Y. 1942.

59. *Detroit Free Press,* July 9, 1929.

60. *The Detroit Tribune,* Oct. 9, 1937, May 22, 1948.

61. *The Detroit Tribune,* Oct. 9, 1937.

62. *The Detroit Tribune,* July 20, 1940.

63. National Housewives' League of America Records. Bentley Historical Library. University of Michigan.

64. *Arsenal of Democracy.* Detroit Historical Society. https://detroithistorical.org/learn/encyclopedia-of-detroit/arsenal-democracy

65. *The Origins of the Urban Crisis: Race and Inequality in Post War Detroit.* Princeton University Press: Princeton, N.J. 2005.

66. Bailer.

67. Lynch, Hollis R., *The Black Urban Condition.* Thomas Y. Crowell Co.: New York. 1973. Appendix A.

68. Boyd. Sugrue, Thomas J. The Origins of the Urban Crisis: Race and Inequality in Post War Detroit. Princeton University Press: Princeton, N.J. 2005.

69. Bailer.

70. Russ, Johanna. *The 1943 Detroit Race Riot.* Walter P. Reuther Library. Wayne State University. 2012.

71. Sugrue.

72. Boyd.

73. *The Daily Boston Globe,* June 22, 1943.

74. *Race Riot of 1943.* Encyclopedia of Detroit. Detroit Historical Society.

75. Dancy, p. 199.

76. *The Detroit Tribune,* July 3, 1943.

77. *The Chicago Defender,* July 10, 1943, Aug. 21, 1943. *The Pittsburgh Courier,* Aug. 21, 1943.

78. Sugrue, p. 43

79. Ibid.

80. Ibid.

81. Dancy, p. 202.

82. Sugrue.

83. *The Detroit Tribune,* Feb. 27. 1943.

84. *The Detroit Tribune,* March 4, 1944.

85. *Manufacturers Record.* Manufacturers Record Publishing Co., Baltimore MD. 1921.

86. *The Detroit Tribune,* April 12, 1947.

87. *The Detroit Tribune,* Jan. 15, 1949. *The Atlanta Daily World,* April 2, 1952.

88. *The Detroit Tribune,* Aug. 5, 1950.

89. *Detroit Free Press,* Dec. 5, 1980.

90. *The Detroit Tribune,* May 2, 1948

91. *The Pittsburgh Courier,* June 18, 1955.

92. Thompson, M. Stewart. Letters to Sens. Robert Griffin and Philip Hart. July 11, 1966. *Congressional Record.* Proceedings and Debates of the 89th Congress. Second Session. Volume 112, Part 14. Aug. 3, 1966 to Aug. 16, 1966. U.S. Government Printing Office: Washington, D.C. 1966.

93. Sugrue.

94. U.S. Congress House Committee on Banking and Currency. Hearings Vol. 1. Eighty-fourth Congress. First Session. 1955.

95. *The Detroit Tribune,* July 5, 1947.

96. *The Detroit Tribune,* Jan. 22, 1949.

97. *Detroit Free Press,* Aug. 11, 1954.

98. Sugrue.

99. *Detroit Free Press,* Aug. 12, 1954.

100. Boyle, Ken. "The Ruins of Detroit: Exploring the Urban Crisis in the Motor City." *Michigan Historical Review.* Vol. 27, No. 1. (Spring 2001) pp. 109-127. Sugrue.

101. Sugrue.

102. Virginia Park Historic District. National Register of Historic Places Inventory – Nomination Form. Nov. 2, 1982.

103. *Report of the National Advisory Commission on Civil Disorders,* March 1, 1968.

104. Dr. Karl Gregory interview. Detroit Historical Society, Detroit, Mich. Sept. 1, 2015. https://detroit1967.detroithistorical.org/items/show/249

105. Ibid.

106. Christian.

107. Sugrue. Fine, Sidney. "Violence in the Model City: The Cavanaugh Administration, Race Relations, and the Detroit Riot of 1967." Michigan State University Press: East Lansing, Mich. 2007.

108. *Detroit Free Press,* July 28, 1967.

109. "By the numbers: Economic devastation of '67 difficult to quantify – but it was massive." *Crain's Detroit Business,* June 25, 2017.

110. *Detroit Free Press,* July 28, 1967.

111. Sugrue, p. 260.

112. Text from the historic marker located in Gordon Park, Detroit, erected and unveiled on July 23, 2017.

113. Fine.

114. Associated Press story as appearing in *The Battle Creek Enquirer,* March 18, 1969.

115. Brodt, Katherine. *Belair at Bowie: Segregated Suburbia.* Boundary Stones. WETA's Local History Blog. June 12, 2020. https://boundarystones.weta.org/2020/06/12/belair-bowie-segregated-suburbia

116. Dr. Karl Gregory interview. Detroit Historical Society.

117. Fine.

118. Gregory, Karl, Daniel Braunstein, Norton Seeber and Walter McMurtry. "Corporate Viewpoints: Interviews with Top Managers: Interview with: Walter McMurtry." *Interfaces.* Vol. 5, No. 2, Part 1 of Two (Feb. 1975), pp. 11-22.

119. UPI story in *The Traverse City Record-Eagle,* July 30, 1973.

120. Ibid.

121. *The Michigan Chronicle,* Dec. 1, 2016.

122. *Detroit Free Press,* Jan. 29, 1969.

123. *Detroit Free Press,* May 4, 1970, March 30, 1971. Ammons.

124. *The Michigan Chronicle,* March 19, 2019.

125. *Detroit Free Press,* March 22, 1970.

126. *Detroit Free Press,* June 20. 1971.

127. Ibid.

128. Beltramini, Enrico. "SCLC Operation Breadbasket: From Economic Civil Rights to Black Economic Power." *Fire!!!* Vol. 2, No. 2. Pp. 5 47.

129. *The Pilgrimage of Jesse Jackson.* Frontline show #1415. April 30, 1995.

130. *Detroit Free Press,* May 25, 1975 and April 30, 1976.

131. *The Hartford Courant,* May 8, 1975.

132. Ibid.

133. *Detroit Free Press,* April 30, 1976.

134. Ibid.

135. *Detroit Free Press,* Aug. 4, 1976.

136. *The St. Louis Post Dispatch,* Nov. 9, 2009.

137. *Detroit Free Press,* July 5, 1981.

138. Quote from Charles Allen appearing in *Detroit Free Press,* May 4, 1970.

139. *Detroit Free Press,* May 22, 1980.

140. Inner City Business Improvement Forum pamphlet.

141. *Detroit Free Press,* May 22, 1980.

142. Don Davis: Electrifying Mojo Interview. Radio interview. Detroit Sound.org. : http://detroitsound.org/artifact/don-davis/

143. *Detroit Free Press,* July 27, 1980. United Sound Systems Museum: History. https://unitedsoundsystemsrecordingstudios.com/museum/

144. Don Davis: Electrifying Mojo Interview.

145. *Detroit Free Press,* May 22, 1980.

146. *Detroit Free Press,* March 11, 1996.

147. Don Davis: Electrifying Mojo Interview. Radio interview. Detroit Sound.org.

148. *Detroit Free Press,* July 5, 1981.

149. *Detroit Free Press,* Nov. 28 ,1983.

150. *Detroit Free Press,* March 22, 1982.

151. Ibid.

152. *Detroit Free Press,* March 30, 1992. Black Enterprise, May 1987.

153. *Detroit Free Press,* July 13, 1986. *Black Enterprise,* May 1987.

154. *Detroit Free Press,* July 13, 1986.

155. *The Christian Science Monitor,* April 3, 1987.

156. Ibid.

157. *Black Enterprise,* May 1987.

158. *The Christian Science Monitor,* April 3, 1987.

159. *Detroit Free Press,* July 27, 1988.

160. *Detroit Free Press,* March 30, 1992.

161. *Detroit Free Press,* July 30 1996, Oct. 10, 1991, Nov. 11, 1990.

162. *Detroit Free Press,* July 10, 1995.

163. *Detroit Free Press,* July 23, 1993.

164. *Detroit Free Press,* July 25, 1993.

165. Ibid.

166. *American Banker,* Dec. 28, 1993.

167. *Detroit Free Press,* Aug. 23, 1996.

168. *Detroit Free Press,* July 10, 1995.

169. *Crain's Detroit Business,* April 13, 1998.

170. *American Banker,* May 8, 1998.

171. *Detroit Free Press,* April 16, 1998.

172. Ibid.

173. *Detroit Free Press,* July 30, 1996. *Crain's Detroit Business,* March 3, 1997.

174. Newberger, Robin. "Capital-raising among minority-owned banks before and after the financial crisis." *ProfitWise News and Views,* No. 4, 2018. Federal Reserve Bank of Chicago: Chicago, Ill.

175. *Bank Failures in Brief – Summary 2001 through 2020.* Federal Deposit Insurance Corporation. https://www.fdic.gov/bank/historical/bank/

176. *Crain's Detroit Business,* March 23, 2009.

177. *Black Enterprise,* Nov. 11, 2009.

178. *Detroit Free Press,* June 7, 1999.

179. *Black Enterprise,* March 2010.

180. Ibid.

181. *Black Enterprise,* Aug. 4, 2020.

182. *Black Enterprise,* March 12, 2018.

183. Testimony of Kenneth Kelly, chairman and CEO, First Independence Bank; Chairman, Board of Directors, National Bankers Association; on behalf of both First Independence Bank and the National Bankers Association; Before the House Financial Services Subcommittee on Consumer Protection and Financial Institutions. "An Examination of the Decline of Minority Depository Institutions and the Impact on Underserved Communities." Oct. 22, 2019.

184. *Crain's Detroit Business,* July 13, 2020.

185. The quotes are combined in the text for clarity, but were made in response to the separate questions about the bank's ability to serve the community in the short and long-term and, separately, issues of economic equality in Detroit as the city's only Black bank. *Crain's Detroit Business,* July 13, 2020.

In Your Hands

1. *USA Today,* July 15, 2016.

2. Gregory, Kia. Banking Black. *The New Republic.* Vol. 249, issue 6. Jan. 2018.

3. *USA Today,* July 15, 2016.

4. CNN Interview, Aug. 20, 2014.

5. *GQ,* July 8, 2020.

6. *Atlanta,* May 2010.

7. Ibid.

8. *GQ,* July 8, 2020.

9. *The New York Times.* "Killer Mike says he has a choice to make." Sway Podcast transcript, Oct. 8, 2020

10. *The Atlanta Journal-Constitution,* Oct. 8, 2020. American Banker, Oct. 9, 2020.

11. Faber, Jacob William. "Segregation and the Cost of Money: Race, Poverty, and the Prevalence of Alternative Financial Institutions." *Social Forces,* Vol. 98, NO. 2. Dec. 2019. Pp. 819-848.

12. Bennett. Jeannette N. "Fast Cash and Payday Loans." *Page One Economics.* Federal Reserve Bank of St. Louis. April 2019.

13. *The New York Times.* "Killer Mike says he has a choice to make."

14. Ibid.

15. *The Los Angeles Times,* Aug. 27, 2020.

16. The Associated Press as appearing in *Chicago Tribune,* Sept. 8, 2020. These comments were in response to separate questions by the reporter, but are combined here for clarity.

17. Sastry, Anjuli and Karen Grigsby Bates. *When L.A. Erupted in Anger: A Look Back at the Rodney King Riots.* NPR. April 26, 2017.

18. *The Washington Post,* Nov. 7, 2011.

19. Quarterly Banking Profile. Third Quarter 2020. Federal Deposit Insurance Corporation.

20. Report on the Economic Well-Being of U.S Households in 2019 – May 2020. Board of the Governors of the Federal Reserve System. https://www.federalreserve.gov/publications/2020-economic-well-being-of-us-households-in-2019-preface.htm

21. Home Mortgage Disclosure Act data in addition to surveys reported by real estate firms and lenders.

22. Report to Congress on the Availability of Credit to Small Business – Sept. 2017. Federal Reserve. https://www.federalreserve.gov/publications/2017-september-availability-of-credit-to-small-businesses.htm

23. Dr. Karl Gregory interview. Detroit Historical Society, Detroit, Mich. Sept. 1, 2015. https://detroit1967.detroithistorical.org/items/show/249

24. The series, "Detroit Banking: The Race for Money," began with multiple stories in the July 24, 1988 edition of *Detroit Free Press* and continued for an additional three days.

25. The study, conducted by the *Atlanta Journal Constitution,* was highlighted in a wire service story appearing in *Detroit Free Press,* Jan. 22, 1989.

26. Among others, see: Mock, Brentin, Disinvestment in Baltimore's Black Neighborhoods." Bloomberg CityLab, Nov. 18, 2015. Coryne, Haru. Tony Briscoe. "These Cities Tried to Tackle Disinvestment. Here are Lessons From What Happened." ProPublica, Dec. 30, 2020.

27. Dr. Karl Gregory interview. Detroit Historical Society, Detroit, Mich. Sept. 1, 2015. https://detroit1967.detroithistorical.org/items/show/249

28. "2019 Minority Depository Institutions: Structure, Performance and Social Impact." Federal Deposit Insurance Corporation

29. *Detroit Free Press,* July 10, 1995.

30. Baradaran, p. 278-279.

31. Saunders, Pete. "Detroit, Five Years After Bankruptcy." *Forbes,* July 19, 2018.

32. *Bloomberg Businessweek,* April 22, 2020.

33. Dr. Karl Gregory interview. Detroit Historical Society, Detroit, Mich. Sept. 1, 2015. https://detroit1967.detroithistorical.org/items/show/249

34. *Detroit Free Press,* May 25, 1975.

35. *Chicago Tribune,* July 22, 1979.

36. *The New York Times,* July 24, 1979.

37. Faber.

38. Aaronson, Daniel. Daniel Hartley and Bhashkar Mazumder. *The Effects of the 1930s HOLC 'Redlining' Maps.* Federal Reserve Bank of Chicago. REVISED Aug. 2020.

39. Bayer, Patrick. Fernando Ferreira and Stephen L. Ross. *What Drives Racial and Ethnic Differences in High Cost Mortgages? The Role of High Risk Lenders.* NBER Working Paper Series. Feb. 2016. McGhee, Heather. *The Sum of Us: What Racism Costs Everyone and How We Can Prosper Together.* One World: New York City, N.Y. 2021.

40. Faber.

41. Faber. In addition to Faber's own findings and conclusions, his paper cites a wealth of additional resources conducted by numerous others.

42. Friedline, Terri, and Nancy Kepple. 2017. "Does Community Access to Alternative Financial Services Relate to Individuals' Use of These Services? Beyond Individual Explanations." *Journal of Consumer Policy,* Vol. 40, No. 1, pp: 51–79.

43. Friedline, Terri and Mathieu Despard. "Life in a Banking Desert." *The Atlantic.* March 13, 2016.

44. Stein, Luke C.D. and Constantine Yannelis. "Financial Inclusion, Human Capital, and Wealth Accumulation: Evidence from the Freedman's Savings Bank." The Review of Financial Studies, Vol 33, Issue 11. Nov. 2020.

45. *Why We Need Black-Owned Banks.* The Indicator from Planet Money. National Public Radio. July 8, 2020. https://www.npr.org/transcripts/889141681

46. *The Christian Science Monitor,* April 3, 1987.

47. The depositor claim is as of September 2020. Fortune. Sept. 21, 2020.

48. Anenberg, Elliot, Andrew C. Chang, Serafin Grundl, Kevin B. Moore, and Richard Windle. *The Branch Puzzle: Why Are there Still Bank Branches?,* FEDS Notes. Washington: Board of Governors of the Federal Reserve System, August 20, 2018, https://doi.org/10.17016/2380-7172.2206

49. Ibid.

50. Fisman, Raymond. Daniel Paravisini and Vikrant Vig. "Cultural Proximity and Loan Outcomes." *The American Economic Review.* Vol. 107, No. 2. (Feb. 2017) pp. 457-492. Fleisher, Chris. "When bankers and borrowers come from the same culture, does everybody win?" *American Economic Association.* March 1, 2017.

51. Nguyen, Hoai-Luu. *Do Bank Branches Still Matter? The Effect of Closings on Local Economic Outcomes.* Department of Economics. Massachusetts Institute of Technology. 2014.

52. *Detroit Free Press,* Nov. 28, 1983.

53. *American Banker,* Oct. 18, 1985.

TODAY'S CHALLENGES, YESTERDAY'S LESSONS

1.   "Report on the Economic Well-Being of U.S. Households in 2019." Board of Governors of the Federal Reserve System. May 2020.

2.   Prager, Robin A. "Determinants of the Locations of Payday Lenders, Pawnshops and Check-Cashing Outlets." Board of Governors of the Federal Reserve System. June 2009.

3.   One example of this is nonbank lending to homebuyers: See American Banker, Nov. 30, 2020.

4.   https://www.wmcactionnews5.com/2021/06/09/tri-state-bank-memphis-be-acquired-by-liberty-bank-trust-new-orleans/

5.   Hanauer, Matt. Brent Lytle, Chis Summers, Stephanie Ziadah. *Community Banks' Ongoing Role in the U.S. Economy.* Federal Reserve Bank of Kansas City. June 2021.

6.   "Charging 589% Interest in the Pandemic is Booming Business: Lenders are Raking in Record Profits in a Controversial Industry that Often Targets Black and Latino Communities." Bloomberg. May 17, 2021. https://www.bloomberg.com/graphics/2021-payday-loan-lenders/

7.   Hanauer, Matt. Brent Lytle. Chis Summers, Stephanie Ziadeh. *Community Banks' Ongoing Role in the U.S. Economy.* Federal Reserve Bank of Kansas City. June 2021.

8.   "Community Bank Access to Innovation through Partnerships." Board of Governors of the Federal Reserve System. September 2021.

9.   For additional details about the characteristics of the various types of CDFIs see: CDFI Organizational Structures. https://www.fdic.gov/consumers/community/CDFI/CDFIs_SectionII.pdf *Strategies for Community Banks to Develop Partnerships with Community Development Financial Institutions.* FDIC. March 2014.

10. Data from U.S. Department of Treasury Community Development Financial Institution Fund reports.

11. 2021 CDFI Survey Key Findings. Federal Reserve. Aug. 12, 2021. https://fedcommunities.org/data/2021-cdfi-survey-key-findings/#organizational-status

12. Bradford, Beth and Patrick Davis. *Scaling Community Finance to Fill a Growing Market Gap.* Stanford Social Innovation Review. June 23, 2021.

13. For examples, see Strength in Numbers: The Growth and Evolution of CDFI Partnerships. *Community Scope.* Vol. 6, Issue 2. Federal Reserve Bank of Richmond. 2019. Bank Think: CDFIs have untapped potential as game changers for minority-owned businesses. *American Banker.* Nov. 18, 2020.

Photo Credits

FRONT COVER: Courtesy of University of Memphis Department of Art. Hooks Brothers collection (1946). The original image has been altered to remove window signage behind the men by the Federal Reserve Bank of Kansas City with permission.

Photo Gallery:

PAGE 59
TOP: Courtesy of the Virginia Museum of History and Culture, VAHM 003.161.75 (circa 1897).
Bottom: Courtesy of Susan Mitchell, great-granddaughter-in-law of Dr. Richard F. and Mary Dade (Lane) Tancil (undated). © 2018, Susan Mitchell.

PAGE 60
TOP: Wikimedia Commons (public domain). Original image via Simmons, William J., and Henry McNeal Turner. *Men of Mark: Eminent, Progressive and Rising.* GM Rewell & Company, pp. 320-321 (1887).
BOTTOM: LC. Souvenir Views: Negro Enterprises & Residences, Richmond, Va., p. 33. Original published by D. A. Ferguson, Richmond. 1907.

PAGE 61 Courtesy of the National Park Service, Maggie L. Walker National Historic Site, MAWA 99-0261 (circa 1910).

Page 62
Top: Oklahoma Historical Society Photograph Collection, Oklahoma Historical Society Research Division. OHS 2012.201.B0096.0300 (undated).
Bottom: Oklahoma Historical Society, Oklahoma Publishing Company Photography Collection. OHS 3377.B.1 (undated).

PAGE 63
TOP: Courtesy of the Tulsa Historical Society & Museum, Mozella Franklin Jones Collection (Catalog Number 1977.046.026) (1915).
BOTTOM: Courtesy of the Tulsa Historical Society & Museum. Mozella Franklin Jones collection (Catalog Number 1977.046.046) (1918).

PAGE 64

TOP: Courtesy of the Tulsa Historical Society & Museum. Tulsa Race Riot collection (Catalog Number
            2002.255.001) (1921).
BOTTOM: Illinois Digital Newspaper Collection, Broad Ax (Chicago, Ill.) (January 1, 1910), p. 2.

PAGE 65

TOP: Courtesy of Chicago History Museum, ICHi-065481; Jun Fujita, photographer (1919).
BOTTOM: The Project Gutenberg EBook (2018), of The Negro in Chicago, by The Chicago Commission
            on Race Relations, Original published by The University of Chicago (1922).

PAGE 66

TOP: Internet Archive (2008). Library of Congress collection. *Beacon Lights of the Race,* p. 216, by
            G.P. Hamilton, Original published by F.H. Clarke & Brother, Memphis (1911).
BOTTOM: Courtesy of the Memphis & Shelby County Room, Memphis Public Library & Information
            Center, Photograph Collection (Digital AAP023) (undated).

PAGE 67

TOP: Courtesy of the Memphis & Shelby County Room, Memphis Public Library & Information
            Center, Photograph Collection (Digital AAP044) (undated).
BOTTOM: Courtesy of the Memphis & Shelby County Room, Memphis Public Library & Information
            Center, Benjamin L. Hooks Collection (Digital BLH0092) (1956).

PAGE 68   Courtesy of the University of North Carolina, Chapel Hill, Wilson Library. Original from
            Sermons, Addresses and Reminiscences..., By E.C. Morris, Published by National Baptist Publication
            Board, Nashville, Tenn. (1901).

PAGE 69

TOP: Courtesy of Nashville Public Library, Special Collections, Photograph Collection, 1930s.
BOTTOM: "People's Savings Bank and Trust Company." Nashville Globe, 12 January 1912, news article
            accessed at https://digital.mtsu.edu/digital/collection/p15838coll7/id/324. Courtesy of the
            Center for Historic Preservation and the James E. Walker Library. " Trials, Triumphs, and
            Transformations: Tennesseans' Search for Citizenship, Community, and Opportunity." Middle
            Tennessee State University, 2014-2017, http://dsi.mtsu.edu/trials

PAGE 70

TOP: © ZUMA Press, Marcin Szczepanski, Detroit Free Press, January 11, 2009, p. 49, via ZUMA Press.
BOTTOM: © ZUMA Press, Hugh Grannum, Detroit Free Press, March 11, 1994, via ZUMA Press.

PAGE 71   © ZUMA Press, David C. Turnley, Detroit Free Press, March 22, 1982, p. 43, via ZUMA Press.

Index

Breedlove, Sarah, 24
Brimmer, Andrew, 144-147
Broadway Federal Bank, 213-214
Broadway Financial Corp., 214
Bronzeville, 80, 121
Brown v. Board of Education, 137, 142
Brown, B.F., 42
Brown, James, 23
Brown, Michael, 211
Browne, William Washington, 5-7, 11-12, *59*
Bureau of Engraving and Printing, 127

C
Calloway, Cab., 23, 80
Canada, 37, 88, 169
Carmichael, Stokely, 29
Carnegie, Andrew, 160
Castille, Philando, 211
Central State Hospital, 9
Central Tennessee College, 157
Chattanooga, Tenn., 150, 153, 156
Chavers, Pearl William, 87-88, 107-110
Chelsea Exchange Bank, 114
Chicago, VII, 25, 57, 73-127, 132, 149, 155, 157-158, 170-172, 177-178, 180, 182, 189, 193, 202, 218, 221 222
Chicago American Giants, 80
Chicago Bee, 110
Chicago Commission on Race Relations, 103, 105
Chicago Defender, 78, 80, 83, 104, 114, 121
Chicago Tribune, 81, 100, 118
Choctaw Nation, 33
Chrysler Corp., 147
Citizens Savings Bank and Trust Co., 149, 152-153, 155-159
Citizens Trust Bank, 147, 211
City First Bank, 213-214
Civil Rights Act of 1964, 143, 167
Civil Rights era, 78, 133, 139, 168
Civil War, 4-6, 17, 30, 33, 35, 37, 54, 77, 108, 126-127, 142, 150, 161, 169-170, 182
Cleveland, 96, 178

Turner, D.J., 41, 44, 48-49, *62*

Turner, Jesse Sr., *67,* 139-140, 222

Tuskegee Institute, 161, 177

U

Underground Railroad, 142, 169, 182

Union Transportation Co., 159

United National Bank, 198

United Order of True Reformers, 6-7, 11-13, 23, 25, 79

United States Department of Commerce, 144

United States Office of the Comptroller of the Currency, 107, 110, 192, 198

United States Treasury, 127, 155, 160, 161

Universal Life Insurance Co., 135-136

University of Chicago, 139, 177

V

Victory Life Insurance Co., 110

Victory Loan and Investment Co., 183

Virginia, 5, 7-9, 13, 18

Virginia Industrial School for Girls, 14

Virginia Park, 187, 190-192

Virginia Passenger and Power Co., 20

Voting Rights Act of 1965, 143, 167

W

Walker, A. Maceo, *67,* 133, 137, 139-140

Walker, Dick, 7, 11

Walker, Joseph, *66,* 133-134, 136-139

Walker, Juliet E.K., 45, 113

Walker, Leila, 66

Walker, Maggie, 4, 13-14, *61,* 222

Walker, Robert, 131

Washburn College, 108

Washington, Booker T., 25, 42, 45, 149-150, 154, 160

Washington, D.C., 9, 38, 132, 183-184, 191-192, 198, 213

Washington Post, 29

Watts, 144

Waycross, Ga.. 183

Wayne State University, 187